HOW TO BUY A
BUSINESS
WITHOUT BEING HAD:

SUCCESSFULLY NEGOTIATING THE PURCHASE OF A
SMALL BUSINESS

Jack (John V. M.) Gibson

PAGE PUBLISHING, INC.
New York, NY

First originally published by Page Publishing, Inc. 2016

ISBN 978-1-68348-592-6 (Paperback)
ISBN 978-1-68348-593-3 (Digital)

Printed in the United States of America

CONTENTS

LIST OF TABLES

CASE HISTORIES

PREFACE

This book has grown over a period of thirty years. During this time, I have represented hundreds of business owners who retained my firm to assist them in the sale of their businesses. And in marketing these businesses, I have met and counseled thousands of individuals who contacted me during their search for a business to buy.

After a few years in business, it occurred to us that it would be useful for prospective buyers to have in our reception room a booklet describing the process that a typical buyer might go through to find and, ultimately, buy that "perfect" business. As the years went by, we added a section to help buyers determine how much a typical small business is worth and how much it really earns (or is capable of earning). As our example, we used a cabinet shop with the fictitious name of Doozy Manufacturing Company, which we came to refer to around the office simply as Doozy.

At first, the booklet was only a few pages long, but over the years, we added stories (case histories) about real-life experiences, things that a buyer should watch out for and ideas about how to avoid making mistakes. When Doozy was first published in 1996, it contained thirty pages. As years went by, new sections were added as I realized that the book didn't contain answers to questions my students or clients were asking. Now, in retirement, I have had time to devote to turning Doozy into a real book. It is my hope that the book will help you be successful in your search.

The examples used in *How to Buy a Business without Being Had* are intended to be relevant during all phases of the business cycle. Doozy's financial history, however, is from a period unaffected by serious swings in the economy or by the recent recession. The conclusions, advice, and recommendations included in the book are wholly those of the author.

ACKNOWLEDGMENTS

The author wants to acknowledge the valuable insights of two longtime colleagues at Allied Business Brokers: Sam Cantor and Charles Clark. Also, it is clear to me that this book could not have been written without the tireless editorial assistance of my good friends, Beverly Williams, Deborah Mathews, and Michael Haviland, who gave me many helpful suggestions. And most important, my wife, Lydia, lovingly listened to me moan about my lack of word-processing skills while she patiently got me out of more problems than I can remember. Thanks to all.

INTRODUCTION

This book is for anyone who has ever dreamed of owning a business. During more than thirty years working in the fields of business development and business brokerage, I have seen many people achieve their financial dreams through buying and operating businesses of their own. This has given me great pleasure. The purpose of this book is to assist you in achieving your financial dream through the successful purchase of your business.

Unfortunately, I have also seen a relatively large number of people who became disappointed with the businesses they bought. Many did not achieve their financial dreams. Some prospective buyers never got to the point of submitting an offer to buy a business. I am not sure why. Perhaps they did not have sufficient confidence in their business judgment or never found a business that seemed to match the business of their dreams. Some (thankfully, a very small number) buyers closed their businesses shortly after buying them. And others talked to me about reselling the businesses before they had owned them for very long, often a sign that they were not entirely pleased with their feelings about the long-term prospects of the businesses they had purchased.

It seems that some buyers and some businesses did not make a good fit. This has troubled and perplexed me. I wanted to know what went wrong so that I could more effectively counsel buyers in the future. Five possible explanations come to mind.

1. *The economy*—was the economy to blame, rising prices or rising interest rates, for example?

2. *The business*—was it the business? Loss of key customers or employees, or weak **cash flow**?[1]

3. *The price*—did a buyer pay too much for the business and thereby take on too much debt?

4. *Misrepresentation*—was the business misrepresented in some way by the seller or broker, particularly with respect to financial stability or profitability?

5. *The Buyer*—or was the disappointment in some other way the fault of the buyer? Inadequate management skills, perhaps, or a poorly drafted purchase contract?

Each of these five factors may have played a role in what went wrong, yet none fully explained why many buyers' expectations were not met. After following up with the buyers of hundreds of businesses, I concluded that some "good" businesses are not good for some people, and conversely, some "not-so-good" businesses are perfect for other people. Two keys to success for the buyer appear to be

(1) discovering why some businesses and some people make a good fit, and

(2) doing some careful homework before buying in order to learn what makes the business run and what would make it run better.

I was also puzzled by the fact that some qualified buyers passed on purchasing businesses that I felt were unusually good financial opportunities for them. One answer to this puzzle turned out to be that some buyers had been advised (by their bankers or other financial advisers) that the businesses they liked and had considered buying were too expensive. This was, of course, easy advice to give and often not very helpful since the advice was usually based largely upon a seller's initial asking price only and not upon any detailed knowledge of the business or of how the business fit into its market or industry.

These buyers often became discouraged and looked no further. They did not have the tools to help them discover what a fair price and terms of purchase might be. Sometimes, the gulf between the values that sellers (and their advisers) put on their businesses and the values that buyers (and their advisers) put on the same businesses seemed too great.

---

[1] Certain terms that have precise meanings in the world of small business (or bookkeeping in general) are in boldface type. Some are also defined in the Glossary of Terms.

It was not unusual, for example, for an appraiser or financial adviser retained by a seller to assign a value of, say, $300,000 to a business, while an appraiser or financial adviser retained by the buyer assigned a value as low as $100,000 to the same business. I began to ask myself how, if these were trained and experienced appraisers or advisers, could the differences be so great? How can we make sense of these disparate opinions of value? It is no wonder that some buyers became discouraged and passed up good opportunities. They did not know whom to trust.

While most buyers had the necessary skills to operate a business, they did not have the skills with which to develop with confidence their own **opinions of value**. I have concluded that the appraisers or advisers, were simply attempting to protect their clients' interests and were therefore sometimes overly cautious in the opinions they offered.

When buyers did decide to explore an opportunity in-depth, often neither the appraisers nor the buyers did adequate homework. They relied much too heavily on a business's federal tax returns and on their year-end financial statements without making adjustments or asking sufficient questions to learn how the statements were prepared. And often, they did not tour the business, meet with the owner, or review the business's monthly financial statements. For me, after many years of experience in the field of "small business," I have learned that it is in the monthly (rather than year-end) statements that the answers to many critical questions concerning the value of a business can be found.

Certainly, in some cases, the **asking price** for the business was too high, particularly the initial asking price. However, as a broker for many years, I can comfortably state that the price at which many (but not all) businesses are sold is considerably less than the initial asking price. It also, sometimes, takes a seller awhile to determine that the initial asking price is too steep. Therefore, the initial price sought by the seller is not always a reliable criterion for selecting a business opportunity to explore (or for not considering an otherwise attractive business).

In other cases, there was genuine misunderstanding regarding the nature of the business or how the business in question kept (or did not keep) its books. In a few cases, there appeared to be a lack of understanding regarding the nature or the quantities of assets that would be included in the sale. For example, the actual value of **inventories on hand** can far exceed their **book value**—that is, the value at which they are carried on a company's balance sheet.

Above all, I learned the importance of writing down clearly and in detail the agreements reached between buyer and seller. Poorly drafted purchase contracts were probably the single greatest source of frustration for buyers of the small businesses that I have worked with. How often have I heard the words, "Don't worry. We can handle that later." Often, *later* is too late to avoid costly business interruptions, such as the search for a knowledgeable attorney or trying to find the seller and pin him down on loose ends not fully spelled out in the purchase contract.

As important as it is to write things down, it is equally important to understand all the provisions set out in the purchase contract. Too many buyers do not read their contracts in full or fully enough to understand their contents. In their enthusiasm to purchase a business, buyers sometimes sign a contract or sign the closing papers without reading them and discover later that "failing to read" is no defense when it comes to the law.[2] Every buyer should be careful to understand each paper he or she signs, why the paper is important, whom it protects, and what the remedies might be if problems or misunderstandings arise.

Of course, often the parties to a contract have no dispute. They simply want to know what the contract says (what it means), so they can fully and properly satisfy its provisions. And believe it or not, a year or two after an agreement is signed, it may be difficult, even for the attorney who drafted it, to interpret the meaning of some provisions.

It is from these observations that the idea of writing a guide for prospective business purchasers arose. I wanted these purchasers to be able to learn *How to Buy a Business without Being Had* and without paying too high a price or being disappointed in the financial results of the business after the purchase. It is my hope and belief that if buyers follow the steps set out in this book, they will avoid buying the wrong business and will avoid passing up some great opportunities as well.

When it comes to finances and the future earnings of a business, the **cardinal rule** for a buyer seems to be summed up in this question:

Will the business, given the skills and other resources that a buyer brings to the acquisition, generate enough **cash flow** to

- pay the new owner (the buyer) a reasonable salary,

---

[2]   There are many good texts on the subject of contracts, including the subject of fraudulent conveyances. One source from which much of the material on these matters is taken is *Business Law* by Louis O. Bergh.

- pay the operating costs (expenses) of the business,
- provide some reserve cash for future working capital, and
- pay interest and principal on the debts of the business, including the debts incurred in purchasing the business?

In the world of small business, banks are often eager to provide loans for **acquisition financing**, but later (after the business has been purchased), even if the business is growing, banks are often reluctant to provide additional loans for **working capital**. Many business owners learn too late that it is best to rely on, and plan around, the working capital provided by the cash flow of their business rather than upon cash obtained later from outside sources.

In learning *How to Buy a Business without Being Had*, we will explore ten distinct steps along the path to success. Each step is important.

Ten Steps to Successfully Buying a Business

1. Find a business you would like to buy *(the search process)*.
2. Study the business, its market, and its industry. Visit the place of business, and meet with the owner *(the study process)*.
3. Review the business's financial statements *(financial review process)*.
4. Adjust, or recast, the financial statements (when needed) *(the recasting process)*.
5. Determine a proper **offering price** and **terms of purchase** (the *valuation process*).
6. Prepare a written offer with price and terms of purchase spelled out in detail *(contract preparation process)*.
7. Submit the offer to the seller and respond to any changes he requests *(negotiating process)*. After the offer has been accepted, is signed by all parties, and becomes a binding contract,
8. Conduct a thorough **due diligence** (the *due diligence process*) including:
   a. inspecting the facilities, inventories, and equipment (and other assets to be included in the purchase of the business),
   b. confirming the owner's financial representations (contained in the contract), including the business's sales history, profitability, inventory levels, and legal matters,
   c. obtaining all licenses and other approvals needed to operate the business, and

    d.   removing or satisfying all "**contingencies**" included in your offer (or purchase contract) such as securing loan approval.

9.   Have a qualified attorney conduct the "lien searches" and oversee the formal closing on the sale and purchase of the business (the *closing process*). Lien searches are necessary for the seller to sell a business (or to sell the assets of a business) free and clear of any indebtedness.

10.   Be sure there is a smooth and successful management transition between you and the former owner after the sale is closed (*management transition process*).

Completing each of these steps might at first seems a little daunting. After finding a business to study, however, the total process moves fairly quick and smoothly. Perhaps it will take a month to complete steps 1–7, the point at which you have in-hand a negotiated and signed purchase agreement. It will usually take another month to complete the **due diligence**, secure a written commitment from a lender (when necessary), and be ready for the closing on the purchase of your business. When purchasing a larger business, it can take longer to complete the *due diligence process* and obtain any necessary loan commitments. Don't rush the process. It's a good time to be careful. Most of all, be careful to protect your capital resources. See tip below.

TIP: More businesses fail because they run out of money than for any other reason. Always learn exactly what it will cost to buy a business—the down payment, the closing costs, your first month's rent, any required deposits, and the amount of **petty cash**, or **working capital**, needed to operate the business from the time you buy it until the cash coming in catches up with the cash going out to pay your expenses.

And if the first business you study does not turn out to be the right one to buy, do not worry. You will be better equipped to spot and quickly value and negotiate the next opportunity.

CHAPTER 1

WHY BUY A BUSINESS?

OVERVIEW OF THE WORLD OF SMALL BUSINESS

People buy businesses because (1) they want to be their own boss, (2) they cannot find a job they like, or (3) they see business ownership as the best path to building wealth. Self-employed people do in fact seem to be wealthier than other folks. It was recently reported in *Money Magazine* that the median net worth for business owners is $497,000 versus $42,000 for nonbusiness owners.[3]

There are several familiar choices available to help you reach your goal of self-employment and business ownership:

1. Start a new venture as a sole proprietor of a home-based business or work as an independent contractor. Both have become more attractive options with the growth of various forms of social media.
2. Start a business by renting an office or other suitable location and leasing or purchasing the necessary equipment and inventory to get started.
3. Go into business with someone else—a partner, your spouse, children, or friends.
4. Form a corporation, prepare a prospectus, and try to raise the necessary capital through the sale of shares of stock.
5. Buy an existing business.

---

[3] *Money Magazine* (April 2011), 68

This book is about this last choice: buying an existing business for yourself. Some existing businesses may be franchised, but the majority will not be. Most will still be operated by their founders; some will have already passed to second-generation owners.

Going into business for oneself is becoming an increasingly popular goal for many people from all walks of life. In fact, more new jobs are created each year by the estimated ten million small businesses in the United States than by all the large corporations in the Fortune 500 or by the ten thousand publicly traded companies in the United States.[4] Small businesses form a dynamic and growing sector of our economy and by some recent estimates provide as many as 70 percent of all new jobs created each year. Current data about small business and the important and expanding role it plays in the economy, even in times of economic uncertainty, can be found by visiting many Web sites—among them *SBA.com, bls.gov* (the US Bureau of Labor Statistics); *huffingtonpost.com/news/smallbusiness-tips/; NFIB.com; CNN.com/smallbusiness; smallbusinessadvocate.com; Smallbusinesstrends.com;* and *Bizbuysell.com.*

Finding a location and starting a new business from scratch often takes a long time and often turns out to require a larger investment than originally anticipated. Of course, people start new businesses all the time, but start-up businesses do not have a great record of success. Some knowledgeable sources believe that 50 percent of all start-ups fail within the first year and 90 percent do not survive beyond the fifth year. Franchised businesses have lower failure rates than stand-alone businesses, but most observers agree that their income potential is lower as well. *CNN.com/smallbusiness* has data on failure rates in various industries. *Sba.gov/moneysmart* and *sba.gov/franchise* can be very helpful sites.

Advantages of Buying an Existing Business

Buying an existing business is less risky and has proven to have other advantages as well.

1. It automatically eliminates a future competitor.
2. It usually saves both time and money.
3. An existing business normally has cash coming in from the first day you take over ownership, so it can pay you a regular salary.

---

[4] Estimates vary: *CreditRiskMonitor.com* reports 14,288 companies in 2015 while the Wall Street Journal reports 5,008 net listings on US stock exchanges in 2013. See US Public Companies Rise Again, WSJ, Feb. 5, 2014.

4.   If you stay on good terms with the former owner, you may glean valuable tips and leads from him or her that will help you guide the business to its next level.
5.   An established business has a credit history; start-ups do not.
6.   There may be experienced employees and established procedures that make an existing business much more efficient than a start-up.

People who want to go into business often think first of starting their own business from scratch. They do so because they believe it is less expensive than buying an existing business. In too many cases, the opposite proves to be true. Starting a business usually entails many costs that the founder does not think of. Even when the founder plans carefully and prepares a start-up budget and seeks professional assistance from a business counselor or from a government-funded agency or organization, such as SBA and SCORE, costs often quickly exceed what has been budgeted. The most overlooked costs are the personal compensation and working capital needed during the start-up period. Said differently, many start-up business owners go broke before the new business grows to the point that it can pay an adequate salary to the owner. *Visit SBA.org* or *SCORE. org* for advice on "prebusiness planning."

A realistic minimum budget for a new venture or a new franchise is $30,000. Some business owners will tell you that they developed a successful business with a smaller initial investment than $30,000, but it is wise to plan conservatively. Even with no start-up costs, someone who needs to pay himself (or herself) a salary of $5,000 per month will have gone through a $30,000 stake after only six months. Your real cost will be (1) the start-up costs, plus (2) salaries of $30,000, plus (3) the working capital necessary to run the business until that magic breakeven point is reached. Few new businesses are able to breakeven after just six months of operation, if the owner's salary is deducted. (*Breakeven* is achieved when a business grows to the point that cash coming in from sales covers the cash going out for expenses. After reaching breakeven, a business has positive cash flow.)

Many profitable small businesses can be purchased with a down payment of as little as $30,000, or 30 % to 40 %, of the purchase price. This means that you can find good businesses with asking prices of $80,000 to $120,000—less than the cost of many franchises and usually less than the cost of starting a new venture. The great majority of sales are installment sales: the seller carries a note for the balance of the purchase price. Of course, many businesses sell for far more than $120,000. Most important is that fact that these "going concerns" are "in operation" and have adequate cash flow to pay their bills, pay your salary, and still show a profit. Only a small percentage of businesses are sold for all cash. See list of some typical types of smaller businesses below:

Typical Small Businesses for Sale for $120,000 or Less

Advertising agency	Subway sandwich shop	Donut shop
Hair salon	Muffler shop	Tuxedo rental shop
Retail travel agency	Collection agency	Print shop
Coin-op laundry	Ice cream parlor	Needle art shop
Wine and liquor store	Pizza parlor	Flower and gift shop
Bicycle sales and repairs	Vending service	Real estate business
Landscape service	Dry cleaners	Pet shop
Convenience store	Transmission	and many other types
Dental laboratory	repair service	

According to the Internal Revenue Service, there are thirty million businesses (or firms) in the United States. This includes **firms with employees** plus the **sole proprietors**, the people that file self-employment tax returns. Only six million firms have employees, and only 8 percent of them have annual revenues of more than $5,000,000; almost 56 percent have annual revenues of less than $500,000. So I suspect that you can find an attractive business for less than you than you thought you would have to pay.

Many people who sell their businesses do so because they are looking forward to retirement, or simply to getting some time off, rather than because the business is failing or has serious problems. In every case, the seller has extensive knowledge of the industry of which the business is a part and should be happy to pass this knowledge along to you.

Former business owners often have well-formulated ideas about how their own businesses could expand and become more profitable. They know their employees', customers', and suppliers' habits, quirks, and preferences and can guide you in how to deal with them effectively. And they can advise you about handling the bumps in the road that every business owner has experienced. Their experience is one of the most valuable assets that a business has.

If a business has a good credit history, suppliers will probably ship goods without requiring payment at time of shipment or requiring your personal guarantee. If the business has been established for several years and has a history of generally paying its suppliers on time (or early, to receive purchase discounts), the business will have a favorable credit history. Do not underestimate the value of this hidden asset.

On the other hand, while starting a new business, it may take a long time to find a suitable location and to develop the facilities and contracts needed to establish a profitable business and achieve a positive **cash flow**.[5] It may be difficult to find trained and reliable employees. With a new business, it may take months or even years before it can pay you a salary that matches the salary you earned in your last position. Generally, when buying an existing business, you will not lose salary during your start-up period, and you may avoid some of the typical start-up costs associated with a new business. Buying one that has been around for a while provides you with a running start.

First-Generation and Second-Generation Business Owners

A business is often called a first-generation business if it was founded by and still managed by its founding owner. Buyers of first-generation businesses become second-generation owners, and the businesses then become second-generation businesses. The differences between the two are instructive.

A first-generation owner typically starts a business with little capital and with little formal business training. It is unusual to find a first-generation owner who has previously worked in "corporate America." For these reasons, the typical first-generation owner has limited management skills and little formal knowledge of accounting or bookkeeping. He or she does not delegate much authority to employees. However, the founder usually has solid technical skills. As the business grows, this first-generation owner goes through a steep learning curve and, over the years, through trial and error, develops the policies, procedures, business forms, job descriptions, and vital contacts that enable his business to survive, operate efficiently, and to become (in most cases) profitable. All of these assets have value because they would cost money to develop, but their value would rarely appear on the balance sheet of the business.

Many times, also, first-generation owners mingle business accounts with their or their family's personal funds. To these owners, there is little distinction between personal and business. What the business earns is what they earn. Many first-generation owners did not incorporate their businesses; they operate as sole

---

[5]   Many of the terms such as "cash flow" which appear in bold face type are defined in the Glossary.

proprietors and file their business tax returns on the schedule C of their individual tax return.

Second-generation owners, by contrast, often have less technical knowledge but extensive business training. They tend to keep business and personal affairs quite separate and, therefore, operate their businesses as corporations. The corporation pays them a salary and employee benefits (funds permitting). One consequence of these differences is that first and second-generation owners speak, quite literally, different languages when it comes to discussing finance and many other business-related matters. A second-generation buyer tends to know precise definitions to common business terminology while a first-generation owner may not. This is no reflection upon intelligence; it is simply a result of different training and experience.

Second-generation buyers may consider buying a particular business because they see better or more efficient ways of making or marketing a business's products or services. This is what makes commerce work; some people can see a better way of doing things and back their ideas (or hunches) by making investments—an investment in purchasing a business or an investment in new equipment, facilities, or personnel.

There are components or procedures in almost every business that can be improved in ways that will make the business stronger, more efficient, and more profitable. Sometimes it is wise to purchase new, state-of-the art equipment; at other times, it is better to operate with fewer assets (fewer trucks or less inventory) and to convert the excess assets to cash.

But it is unwise for buyers (who become the second-generation owners) to discard too many of the old ways too quickly. Some were learned through painful and costly experience. Second-generation owners should attempt not to repeat the learning curve of the previous owner who is usually quite proud of the business he has created. It is often wise to learn why the owner is interested in selling. There are many predictable reasons, but in my experience, they boil down to one common denominator; the business has grown beyond the skills, or game plan, of the founding owner and needs fresh ideas or energy, or both, to grow to the next level. Be careful not to discard the old game plan too quickly. The following story gives one reason why.

Case History – MISMANAGING ACCOUNTS RECEIVABLE

The buyer of a company with annual sales of $4,000,000 had accounts receivable aged on average to 90 days, longer than had been acceptable in his previous place of employment. He felt he could improve cash flow by implementing some new measures. So, against the seller's advice, he began to add late fees and interest to the overdue accounts. Before long many older customers canceled their accounts. The buyer did not understand the relationship that the seller had built with them.

What the buyer did not know was that years earlier, the seller, who shipped orders in his company trucks, asked customers if he could ship by the truckload even when they had only ordered a partial load. Many customers agreed to do this, provided they could pay as they used the product. The seller readily agreed, because truckload shipping was more efficient. However, when product left the plant, the seller booked each truckload as a sale and left the full trailers on his customers' lots. Each truckload was also booked as an account receivable, so it appeared on paper that the accounts were older than they really were.

Moral – Understanding what has been responsible for success in the past is as important as a buyer's new ideas.

Unscrupulous Business Owners

Yes, there are some unscrupulous business owners. In the course of assisting buyers and sellers over thirty years, I have met very few owners whom I would call unscrupulous and, happily, fewer still that take advantage of an unsuspecting buyer. Far more often, when a buyer senses that something is wrong with a business, the problems are the result of employee misdeeds. If an owner does not seem able to explain satisfactorily, for example, why the reported revenue or margins seem low or why certain expenses seem unrealistically high, he may not be equivocating, or attempting to mislead. He may simply not know. The problems may be the result of employee theft that the owner is not aware of. Or the problems may be the result of bookkeeping errors, such as an expense item posted to the incorrect account. Be cautious in jumping to conclusions.

Most small business owners are simply trying to feed their families and build up enough equity to retire comfortably. Many spend as little time as possible in record keeping and, as a result, may not have at their fingertips much of the kind of data or answers that you, as a potential buyer, might expect. Moreover, it is natural for an owner to want to make his business appear attractive to a buyer. So some owners will embellish their financial success. They might boldly tell a buyer how much money their businesses have earned (or is capable of earning) even when the financial statements seem to tell a different story.

It is difficult for someone not walking in the seller's shoes to be able to say with certainty that some practice was unscrupulous. There are more often gray areas that make managing a business with absolute fairness to all virtually impossible. Take the issue of calculating employee bonuses or profit sharing as an example. If employees are to receive 10 percent of pretax profit, how is that profit to be calculated? The parties to such an agreement may have quite different views of what is considered profit. The problem results from the fact that no agreement has been spelled out in writing. One of the things every buyer should learn is that in the world of small business, many things never get written down.

If an owner has repeatedly engaged in practices that appear improper or were calculated to take advantage of someone, walking away might be the best response for any buyer. A bad reputation could be expensive to repair. In their enthusiasm to grow their businesses, sometimes owners do promise more than they can deliver or may exaggerate certain aspects of their business's condition. Perhaps a supplier has told the owner that a qualified business must have a $1,000,000 net worth in order to get exclusive rights to some product line. An owner may make some adjustments to his balance sheet in an effort to get his business qualified.

The question for the business buyer is to determine if some practice, current or past, has damaged the reputation of the business. If the determination is that, no, neither the business nor its reputation has been damaged, the prudent buyer should continue to find a fair purchase price and resolve to address any issues that have come to light in his **purchase contract**.

Obviously, some businesses are not worth pursuing. They may have myriad incurable problems. Their financial statements may be badly messed up. New technologies may have passed them by. And yes, some owners may not negotiate with every buyer in good faith or ever agree to accept a price that is a true reflection of a business's worth. For whatever reason, over one-half of the small businesses on the market never sell. Some have not grown to the point that they can pay a buyer a reasonable salary. Others may have problems that are terminal: obsolete equipment, poor location, a history of poor customer service, and in many cases, too much debt or overhead.

HOW TO GET STARTED

While getting started, take time to do some financial housekeeping. Carefully check your personal credit score with the three credit reporting bureaus or at complimentary web sites such as CreditKarma.com. Most credit reports contain errors. For this reason, it is important to review yours carefully before banks, suppliers or business owners have to determine whether they want to extend credit to you. At this time, also, prepare or update your personal financial statement. Creditors and potential creditors always want to see a current statement, so I recommend that you update yours every ninety days.

The majority of small business owners will agree with the sentiment that "there's nothing like being your own boss." So, be sure that you have that strong desire—to head out on your own into a world where there is no personnel department, no rules and regulations, and no coworkers to chat with when you take a break or need someone else's opinion. Some buyers tell me that another strong motivator in wanting to buy a business is to be free of the restrictions, frustrations, the sometimes-endless meetings and other seemingly unfulfilling activities that were part of their present employment. For millions of people, business ownership has been the best investment of their lives and a major step toward achieving their goal of financial independence. If any of these reasons fit you, you are in the company of thousands of Americans who buy or start new businesses each year because they want more control over their lives and their economic future.

Some small business owners tell me that they never doubted that one day they would be in business for themselves. When the opportunity arose, they jumped in with little hesitation. Others tell me that they agonized for months or even years while wondering if they were cut out for self-employment, or to be entrepreneurs, before deciding to buy a business. To help you make this decision, review some of the good sources of information on the Web, such as the website of the Small Business Administration of the U.S. Department of Commerce (*www. sba.gov/smallbusinessplanner/index.html*). Other helpful websites are *Bizbuysell. com*, *bizquest.com*, and *diomo.com*.

Let's say that you're convinced that it is more prudent to buy an existing business than to start to build a new business from scratch. Now, you want to know how to get started. Buyers normally have two big questions. First, where do I find an attractive business for sale? Second, what is it worth? Regarding the first question, if you haven't found one, there are three main resources:

Where to Find a Business for Sale

1. Conversations with people experienced in the field: accountants, bankers, lawyers, business owners, and of course, business brokers and leasing agents—specialists who earn their living representing or assisting business owners.

2. Reviewing the "Business for Sale" column in local and national newspapers and trade magazines. In the papers, some "businesses for sale" are offered through brokers and some are "for sale by owner."

3. In more recent years, looking through Internet websites devoted to buying and selling businesses, such as Bizbuysell.com, you will find sites that specialize in the type of business or franchise you are considering buying. In addition to the sites mentioned above, look at *www. franchise@coolshoppers.com.*

After you have found a business, or perhaps two or three businesses, that appear attractive, it is time to move to step 2, the *study process,* and learn "how to buy a business without being had." For each business, "study" involves learning something about its history, its customers, its industry, and the niche each occupies within its industry. Try also to learn something about the market(s) served by each of the businesses that you have uncovered. It is often helpful at this stage to learn why a seller has put his business "on the market" or, if the business is not formally listed for sale, why an owner is interested in selling.

First, arrange to meet with the owner, or his agent, probably away from the place of business to avoid alarming employees or revealing to others that the business may be for sale.[6] During this initial meeting, try not to sound critical or skeptical. You want the owner to like you and, over time, to take you into his or her confidence. Then, take a tour of the plant or place of business (this will probably occur outside of business hours), and jot down all questions that pop into your mind, however inconsequential they may seem.

When meeting the business owner, respect his or her time because time taken away from running the business may be costly to the owner. Remember also that he or she may have other prospective (and qualified) buyers who are studying the business as well.

---

[6] Confidentiality during this process is very important to the buyer and to the seller. Many things that can be damaging to a business often occur when word gets "out on the street" that a business is for sale.

The object of your "study" is simply to discover if a business is worth further time and effort on your part. There is no point in getting bogged down in too much study before you have had a chance to complete steps 3 and 4 (the *review process and* the *recasting process*). Some buyers may be tempted to discard a business from further consideration after meeting the owner and touring the premises, but in most cases, I recommend "hanging in there" until you complete your review of each business's financial records.

TIP: There are many sources of information in addition to the owner and the broker, who want to put the best face possible on a business. It is natural for you to want to learn more from, hopefully, objective sources. If you are constrained by having agreed to protect the owner's confidentiality, where can you turn? In most communities, there are secondary sources available: the Chamber of Commerce, the Better Business Bureau, or a trade association. You might check the yellow pages directory and trade publications, and you might speak to other business brokers in the area. In some cases, you can pose as a potential customer. In other situations, you might contact a supplier about becoming a dealer or contact a franchiser about buying a similar franchise.

A Word about Small Businesses

Businesses with fewer than fifty employees are considered small. Some economists define *small* as a business with fewer than a hundred employees. Government statistics generally classify *small* as a business with fewer than five hundred employees. In addition to the six million businesses (firms) that have employees, there are twenty-two million that are sole proprietorships.

A small retail establishment might have annual sales (revenue) of $100,000 per employee. A distributorship might have revenue of $1 million per employee. So a business with ten employees might have revenue of $1 million to $10 million. With fifty employees, revenue could range from $5 to $50 million. Most small businesses, however, have fewer than ten employees and revenue of less than $1 million.

Size of Firm	Number of Firms	Employees	Employees per Firm
1–4 employees	3,600,000	6,100,000	1.7
5–9 employees	1,000,000	6,900,000	6.9
10–19 employees	635,000	8,500,000	13.4
20–99 employees	530,000	21,000,000	39.6
100–499 employees	90,000	17,500,000	194.5

Of the roughly 125 million persons employed in the private sector in the United States, 50 percent work for "big business" firms, those with five hundred or more employees. If all the sole proprietors (including those who do not file tax returns) are included in this calculation, it is estimated that the number people working for "big business" falls to 43 percent. So the majority of us work for small business. A breakdown of businesses ranked by size follows. The data comes from the 2008 Economic Census. All numbers have been rounded.

The U.S. Census also tracks receipts for each category of firm. A simplified breakdown from 2008 data is shown below. The key figure to remember is the annual receipts per employee. Bigger businesses generate ten times the receipts per employee that the sole proprietors generate. This explains to a large degree why the owner of a small business must be prepared to "wear several hats." He cannot sit in an office and expect his business to operate efficiently without his participation in every facet of the business. Businesses with five hundred employees or more regularly generate between $500,000 and $1 million in receipts per employee. Many firms in the field of social media and IT (Google and Yahoo) in 2014 had over $1 million per employee. Exxon had over $4 million!

	Number of Firms	Total Receipts	Receipts per Employee
Nonemployee firms	21.7 million	$991 million	$46,000
Firms with employees	6.1 million	$30 trillion	$492,000
All firms	27.8 million	$31 trillion	$111,000

Small businesses are different from their larger corporate counterparts in other important ways as well. The financial press and even some university curricula now recognize them as different. They have fewer administrative personnel. Their owners have little time to study problems; decisions often must be made quickly. This includes being able to spot a good business when it comes on the market and move decisively if the business seems right for you. And small businesses are usually thinly capitalized. They have few lines of credit or capital reserves.

Because of these factors, small businesses usually have a different style of management, very hands-on management. Owners may have to participate in every facet—from handling sales, to greeting customers, meeting their bankers, loading trucks, and sweeping the floors. The good news is that the small business sector of our economy is vibrant and growing. According to the 2013 annual report, since 1990 big business has eliminated four million jobs while small businesses have added eight million.

A Word about Business Brokers

Business brokers generally represent business owners, not the buyers. The owners pay the brokerage fees when a sale is consummated. This means that most brokers have a strong incentive to assist buyers whenever they can. While learning about a business you find through a broker, most of your contact will be with the broker or agent (or perhaps the Seller's lawyer or accountant), who will get answers to your questions. Contact with the owner is usually limited because he (or she) is busy running the business and, at first at least, does not know if your interest is serious enough to justify taking time away from the business. He is also inclined to protect his business secrets and any information that might assist a potential competitor.

The brokers' job is to save their clients time and money by presenting their businesses to interested parties and, by screening, to determine if buyers are financially qualified. Business owners do not want to spend much time with buyers who are not financially qualified—they are easy to find. And if word gets out that a business might be for sale, a seemingly endless stream of buyers often appears at every seller's door, interrupting the business and alarming employees.

At first, brokers, like owners, may be hesitant to reveal much about a business. Owners and brokers both want to know that you have a genuine interest before dedicating large amounts of time to answering your questions. In fact, the best way to get questions answered is to show interest. This is not a time to act coy. At some point, fairly early in the conversation, most brokers will ask you to sign a **buyers agreement** (**nondisclosure**, or **confidentiality**, **agreement**), stating that you will keep all information in strict confidence. See Appendix for a sample.

Only after you sign will the broker or agent reveal the identity of the business. This is perfectly normal and does not obligate you, as a potential buyer, in any way except to keep all information in confidence, including the fact that a business may be available for purchase.

A broker will also probably ask you to list what are called **acquisition criteria.** Sometimes, these are referred to as **search criteria**, or purchase criteria. These criteria describe the kind and size of business you would like to buy. Some of the criteria are financial (I want a business that earns $100,000 a year and can pay me a salary of $60,000), and some are nonfinancial but equally important (I want a business that is located near my home). I urge every buyer to write down a list of specific characteristics that would make a business attractive as well as make it unattractive. Your list should include several "financial" and several "nonfinancial" criteria.

Buying a business without the assistance of a broker or other experienced professional can be a slow, drawn-out process. When you find a potentially attractive business on your own (familiar industry, good location, about the right size), the owner may not have available for your review any of the documents listed above. In fact, the owner may not have in mind either a selling price or a clear picture of what assets would be included in a sale. Many months can elapse while the seller struggles to find time to assemble the information a buyer needs to determine the value of a business and set a firm asking price and terms. When a buyer contacts a broker, the broker should be able to provide what is needed, since the broker has already spent hours with the seller telling him (or her) what is needed and then putting offering documents together into a prospectus.

Profiles, Prospectuses, and Offering Documents

Brokers can and should provide you with a fact sheet, or **profile**, of any business you want to look at or study. A good broker should become very familiar with the "product" he is offering for sale. A key piece of information to look for at this stage is owner compensation—that is, how much money the owner is taking home each year.

A good broker will also have for each business, particularly businesses with annual sales of $1 million or more, a more detailed write-up called a **prospectus**. That document will contain a description and financial analysis of the business, as well as copies of the Seller's financial statements for several years of operations. The analysis will probably include a **spreadsheet**, showing operating results from several years on one page, making the year-over-year review and analysis much easier. A broker may also provide the following documents. Customer lists and tax returns will probably not be available at this early stage for most small businesses.

- Summary of monthly sales (for five years)
- List of employees (with date of hire, compensation, and title)
- List of suppliers (with dollars amount of annual purchases)
- Schedule of accounts receivable (with aging)
- Schedule of furniture, fixtures, and equipment (with original cost and estimated present market value of each item)
- Listing of products and services offered for sale
- A spreadsheet showing reported financial results for the past five years

Spreadsheets sometimes show adjustments to reported income, but the one below shows revenue and expenses exactly as reported by the owner. There are two sample spreadsheets in this book, one for the day care business shown below and one for a cabinet manufacturer in the Appendix.

Day Care Business—Spreadsheet without Adjustments

		2009	**2008**	**2007**	**2006**	**2005**
Total sales (revenue)		**$185,514**	**$194,366**	**$190,488**	**$175,608**	**$140,589**
	Average sales per month	15,459	16,197	15,874	14,634	14,059
Account no. and name						
515	Day care supplies	6,093	7,527	8,856	4,921	2,776
525	Day care food	4,290	1,987	1,643	1,009	1,714
535	Equipment rental	10,662	17,186	437	3,622	307
610	Employee payroll	77,000	80,422	90,157	86,791	56,505
615	Employee advance	0	0	0	0	1,232
620	Contract labor	0	0	0	0	358
630	Payroll taxes	7,444	8,935	10,017	9,643	15,293
700	Rent paid to owner	39,683	41,950	76,500	48,500	41,940
705	Utilities	4,618	5,006	4,010	6,042	3,388
710	Telephone	4,424	4,465	4,113	3,583	4,532
712	Security	4,481	2,635	877	1,131	759
715	Maintenance & repairs	4,181	4,922	6,109	3,810	1,033
720	Office supplies	557	664	98	43	491
760	Transportation	2,162	3,319	1,363	849	847
805	Professional fees	1,700	2,125	2,343	2,194	2,083
815	Bank charges	183	323	304	397	244

820	Bounced checks	1,317	348	0	282	2,514
835	Taxes, licenses, & fees	2,940	5,809	6,705	3,248	7,583
840	Insurance	1,327	1,094	1,654	3,517	554
850	Ads, publications, dues	204	215	596	334	523
855	Interest	83	0	671	0	0
860	Student recognition	0	972	0	0	0
865	Postage	58	64	0	32	0
870	Depreciation	10,647	2,638	0	0	0
875	Contributions	0	50	0	0	0
880	Miscellaneous	0	1,430	0	535	225
	Total Expenses	184,414	194,086	207,453	180,483	145,406
	Income (Pretax) Reported	**$1,145**	**$447**	**-$16,717**	**-$4,867**	**$4,183**

Suggestion—if the broker does not provide spreadsheets, make one for revenue and expenses and another for balance sheet data. Use of spreadsheets makes the financial review of a business much easier. Check the "reported" results above for accuracy and for consistency. How can the inconsistency in account 700 be explained?

After reviewing the Day Care spreadsheet carefully, try to determine what "adjustments" you might make to the reported income. How would you "recast" the reported expenses? Could the cost of day care food (account 525) double in one year? Could taxes, licenses, and fees (account 835) decline by 50 percent in one year? There must be explanations. Look for "lumpy" expenses. These may be for non-operating expenses or, perhaps, for large expenses that should be spread over several years. Look at account 535 Equipment rental: what kind of equipment does a day care rent? Why is the reported income such a low percentage (%) of revenue?

The important question always is: **"Will there be enough income for me to make a living from this business?"** Be sure to review the "top line" results, **Total Sales**, as well as the various expense accounts. Try to determine if there is a trend. And, if the trend is broken (as occurred in the Day Care business between 2008 and 2009), try to determine why. The 2009-2012 recession may provide the explanation.

The prospectus or profile should always include a description of the assets that are, or will be, included with the business being offered for sale: the furniture, fixtures, and equipment (the FF&E) plus tools and leasehold improvements, with the original cost of each item and its estimated current value. These lists are not always as detailed as the following two abbreviated examples (one for the Day Care profiled above and one for a large industrial equipment sales and rental company) and may not include values, original cost or date purchased, but simply the number and type of items that a seller intends to include in a sale.

Schedule 1. Day Care FF&E—Manager/Owner's Office

No. and Description of Items	Original Cost	Estimated Current Value
1 3×6 walnut executive desk	$1,200	$400
1 matching walnut credenza	995	400
2 4-drawer legal file cabinets	140 ea.	160
1 leather high back desk chair	550	250
2 upholstered side chairs w/arms	225 ea.	200
1 fireproof 2-drawer legal file cabinet	500	300
1 HP flat screen 22" monitor (new)	240	150

Schedule 2. FF&E Industrial Sales Co.—Rental Department

	Serial No.	Date Bought	Original Cost	8/31/04 Book Value	Estimated Market Value	Remaining Economic Life
CDI Forklift	4095	11/94	$25,380	$14,530	$16,500	4–6 yrs.
CDI Forklift	4169	11/96	25,380	15,150	16,500	4–6 yrs.
Manlift SM31RT	11062	10/97	18,130	7,645	12,500	6–8 yrs.
A/C Forklift	2310	10/98	24,490	6,910	12,500	6–8 yrs.
LManlift SM42	36146	05/98	19,345	7,555	13,000	6–8 yrs.
Boomlift MZ50	85165	06/02	38,575	12,000	21,000	8–10 yrs.
JCB Backhoe	13230	18/04	26, 030	25, 230	25, 000	9-12 yrs.

Whether you are working with a broker or not, check the offering documents to be sure they include detailed financial statements. If not, ask the seller or his agent to provide them for four full years, plus monthly statements for the current year. Later (after you have decided to make an offer to buy a business), ask for federal tax returns as well. It is a big red flag if a seller hesitates to provide any of this information. And it might also be a red flag if the data contained in the tax returns differ substantially from the data shown in the financial statements.

Since it is the broker's job to show each business in its best light, these offering documents usually include a "recasting" of each business's financial statements. This recasting includes adding back any non-operating expenses to the reported income and making other adjustments necessary to indicate what the broker (or owner) believes each business has truly earned or is capable of earning. Sometimes it is more and sometimes less than the income that has been reported.

The majority of small businesses are not sold through brokers. They are sold through word of mouth. Whether a business owner is represented or not, it is still important to be careful about not abridging confidentiality and respecting his or her time. Brokers can be useful in helping you, even when you have found a business on your own. But be aware that the experience and knowledge of business brokers varies greatly. Some states require that brokers be licensed; others do not. All things considered, it is wise to use a broker who has some licensure or other professional credentials under his belt.

A sample **profile** is included in the Appendix. It includes a short history of the business, the owners' reasons for offering their business for sale, and a market (industry) analysis. This detail of information should prepare a buyer to have a productive conversation with the sellers and to undertake his own research into the feasibility of buying the business. For larger businesses, the offering document will include financial statements for the past four or five years as well as employee rosters (with compensation, title, and year hired); a complete listing of assets included in the intended sale (with purchase price and current estimate of value); a summary of monthly sales (often broken down by department); and various spreadsheets. Federal tax returns will probably not be available even for larger businesses at this stage.

A Word about Financial Statements[7]

Formats differ considerably. Nomenclature differs as well. Sales can be referred as revenue and earnings as income. Within the expense accounts, distinct accounts are grouped together as seen on the day care spreadsheet shown above. See accounts 715, 835, and 850. At times, "grouping" can be misleading. For example, equipment rental and rent may be shown as a single account called leases. In other cases, nonbusiness related expenses are grouped with business expenses. Account 840 insurance may include premiums for personal auto insurance as well as employee health insurance premiums. In larger businesses, there are many more expense accounts than are included in the day care spreadsheet, and they are often divided into several groups (departments), such as,

---

[7]   See Glossary of Terms for definition of a financial statement.

- Cost of Sales (production costs)
- Research and Development
- General and Administrative Expenses
- Selling and Marketing

The normal expenses involved in running a business are called operating expenses. Certain other expenses, especially certain interest expenses, are not considered operating expenses even though they appear to be on some statements of income. So it is always important when analyzing a business (or comparing the results of several businesses) to learn how the statements are formatted and check to see if the format is consistent for the years under review.

In the world of small business, financial statements are rarely audited. Most will contain fairly obvious errors. Sometimes, you may discover that the value of inventories on the balance sheet has not changed in several years. Sometimes, there appear to be discrepancies between the financial results shown on the federal tax returns and the internal statements prepared by the owner. One fairly common practice is not to include the **depreciation schedule** in the internal statements[8]. The depreciation is calculated at the end of the year by the person who prepares the tax returns. Sometimes also, owners say they do not have time to prepare timely monthly financial statements. So while doing your review, list the questions that come up and ask the broker to find the answers.

Financial Red Flags

Red flags can take many forms. For me, declining sales would be a red flag. Declining gross profit margins would be of concern. Some of the entries on the day care spreadsheet are certainly potential red flags, but they are not "deal killers." They require explanations. Perhaps there were no financial statements. For me, this would be a serious "red flag." Buyers should always be cautious when red flags appear. Some have been discussed above, and some can be resolved through the *recasting process* discussed in detail in Chapter 4. Others might be critical to placing a fair value on a business. The subject of missing documents at the time of the closing is discussed in Chapter 7.

---

[8] Financial statements that are prepared by an employee instead of an outside accountant or tax preparer are referred to as 'internal statements.'

Listed below are some typical red flags to watch for. But since each business is unique, every buyer should be alert to the possibility of the existence of other red flags that are not listed.

Red Flags Concerning All Financial Statements

1. No statements are available for a business you are looking at, or the statements you have been provided are not up-to-date, or statements for certain reporting periods are missing.
2. Incomplete financial statements (perhaps the balance sheet, cash flow statement, or accountant's opinion letter is missing).
3. The statements are not prepared (formatted) in a consistent manner from year to year or from month to month.
4. The CPA (accountant or bookkeeper) did not attach an opinion letter to the financial statement—or the opinion letter stated, in essence, that he could not offer an opinion regarding the accuracy of the statement.

Red Flags Found on Income Statements (the P&L)

1. Declining year-over-year sales.
2. Declining gross profit margins in recent years (or months).
3. Recent increase in cost of labor (measured as a percent of sales).
4. Lumpy expenses in certain accounts (large changes in reported expenses between reporting periods).
5. Unpaid expenses in certain months, such as rent or payroll taxes.
6. No depreciation has been taken in the current reporting period.
7. The gross profit margins and the net profit margins vary substantially from year to year. You can determine this by calculating the percentages for both margins on a spreadsheet of annual (and monthly) results.

Red Flags Found on Balance Sheets

1. Little or negative retained earnings (which may suggest that the business has operated at a loss for many years or that the owner has expensive tastes and frequently has made foolishly large expenditures).
2. Aging accounts receivable (as a multiple of monthly sales).
3. Accounts payable and other current liabilities are increasing (as a percent of sales).

4. It appears that certain unpaid expenses (that you have spotted on the income statement) have not been added to the accounts payable.
5. No new fixed assets (equipment) has been added for a while.
6. Changes in equity (net worth) on the balance sheet do not match changes in income shown on the income statement.

Not all red flags are serious. Some may be, certainly. All are not deal killers either, but all require investigation as well as satisfactory explanations. But proceed with caution. Remember that the business owners may not have reviewed their own statements and may be offended if you challenge their accuracy or say things that sound overly critical about the business. Finally, while you are studying a business, be alert to other potential red flags, such as anticipated future increases in some "cost of doing business" or things that have nothing to do with financial statements, such as changing markets or changes in technology.

Case Histories

Throughout this book are actual stories of real buyers and the experiences and challenges that they faced. All stories are abridged or edited to reduce the possibility of disclosing the identity of either the businesses or their owners. To begin, let me share two case histories—one a success story and one a story that was not so successful.

Case History – LANDSCAPE CONTRACTOR—A WINNER

This company had won many awards for excellence in landscape design but had not made much money despite growing sales. The buyer, a banker, spotted three things that encouraged him to believe the business could be quite profitable: (1) the large cost of (and lost revenue from time spent) preparing for the awards, (2) the interest the seller was paying on several accounts payable, and (3) the frequent use of credit cards to pay for routine purchases. The banker bought the company, sold it four years later for a considerable profit, and retired at a very young age to a mountaintop in the Smoky Mountains.

Moral – don't overlook good companies with a disappointing earnings history.

Case History – DRIVE-THRU PHOTO PROCESSOR
AN UNFORTUNATE STORY

A former store manager, a hard-working and talented guy, was able to buy a shop with a modest down payment. Because of rapidly changing technology, he shortly thereafter had to purchase new equipment. Debt service on the equipment was expensive. To help the buyer, the seller reduced the monthly note payments the buyer owed him, but the buyer still couldn't make an adequate living. Chain drugstores began to go into photo processing. Revenue at the photo shop began to decline, and the buyer decided to throw in the towel when his lease expired. In view of changes in the industry, the buyer no doubt paid too much, as is often the case when a buyer can only make a small down payment.

Moral – be sure you can afford the business you want to buy.

Perhaps a third case history, one about a business that was never sold, would be appropriate also because many businesses never sell. They seem to have one of three problems: they are overpriced, have poor financial records, or the seller is just on a fishing expedition and not really interested in selling. With some careful homework, you can determine a fair price and reconstruct reasonably accurate financial statements and overcome the first two problems. I hope this book will give you the tools to do so with confidence.

Some few businesses, however, do not sell because the seller cannot obtain the necessary authority from the board of directors, from shareholders, or from other third parties—such as a government agency or family members.

Case History – A BUSINESS THAT WAS NEVER SOLD

This brief story is about a man who was at retirement age and was fully committed to selling in every way I could discern but, without realizing it, needed his family's approval. He entered into a purchase contract with a capable and financially qualified buyer. However, two days before the closing, his two sons approached him and, in essence, said, "Dad, you can't do this to us." The father, with tears in his eyes, asked me if there were some way he could get out of his contract. Luckily, the buyer and seller worked something out, and the sons took over the business.

Moral – all buyers, sellers and brokers should be sure they have not overlooked the need to obtain some third party approvals

---

CHAPTER 2

WHAT KIND OF BUSINESS TO BUY?

Would you have ever thought of buying a cricket farm? A manufacturer of stained glass windows? A school that trains riverboat captains? A company that makes and installs seamless gutters? All are businesses our company has represented and sold in recent years. When thinking about what kind of business to buy, more often we think of traditional businesses—hardware stores, florists, restaurants, or dry cleaners—businesses that have been around for a while and that are part of the fabric of a community.

What would make a business attractive to you? There is an almost infinite variety to choose from. Houses and cars have personalities. We easily fall in love with them. Businesses also have personalities. Therefore, the business that is right for you may be totally wrong for someone else. This is true even when both the "price" and the "financial condition" of a business seem attractive. So before you buy, consider carefully the noneconomic characteristics of any business you are looking at.

As we will learn in Chapters 3, 4, and 5, "numbers" are important, and understanding them is even more important. However, all truth is not in the numbers. We can "spreadsheet" a business to death doing forecasts and making adjustments to financial statements and still not understand the core business. Many successful buyers focus more on their strategic vision, or game plan, for the business they want to buy. They constantly ask themselves how this "collection of assets" can be deployed to yield greater returns in the future and to meet life objectives. This chapter deals with the nonfinancial aspects of determining if a business is right for you.

There are four broad categories of business in almost every community: **wholesale**, **retail**, **manufacturing**, and **service**.[9] Each type relates to almost every industry. Use the apparel industry as an example. We can sell wholesale clothing. We can sell clothing retail; we can manufacture clothing, and we can "service," or repair, it as in a dry cleaners or tailor shop. There are also some so-called "integrated" businesses—that is, businesses that make, sell, and service their products. A picture frame shop may be a good example. GE may be another example.

Each category has unique characteristics. The "service sector" is the most rapidly growing. It includes **personal services**, **business services**, **repair services**, **professional services**, and many others. In metropolitan Memphis, for example, 62 percent of the businesses listed in a local directory were in the service sector in 2003, up from 60 percent in 2000.[10] If every new business has found its way into a directory, I suspect that the service sector today would include over 70 percent of all businesses. However, since service businesses may have only a few employees, the service sector had a smaller percent of total employment— around 64 percent of nonfarm employment in 2009.[11]

Manufacturing employment has declined fairly rapidly in many parts of the United States but still forms the economic base of many cities in the northeast and midwest. Nationally, manufacturing accounts for only 9 percent of employment today, down from 12.5 percent as recently as 2000. Employment in wholesale businesses has declined slightly, primarily as a result of automation, from 4.1 percent in 2000 to 4.0 percent in 2009.

In the retail sector, products are sold to the public. Wholesale businesses sell products to the retailers and to other businesses. Manufacturers make the products that we sell or service. Some manufacturers are called "primary" because they process raw materials into such basic products as steel, plastics, and lumber. Other so-called "secondary" manufacturers use the steel, plastics, and wood, for example, to manufacture furniture or cabinets. Some manufacturers simply assemble products from parts that were made by other manufacturers.

Service businesses, unlike businesses in the other three sectors, have few tangible products to sell; they generally work on other people's products. They provide services to businesses and to individuals. They repair or clean cars, furni-

---

[9]   Not included are extraction (mining), food production (farming), and real estate–related businesses, such as motels and hotels.

[10] "Who's Who In Memphis Business, Rodney Baber and Company," *www.baberweb.com*

[11] Employment data, broken down by industry, is compiled by the Bureau of Labor Statistics and may be viewed by visiting *www.bls.gov.ces/home.htm*.

ture, and clothes. They fix broken bones and windows, test air quality emissions, train and test persons who wish to become licensed, prepare our tax returns, offer financial advice, and provide many other services that we all need.

The service sector has grown most rapidly in recent decades and now constitutes the largest sector in the U.S. economy in terms of **number of total jobs**, **number of new jobs added** each year, as well as the **number of businesses**. It is broken down below into five separate categories below. Professional services may seem to overlap business services. The distinction is that they usually require formal training and licensing of some kind. In some states, persons without professional degrees or certification are barred from owning or operating certain businesses such as a real estate practice. It is wise to check if any certifications are required in your state.

Changing Industrial Landscape

The landscape is changing more rapidly today than ever before: rapid growth in some industries and decline in others, even the disappearance of traditional businesses in some smaller neighborhoods and cities. Independently owned hardware and drugstores come to mind; many have not been able to compete successfully with the chains. In business, change is a constant. Car dealerships, which were fixtures for years in most small cities, are disappearing because of economies of scale.

Some businesses are declining as a result of changing technology, improvements in labor force productivity, and a more mobile labor force. Other businesses have been able to change the way they make or market their products by adopting more cost effective and less labor-intensive technologies. And some businesses, veterinary practices for example, seem relatively immune to the ups and downs in the economy. People like their pets.

The Information Age

The "old economy" was defined by assets. We could see, feel, touch, and even smell the buildings, smokestacks, equipment, trucks, and storage yards. A business was defined by (and in many cases valued by) the quantity of physical (tangible) assets that it owned. Today, often the most valuable assets a business owns are its data (information) and other assets, such as trademarks, patents, or goodwill—assets that cannot be so readily seen, measured, or valued.

Many neighborhood businesses and other traditional businesses will always continue to be attractive acquisition targets and will continue to generate attractive returns to buyers. If well managed, the returns can often be very attractive, since they are sometimes overlooked and may sell for very reasonable prices compared to the prices that "information age" companies sell for.

In the "new" economy, businesses that rely upon specialized knowledge, use of computer technology and software (but own quite little in the way of furniture, fixture, equipment, or real estate) often offer greater growth and more attractive returns. Tangible assets defined the "old" economy. In today's service-oriented and information economy, tangible assets are passé. Knowledge (information) can be your most important asset. Information has other benefits: (1) it is cheap to store so your cost of rent may be less or virtually nonexistent, and (2) it is cheap to move, install, maintain, and repair, unlike equipment, raw materials, and supplies.

A listing of some frequently seen businesses is shown below. A detailed list of all business types is compiled by the U.S. Securities and Exchange Commission in what is called the SIC (or Standard Industrial Classification) code. The system of SIC codes was replaced in 1997 by a more detailed classification system maintained by the census bureau called the North American Industry Classification System, or NAICS. Both systems may be accessed online.

Traditional Businesses

Retailer	**Manufacturing/Assembly**
Convenience store	Bakery
Liquor store	Cabinetmaker
Fast food restaurant	Awning and blinds manufacturer
Florist	Picture framing manufacturer
Apparel shop	Conveyor system manufacturer
Dealerships (cars, appliances)	Wood pallet manufacturer
Coffee shop	Armored truck bodies
Bike shop	Printing company
Sandwich shop/deli	Funeral caskets and casings
Travel agency	Stained glass windows
Furniture store	Mattresses and bedding
Floor covering	
Lumber yard	**Personal Services**
	Personnel agency

Wholesale Distributor
Beer distributor
Grocery products
Building supplies
HVAC equipment
Auto parts
Plumbing supplies
Marble and tile products

Repair & Cleaning Services
HVAC repair business
Auto repair shop
Roofing/reroofing company
Shoe repair business
Muffler shop
Self-help car wash

Security Services
Armored truck service
Guard (armed) service

Day care center
Hair dresser/beauty parlor
Dry cleaners/coin-op laundry
Landscape services and lawn care

Business Services
Newspaper publisher
Photography shop
Employment agency
Coupon advertising
Quick print shop
Cleaning Services

Professional Services
Veterinary practice
Insurance agency
Real estate office
School of cosmetology
Optical dispensary
Accounting practice

The specific product or industry (e.g., chemicals, dry goods, building materials, personnel) probably doesn't matter to the typical buyer, but it seems advisable to find one that your skills and knowledge complement in some way.

Non-financial Criteria

Try to think of which non-financial criteria would make a business attractive to you (and to your family) and which would make a business seem unattractive to you. Some such criteria to consider in determining if an opportunity is right for you might include the following six:

- **Complementary skills**—do you bring any needed or complementary skills to the business, skills that seem to be lacking among the present ownership and employee base? **If you bring something to the business that is lacking, you will "add value"** when you buy it. This is a key to many successful acquisitions.

- **Management assistance and noncompetition**—will the seller of the business stick around after the sale to show you the ropes? How long will he stay and in what capacity? It's always a plus if the former owner will (1) sign an **agreement not to compete** with you after the sale in any significant way for several years and (2) agree to provide **management transition assistance** for a definite period of time after the sale. Make the seller your friend since these two factors can be very important to your success. These topics will be discussed in more detail in Chapter 6.

- **Customer base**—how many long-term customers does the business have? Can you determine how loyal they are to the current owner? Be careful about buying a business that has only a few customers. If one large customer leaves when he learns the business has been sold, you could be in trouble. However, if you feel you could bring new customers to the business, it may be just the right one to purchase.

- **Owner's management role**—how would you spend your time if you bought a business? Would you be on an assembly line? Would you spend all day preparing financial forms and reports? Would you spend time calling on customers or solving customer problems? Or in a business like Doozy (which is profiled in the next chapter), would you be on the drawing board designing new cabinets, or perhaps, new product lines? An important consideration is to be able to fill or delegate essential functions that you are not comfortable with. In any event, you will probably perform many different tasks each day.

- **Work environment**—do you like the work environment? The work environment is very important because some of us just work better in certain environments. And some work environments are, frankly, dirty, smelly, or hazardous places to be. Work environment includes considerations, such as the quality and cleanliness of the facilities, your office environment, and the types of customers, suppliers, and employees you will be dealing with. It also includes thoughts about the way the business does business. Are you comfortable with the way the business markets its products or services? Would you really be comfortable working in the work environment of the business you are looking at?

- **Business location**—it involves access to markets, customers, and transportation. It also involves distance from home, that is, how long would the commute be. Some people enjoy the drive to work; it is their private time. Others are tired of commuting and want to get home for lunch or be near their church or club.

These are important criteria, but when the *study process* is over, a business's financial characteristics will probably be the most important. You have to decide if an opportunity, whether it is Doozy or some other, will over time meet your income and other financial objectives. However, if you determine that the business will meet your financial objectives but will not meet your nonfinancial needs, you should be cautious. Certainly, if two businesses appear to offer equal returns, the nonfinancial considerations should be looked at in some depth.

It is also important to give some consideration to what is called an "exit strategy." Can a business easily be resold? To whom would you sell it? What would make the business more salable in the future? Can you pass it along to other family members? Perhaps the exit strategy may be eventually to sell the business to its employees or to a competitor. Two brief words of advice: (1) don't let the place run down, and (2) maintain accurate and current financial records.

Most importantly, do not buy a business only because it seems attractive to someone else, even if that "someone" is your banker or your accountant. You will spend more time at the business you buy than you spent working at your last place of employment, so the business must first of all fit your criteria.

When buyers begin looking for a business, they generally look for a particular type of business—a custom cabinet shop, let's say, or a motorcycle shop. But when the time comes to decide what to buy, experience indicates that buyers rarely buy what they originally were looking for. The *search process* opens their eyes to exciting businesses in other industries, ones they had never heard or thought of. There is almost an infinite variety.

Businesses in newer or nontraditional industries often intimidate buyers. Some buyers feel such businesses require unique knowledge or skills and therefore decline to look at these opportunities. But buyers that do look often find that they are easy to manage and utilize skills they already have. Perhaps more importantly, they find these businesses are in rapidly growing fields. Look at the list below. Some of these "industries" did not exist a few years ago. Some have been around for decades. Some are already in danger of disappearing, replaced by newer technologies and changing consumer preferences. Some are sophisticated, some mundane. Few are on the average buyer's radar screen or wish list, yet buyers in each industry are happy with their acquisition.

Nontraditional Businesses

Retailers

Computers and accessories
Reseller of ladies' apparel
Pet food store
Health food store
Bonsai products
Aluminum can recycling
RV and mobile home dealer

Business Services

Microfilm record storage
Toner cartridge refiller
Security guard service
Commuter jet booking
Mailbox rental

Professional Services

Business brokerage
Appraisal service
Auctioneer
Dental laboratory

Security Services

Home alarm service
Security software service

Manufacturers

Fishing lures
Software designer
Spray wash equipment
Dry mix food additives
Neon signs

Wholesalers/Distributors

Hotel supplies
Material handling equipment
Marble and tile products
Janitorial supplies
Aviation parts supply house
Jewelry supplies
Tour packager

Personal Services

Health and fitness center
Check cashing service
Home cleaning/maid service
Food delivery service
Home health care service
Weight reduction clinic

Repair & Cleaning Services

Computer repairs
Vehicle upholstery repair
Seamless "no drip" gutters
Transmission rebuilder
Book rebinding
Automated car wash

Hard to Classify

Catfish farm
Custom van conversions
Bottler of bottled water
Cricket farm (for medical labs)
Marina

Failure Rates

As mentioned in Chapter 1, knowledgeable sources suggest that over time, maybe 50 percent—or even as many as 90 percent—of start-up businesses fail, while a far greater percent of second-generation businesses succeed. However, among different industries, the rates of success vary considerably. Some businesses seem almost indestructible. Others seem quite fragile.

It has been observed by many brokers that non–chain restaurants do not survive a change of ownership easily. Many customers are loyal to the former owner who, in many cases, was quite a personality. The rates of survival, ranked by industry, are hard to find, but buying any business strongly identified with the owner could be risky. Mamie's Restaurant or Bob's Auto Repair are often not the same without Mamie or Bob. In fact, some owners are advised to depersonalize their businesses as an exit strategy, perhaps even to the point of changing the business name.

Among franchised businesses, growth and success may depend on how many franchises the franchiser licenses within a trade area. Other businesses, photo shops, and video rental shops for example, may be victims of new technologies. Neighborhood drugstores find it hard to compete with large chain operations. Neighborhood businesses are always dependent to a large degree upon what happens in the surrounding neighborhood. Sometimes neighborhoods have room to grow while others are losing population as a result of commercial development or highway construction. Businesses serving a larger market generally reflect trends within the industry of which they are part. Learn if the rate of growth in the industry has been increasing recently or has begun to slow. These factors are as important as either the financial history of a business or the price and terms a seller is willing to accept.

TIP: Many failed businesses (especially those identified with strong owners like Mamie or Bob in the paragraph above) spent unwisely or overspent for furniture and fixtures. See schedule 1 in Chapter 1 for some examples. This overspending is really hidden profit. When you offer to buy such a business, let the owner keep these personal items and reduce the price you offer by the amount of the overspending (or value of the items the owner keeps).

Some things that are beyond the control of a business owner can play a large role in the success or failure of any business in any industry. However, more often, the success or failure results directly from actions taken by the purchaser after the business has been acquired. The following case history gives us a good example.

Case History – MANAGING WORKING CAPITAL

A man with many years of industry experience purchased a woodworking shop with annual revenues of around $2 million. He immediately moved the shop to a larger, more modern building. It had several loading docks, something that was lacking in the former facility, and was closer to the customer base. The move seemed highly justified. The landlord offered to (1) build out the office space and make other renovations and to add the cost to the rent or (2) let the purchaser have the building "as is" at the current rent. Purchaser felt he could do the work more economically than the landlord by using company labor, so he took the second option.

During the remodeling, the business did not bill out much work, but since the business had brought in several fairly large contracts, the purchaser was not concerned. After the first year of operations, it was obvious that several customers were slow in paying and cash flow dried up. The owner wished he had reserved more cash to cover this kind of situation instead of using so much of his reserves on the remodeling. Although the business was making money "on paper," it became obvious after several more months that the owner would have to shut down operations and liquidate the assets.

Moral – be very conservative when you project your working capital requirements.

Financial Criteria

If you visit a broker during your search for a business, you will be asked to list (or write down on a form) what your purchase criteria are. Some criteria are "financial," and some are "nonfinancial." The financial criteria are the tougher of the two because they require some experience to be able to list with any precision. Let me list some that you should think about and be ready to discuss with your broker, accountant, and potential investors or partners.

1. How much compensation or salary you need to take home
2. How much down payment you can afford to pay
3. How much working capital you will have left after down payment
4. What is the minimum "return" on your investment (the down payment, closing costs, and working capital) you will accept

5. How big a business you want (described in terms of annual sales)
6. What annual growth rate (in terms of annual sales) is acceptable

Now for the second big question: how to figure out what a business opportunity is worth.[12] Let's look at a fairly typical small business, a custom cabinet shop. After many years of successful operation, the owner is ready to retire. If you are ready to learn more, let's try to calculate the value of this business in the next chapter. In this chapter, there will be discussions on financial criteria as well. See in particular the discussion on ratios and returns.

---

[12] Regardless of price, every business should have extensive financial statements (see Glossary of Terms), and the owner should make these available to you after you sign a buyer's, or confidentiality, agreement. Be sure to learn if the statements are "originals" or copies and if the owner expects them to be returned.

CHAPTER 3

BUSINESS VALUATIONS

Stock Versus Asset Sale

The value of a business is its **fair market value**. That value should be close to the value at which a business can be bought or sold. Since this book deals primarily with "small" businesses, many of which are unincorporated, the valuations are based almost exclusively upon determining the price at which the "assets" of a business can be bought or sold. In the case of larger incorporated businesses, a valuation might be based upon its net worth—that is, the price at which the "shares of outstanding stock" of the business could be bought or sold. This is an important distinction.

Look at the table below. The market value of the assets of this hypothetical business is $800,000 while the market value of the stock is $500,000. The book values are the values shown on the books or financial records of a business.

	Book Value	Value over Book Value	Market Value
Assets	$500,000	300,000	$800,000
Liabilities	-300,000	-0-	-300,000
Net worth	$200,000	300,000	$500,000

When someone refers to the value of a business, you must learn whether the value is based upon selling the assets or upon selling shares of stock. The discussion that follows concerning the value of Doozy Manufacturing Company is based upon a sale of assets. A discussion of the merits of buying "stock" in lieu of "assets" is included in Chapter 6.

PART I.
THE ELEMENTS OF VALUE

One of the keys to "not being had" is to understand the "elements of value" and how they are calculated. There are many approaches to determining the worth (or value) of a business; some are appropriate in some situations and some in others. We will look at three commonly accepted approaches (or methods) in this chapter, especially the first two named below. Some other approaches to valuing small businesses are discussed later in Chapter 4 Part III.

- Income or earnings approach
- Asset valuation approach
- Market valuation, or "comparables," approach

Because valuing (or appraising) is more an art than a science, the values found are considered "opinions of value" rather than scientific fact. Also, when we start a valuation assignment, we do not know what valuation method is best suited to a given business, but we do know that the use of several different methods is usually advisable. If two methods yield fairly similar results, we can usually feel comfortable that the values found are pretty close to a meaningful or reliable valuation. However, if the results differ significantly, it is wise to either (1) employ some other valuation methods or (2) carefully check the data and assumptions used in the methods initially employed.

To help us understand these "elements of value," we will examine in detail a small custom cabinet shop called Doozy Manufacturing Company. It could be located anywhere in the United States. Doozy is "on the market" and has retained a broker to help its owner sell the assets of the company for $160,000. The broker has released the following brief profile.[13]

---

[13] The profile of a business offered for sale would not normally include the name of the business in order to protect the seller's confidentiality.

Company Profile

CUSTOM CABINET MANUFACTURER

Doozy Manufacturing Company has been in business for fifteen years. The company is incorporated as a *C* (or regular) corporation and reports its earnings to the IRS on a calendar year basis. Last year, Doozy reported earnings (before taxes) of $12,000 after paying the owner a salary of $48,000 and paying his family's medical insurance premiums. Annual sales reported in Doozy's latest financial statement were $300,000.

Profits and sales have shown no meaningful growth in recent years and, in fact, have declined slightly. Three years ago, Doozy earned $34,000 on annual sales of $340,000.

The company appears clean and well organized. The owner values Doozy's hard assets at $100,000.[14] Doozy currently has four full-time employees plus the owner. The owner's wife works part-time doing bookkeeping. Doozy keeps books on the "cash" method.

ASKING PRICE: $160,000

Based on this brief profile, can we determine how much Doozy is worth? Is it worth the asking price? How much would you pay for a "job" that pays you a salary of $48,000 a year, plus pays your family's health insurance premiums and last year's reported earnings of $12,000?

The first reaction of many prospective buyers is that earnings of only $12,000 do not seem like very much. Some buyers also wonder why they should pay $160,000 for a business that has only $100,000 in hard assets. These buyers are discouraged and often look no further. Some buyers even feel that they "are being had" because the asking price seems too high.

The prudent buyer chooses to dig a little deeper because he or she senses that the "reported" earnings may not tell the whole story about this company's true profitability. Some buyers like the cabinet manufacturing industry and like

---

14   The term *hard assets* generally refers to the things you can touch: inventories, real estate, and furniture, fixtures, and equipment (FF&E).

the products that Doozy makes. They feel comfortable with the business. For these reasons, they want to learn more.

Business Sale Prices

It is difficult to find the prices at which small businesses are sold. The sale prices are not published in the local newspaper or recorded at the courthouse, as are the sale prices of homes. Most information regarding the sale prices of small businesses is anecdotal. Some pricing information may be learned from attorneys or from brokers. But because it is difficult to compare one business to another, the conflicting sale prices and **opinions of value** may seem confusing. However, the value of a business and the price at which it will sell is generally closely related to one of two things (1) its **earnings value** or (2) its **asset value**.

When the actual prices at which small businesses change hands are available, they seem, at first glance, to vary as broadly as the motives and experiences of the potential buyers. The important thing to remember is that what someone pays for a business is usually more closely related to what a buyer feels it can earn—that is, to its projected earnings or its earnings value, than to its asset value.[15] When looking at quite similar businesses, the better one may turn out be the one with the fewer assets. Let's review three hypothetical examples of businesses in the same industry: Which business should sell for the higher price?

	Business 1	Business 2	Business 3
Annual Sales	$1,000,000	$1,200,000	$1,400,000
Number of Employees	4	6	8
Inventory Value	200,000	300,000	400,000
Sales per Employee	250,000	200,000	175,000

It might seem at first glance that Business 3 is more valuable. After all, it has greater sales than Business 1 or Business 2 and it has double the inventory of Business 1. But, looking more carefully, we see that Business 1 has sales of $250,000 per employee, while Business 3 has sales of only $175,000 per employee. More importantly, every $1 in inventory value in Business 1 seems to generate

---

[15] The term *earnings* used herein is defined as earnings after paying (or deducting) a salary for the business owner that is consistent with present market salaries for persons in similar positions. The terms *earnings, income,* and *profit* are generally interchangeable. *Net profit,* or *net income,* is the earnings remaining after deducting the cost of any corporate income taxes due. Income value and earnings value are also interchangeable. See Glossary.

$5 in annual sales. In sharp contrast, each $1 in inventory in Business 3 generates only $3.50 in sales. This means that business 1 might generate $2,000,000 in annual sales if its inventory were increased to $400,000. (Of course, double inventory does not always mean double sales—these examples are hypothetical.)

Of the three businesses, I suspect business 1 is the most profitable and therefore more valuable because of three factors important to the success of any business: (1) lower payroll costs (fewer employees), (2) lower rent (it doesn't have to house the additional $200,000 in inventory), and (3) lower interest costs (it doesn't have to pay interest on the additional inventory).

There are several useful shorthand ways to describe the earnings (historic or projected) and the price of a business. For example, they can be expressed as the following:

1. A percent of projected or historic annual sales
2. A percent of the asking price of the business
3. A percent of the value of the assets in use (return on assets, or **ROA**)
4. A percent of the book value of business (return on equity, or **ROE**)
5. A percent of owner's or buyer's investment (return on investment, or **ROI**)

Such analytical tools are particularly useful when comparing one business opportunity to another. For example, we can say that one car wash (to use a type of business reasonably easy to compare) shows earnings of 10 percent of sales while another shows earnings of 15 percent of sales. Or we can say that a business is on the market at a price equal to five times or six times last year's reported earnings. We can speak the same way about the **asking price** of different businesses: one has an asking price of 30 percent of sales, and another has an asking price of 40 percent or 50 percent of sales.

Remember, two businesses at first may seem similar (similar annual sales and pretax earnings), but few businesses are exactly comparable. Some may own their service vehicles while others choose to lease them. One may have taken accelerated depreciation while another has used straight line depreciation. In other cases, the more profitable-looking business may not have accrued all expenses (because it keeps books on the cash basis), or it may not have purchased adequate insurance coverage.

Using the five measurements of earnings set out above, let's see what we have learned about Doozy so far. The broker has made some representations about Doozy's performance from the past year and, optimistically, has given us his opinion of what he feels **Doozy** might do next year. (Of course, we do not know yet if his opinion is correct.)

Attachment to Doozy Profile	Last Year Actual	Next Year Projected
Earnings (before deducting income taxes)	$12,000	$24,000
Annual Sales	300,000	340,000
Asking Price	160,000	160,000
Estimated Down Payment/Investment	60,000	60,000
Estimated Value of Hard Assets	100,000	100,000
ROA	12%	24%
ROE	Unknown	Unknown
ROI	20%	40%
Earnings as % of Annual Sales	4%	7.06%
Asking Price as % of Annual Sales	53%	47%

Looking at last year's reported financial results, it appears that Doozy is earning (before paying income taxes) 4 percent of annual sales and that the asking price is 53 percent of sales. Also, before additional analysis, it appears that earnings are 12 percent of the estimated value of hard assets and that the asking price is 60 percent greater than the estimated hard asset value.

Return on Investment

The future, or projected, earnings are also referred to as a buyer's return on investment, or ROI. This is expressed as a percent (%) of the money you invest when you buy a business. Your future profit is the "return," whether your business earns $5,000; $50,000; or $500,000 or more. The "rate of return" can be expressed by dividing the actual or anticipated earnings by the investment (which, in most cases, is the **down payment** paid to the Seller) at the time of purchase. The investment is not the full purchase price unless the full price was paid "in cash."

Example: $12,000 ÷ $60,000 = .20 or 20% **ROI**

Down Payment

The larger the down payment, the lower the ROI, and the smaller the down payment, the greater the ROI. If Doozy's earnings are actually $12,000, all things being equal, the ROI on a $100,000 investment is only 12 percent. By contrast, the $12,000 return on a $24,000 investment is 50 percent, if Doozy's earnings are exactly $12,000. In this paragraph, the "investment" is the buyer's down payment.

In the illustration above, the $60,000 down payment equals the "cash available," which you indicate you can afford to invest. However, the profile is silent on the matter of down payment, so it is not known if the Seller would accept anything other than an "all-cash" offer. And it is not known if you, or any buyer, could borrow the balance of the $160,000 asking price by offering the "hard assets" to a bank as collateral. If either the Seller or a bank will offer partial financing, both will require interest payments. Thus, your future ROI will be the anticipated earnings less the interest charged.

At a price of $160,000 and a down payment of $60,000, the buyer will have to finance $100,000. If the cost of money (interest) is 8 percent annual percentage rate (APR), the interest cost will be $8,000 and the **ROI** (based on next year's anticipated earnings of $24,000) will be only $16,000, or 26.7 percent.[16]

Calculate: $24,000 - 8,000 = $16,000 ÷ 60,000 = 26.7% **ROI**

Pretax and After-Tax Profit

A word of caution—generally, when discussing the profit (or earnings or income) of a small business—brokers, accountants, owners, and others are referring to the "before tax" profit. There are several reasons why this is appropriate in valuing a small business or in determining how much to pay for a small business. One reason is that buyers can deduct interest payments (and other expenses) associated with buying a business from their anticipated profit before calculating their taxable income. Many buyers discover that during the first several years after buying a business, there are enough deductions to almost eliminate federal income taxes. In the case of Doozy, it appears that there may be no income tax due from the buyer's first year of ownership. See Table 17 in Chapter 8.

---

[16]   The actual first year interest will be less than $8,000 if the buyer makes monthly principal payments.

In discussing larger businesses and publicly traded businesses, on the other hand, people usually speak about "after tax" profit when they use the terms profit, earnings, or income. To calculate after-tax profit, we deduct estimated federal income taxes from the pretax profit. When making comparisons between businesses, always use the same "profit" figure.

The percent "return" that you (or any investor) will find attractive may vary considerably, but it will usually revolve around the questions of "risk" and "liquidity."[17] For small businesses, the minimum acceptable ROI is usually thought to be 20 percent per year or more. Thus, if you made a down payment of $100,000, you might expect your new business to produce pretax earnings (after making interest payments and paying you a salary) the first year of $20,000.[18]

Calculate: $20,000 ÷ $100,000 = .20, or 20% **ROI**

An ROI somewhat lower than 20 percent might be acceptable for an established business with very stable and predictable earnings. A higher ROI should be sought for a business with less predictable earnings, fewer assets, and fewer years of successful operation. And a much higher ROI would be sought for less stable businesses and those with a high degree of risk.

Risk Factors

This brief paragraph cannot touch on all potential risk factors that might exist with a given business. Each business is different, even when two businesses are in the same industry and located in the same market. Even the safest-looking investments involve some type of risk, such as one or more of the following. Each could be damaging to the average small business.

- Bank lines of credit are cancelled.
- Interest rates increase significantly.
- Key employee leaves business with little notice.
- Government regulations change, or new ones are imposed.
- An important customer decides to do business with a competitor.
- A well-financed new competitor enters market.

---

17   For more precise definitions of the terms used, refer to the Glossary.

18   Throughout this book, we use "pretax" earnings rather than "after-tax" earnings as our benchmark. Most purchasers of small businesses will have enough depreciation, interest, and other acquisition-related expenses to reduce taxable income to a minimum for several years.

- Lease expires, and landlord wants a 20 percent increase in rent.
- A major customer declares bankruptcy, leaving you with an uncollect-ible account receivable of $100,000.

As a practical matter, the prices at which businesses exchange hands usually range from the value of a business's hard assets (the **asset value**) to ten times the average pretax earnings (the **earnings or income value**).[19] It is important to realize that most businesses consist of many different types and quantities of assets. And of course, a prudent buyer should learn them because much of an established business's value is created through the wise use of the business's assets.

Types of Assets

There are two broad types of assets: **tangible assets** (sometimes referred to as hard assets) and **intangible assets**. The former, which are shown on the balance sheet of a business, are those things that we can easily see and touch—such as cash, buildings, equipment, furniture, and inventories. The original cost, or current book value, of these assets appears on most balance sheets. See Doozy's simplified balance sheet in Table 8 in Chapter 4. There, the tangible assets are divided into two important categories: **current assets** (such as cash, accounts receivable and supplies) and **fixed (or long-term) assets**, usually things with a useful life of one year or more, such as the FF&E.

In contrast, the value or cost of intangible assets rarely appears on the books of small companies. Their "cost" is normally expensed, or written off, when they are purchased or created. Sometimes, there are no specific intangible assets that can readily be identified. They may be collectively referred to simply as the "goodwill," or "going concern," value of a company. These intangible assets form the "know-how," or intellectual property, of a going concern, so they are often very important—in fact, essential—to the successful and profitable operation of a business. Think of how costly it could be to a business if it lost such assets as its customer or employee contracts, service agreements, dealership agreements, marketing materials (such as brochures, business plans, customer lists, and appraisals, or telephone numbers, trade names, and logos). In the case of Doozy, what would it cost to replace all the cost sheets and shop drawings for the various

---

[19] A third useful valuation tool is a review of the sale prices of comparable companies (similar-sized companies in comparable industries). Using "comparables" is referred to as the market approach to business valuation. Most valuation experts recommend using at least three different valuation methods before concluding what a particular business might be worth.

cabinets that Doozy manufactures? It is important to remember that intangible assets can and do have substantial value particularly in an economy increasingly dominated by service industries.

The **earnings value** of a business usually exceeds its **asset value**. This is certainly true of publicly traded companies that, year in and year out, have **market values** of twice their **book values** or more. See examples using Price Per Share data from the close of the New York Stock Exchange on September 17, 2008. Each stock shown is considered "blue chip." Only one, QCOM, which had 24 percent growth in sales the prior year, is considered a "growth" company. The two bank stocks were trading below their **book values**, which is unusual. It is a temporary situation and a reflection of the recent strong decline in housing values and foreclosures across the United States.

The average ratio of market value to book value for the companies shown is 1.93 to 1. Stated differently, the market values exceeded the book values by 93 percent, a ratio of 1.93:1. By comparison, on the first trading day of the year, January 2, 2008, the ratio for these seven companies was 2.26:1. By 2015, the price/share, market value, and book value had increased in most cases, but the ratios have remained relatively constant.

COMPARISON OF MARKET AND BOOK VALUES
(No. Shares Outstanding and Market Value and Book Value are in *billions of dollars*)

Symbol	Company Name	No. Shares Outstanding	×	Price Per Share	=	Market Value	Book Value	Ratio
JPM	JP Morgan	3.90	×	$36	=	$140	$150	.93
C	Citicorp	8.45	×	19	=	160	190	.84
T	AT&T	5.89	×	28	=	165	110	1.50
FDX	FedEx	.31	×	88	=	27	15	1.80
GE	GE	9.95	×	24	=	239	127	1.90
FPL	Florida Power	.41	×	53	=	22	10.5	2.10
QCOM	Qualcomm	1.64	×	45	=	74	17	4.40
Average								1.93

Goodwill

The difference between **asset value** and **earnings value** (the price or value of a company in excess of the market value of its assets) is generally known as goodwill. So when people ask how much are you paying for goodwill, they are really asking, "How much over asset value are you paying?" or "What is the excess value above the book value or asset value of the company being acquired?" A helpful article, "Notes on the Value of Goodwill in Small Businesses," is included in the Appendix.

It is normal the goodwill portion of the purchase price of a manufacturing company, like Doozy, to range from 25 percent to 50 percent.[20] Even though it may not appear that way, no two businesses are identical, so the **goodwill value** may be less than 25 percent in some and more than 50 percent in other perfectly normal businesses. The recent sale of a heating and air-conditioning business illustrates this point. It is profiled below using year-to-date financial data.

HVAC SERVICE CO.—SUMMARY OF FINANCIAL DATA

Sales/Revenue (most recent 6 months only)	$250,427
Growth in Sales (over prior 6 month period)	44.2%
No. of Employees (including the owner)	2.5
Pretax Income (most recent 6 months only)	$62,677
Estimated Market Value of Tangible Assets	$46,875
Estimated Goodwill Value	$189,125
Goodwill as Percentage of Selling Price	**80.1%**
ROA (assume 12 mo. income of $125,354)	268%
Calculate $125,354 ÷ $46,875 = 2.68	

This HVAC company seems to be able to generate an annualized revenue of around $500,000 ($250,427 × 2) with tangible assets valued at only $46,875. And therefore, it seems to have lots of goodwill, probably the result of high customer retention and the very strong ROA. In a good service company, a few tangible assets can generate a lot of income. By contrast, a company like Doozy (or a traditional retail business) will require substantially more tangible assets to generate the same sales volume. A good yardstick to use with small businesses is that each $1 in tangible assets (inventory + FF&E) could produce $3 in revenue. For larger, more capital intensive businesses, it might require $3 in assets to produce $3 in revenue.

---

[20] Many businesses, particularly newer businesses that rely heavily on the skills of the owner, may have no goodwill value. In cases in which the asset value exceeds the earnings value, there is "negative" goodwill. You will also find that there are industry standards relating to the goodwill values in many types of business. While these "standards" may be helpful to you, remember that each business is unique and the standard may not always fit.

Doozy's Goodwill

Let's again look at what Doozy is offering for sale. If Doozy is worth the asking price of $160,000, it appears that the goodwill portion of its value is $60,000, or 37.5 %. At a selling price of $150,000, the goodwill value would be only $50,000, or 33.3 %.

CALCULATION OF GOODWILL

Book value of Doozy's hard assets	$ 62,000
Estimated market value of hard assets	100,000
Asking price	160,000
Anticipated selling price	150,000
Goodwill (price less market value of assets)	$ 50-60,000

Calculate: $60,000 ÷ $160,000 = **37.5%**

The amount of goodwill is also related to a company's rate of growth or prospects for future growth. Note that one of the publicly traded companies shown above, QCOM, is felt to have a market value that is 335 percent greater than (or over three times) its book value.[21]

Calculate: $74 billion - 17 billion = $57 billion - 17 billion = 35%

Many buyers and their advisers feel it is wrong to pay much for **goodwill.** But good businesses have more goodwill because they make more efficient use of their assets like business 4 below. It generated $600,000 in revenue on only $150,000 in inventory (Business1 shown in the chart several pages earlier, generated revenue of $1,000,000 with only $200,000 in inventory). Goodwill might be summed up as a business's general reputation, or degree of name recognition, in its market. Goodwill is often what really makes a business run successfully. This is why, when attempting to value two quite comparable businesses, it is often correct to conclude that the one with the fewer assets is the more valuable and, therefore, has more goodwill.

So as a potential buyer, it is important for you to learn what makes up the goodwill of any business you are interested in. Just because you cannot see these goodwill assets on a company's financial statement does not mean they do not

---

[21] Remember that in talking about a publicly traded company, the market value is the value of its stock (the value of all outstanding shares of stock) and not the value of its assets.

exist and have value. Of course, after some research, you may conclude, quite correctly, that a given business has no goodwill **value** or even has negative goodwill. Look as these examples:

COMPARISON OF GOODWILL VALUES

Typical Retail Business	Business 4	Business 5
Annual sales (revenue)	$600,000	$800,000
Inventory at book value	150,000	300,000
Fixed assets at market value	60,000	100,000
Asset value	$210,000	$400,000
Pretax income	60,000	72,000
Income as percentage of sales	10%	9%
Asking price	$300,000	$400,000
Goodwill value (at full price)	90,000	0
Goodwill as percentage of asking price	30%	0%
Return on assets (ROA)	29%	19%

At first glance, the businesses seem comparable: both are offered for sale at a price equal to 50 percent of annual sales. However, the asking price of number 4 includes $90,000 in goodwill. Is this just "blue sky," or does number 4 merit this premium over asset value? At the asking price of $400,000, number 5 has no goodwill value, perhaps because it has more assets in relation to annual revenue than its competitor. Its assets equal 50 percent of revenue ([$300,000 + 100,000] ÷ $800,000 = .5), while business 4 operates with assets equal in value to only 35 percent of revenue. Unless some reasonable explanation can be found for this disparity, business 4 seems to have earned its goodwill. Notice also that business 4 has achieved a very respectable ROA of 29 %.

Calculate: $60,000 (pretax income) ÷ $210,000 (asset value) = 29%

However, some businesses for a variety of reasons do not merit any goodwill value. It is important to explore these reasons. If a business has negative goodwill, it is generally felt that its value (and selling price) will be less than the value of its tangible assets. Let's look at the same two businesses again.

Inventory Turnover

Businesses with a good product mix and eager customers are expected to have a better (higher) rate of inventory turnover. This is desirable and is often a component in determining the existence of goodwill, because these businesses will need less inventory to operate profitably. This means that less capital will be needed. Looking at the snapshot below, we can see that business 4 achieved 3 turns on its inventory while business 5 achieved only 2 turns. To calculate the turnover rate, simply divide Cost of Goods Sold by Value of Inventory. If we use **Purchases** instead of **COGS** to calculate turnover, we are not taking into account changes in Value of Inventory, Purchase. See Glossary for a further discussion of this point.

CALCULATION OF INVENTORY TURNOVER

Annual sales (revenue)	$600,000	$800,000
Purchases (costs of goods sold)	450,000	600,000
Gross profit	150,000	200,000
Gross profit margin	25%	25%
Value of inventory (see above)	150,000	300,000
Inventory turns	3 turns	2 turns

Since inventory turnover is one measure of how current the inventories are, we may discover that business 5 has experienced declining sales and, as a result, has some "dead" inventory. If these factors are true (declining sales and slow inventory turnover), a prudent buyer may conclude that business 5 has, in fact, some negative goodwill even though the two businesses at first glance appear quite similar. Of course, the "excess" inventory may have recently been purchased.

PART II.
EARNINGS MULTIPLES AND CAP RATES

If you invest in long-term U.S. Treasury obligations, you will usually earn about 5 percent annual interest. Therefore, since 5 percent interest is the "going rate of return" for the safest and most predictable investment, you would expect business investments to give you a greater return. This "rate of return" is sometimes referred to as the capitalization rate, or cap rate.

At a **cap rate** of 5 percent, the value, or price, of Doozy would be $240,000, or twenty times its reported earnings of $12,000. Note that this value is more than twice the reported value of the hard assets.

Calculate: If price (value) × 5% = $12,000 reported earnings, then $12,000 (earnings) ÷ .05 (cap rate) = $240,000 indicated earnings value, or price of business

Is $240,000 a fair price to pay for Doozy? It is certainly not fair if the reported sales and recent earning are the only considerations. Such a high value for Doozy, a multiple of twenty times reported earnings, or 20:1, would assume that U.S. Treasury obligations and Doozy—a fairly typical small business—are both of equal risk and liquidity. Simple logic tells us that this cannot be so. All businesses are much more risky and far less liquid than treasury bills. Let's look at the effect of higher risk and lower liquidity on the **price to earnings multiple.**

The **earnings multiple** is generally referred to as the **P:E** or price-to- earnings ratio. One of the first questions brokers and others ask about a small business is, "What's the P:E?" You should ask that too. Remember that the P in the case of privately held businesses is the asking price, not the market price.

Today, some fixed income investments and publicly traded stocks and bonds have yields as high as 10 percent or more per year. These investments yield more than the treasury obligations, or bank certificates of deposit, because they are somewhat riskier. Corporations may fail, or they may cut or suspend their dividends, but most of them do not have nearly the same risks as the typical small business.

Publicly traded companies can lose market value quickly in a recession or when problems arise. But publicly traded stocks and bonds can be sold at virtually any time, so they are quite liquid. And when the end of a recession is in sight, stocks often rebound in value quickly. It may take many months (or longer) to sell a small, privately held business of any size. The lesson to remember is: **small businesses are not very liquid.**

U.S. Treasury obligations, on the other hand, are both safe and highly liquid. Their yield (return) is highly predictable; in fact, it is guaranteed. This means two things: (1) that there is little risk that your investment will decline in value (safety) and (2) that your investment can be withdrawn at almost any time (liquidity).

Because of the *higher risk, lower liquidity,* and *unpredictable earnings,* you (and any other reasonable investor in a small business like Doozy) would seek a return that is higher than the typical return you can find in the stock or bond markets. After all, many small businesses fail each year, and very few can be sold quickly enough to raise cash if a sudden financial need were to arise. Based on these factors, **an earnings multiple, or P:E, of 20:1 (or even 10:1) is clearly too high for most small businesses.**

Let's look at some lower earnings multiples and see what effect they would have on the value of Doozy. At a multiple of 8:1, for example, Doozy's earnings value would be only $96,000, much closer to the reported $100,000 value of Doozy's hard assets. At a multiple of 4:1, Doozy would be worth only $48,000.

Calculate: $12,000 × 8 = $96,000 indicated earnings value
$12,000 × 4 = $48,000 indicated earnings value

Assets Included in a Typical Sale

Not all classes of assets that may be owned by a small business exchange hands when the business is sold. Unlike many larger businesses, the typical small business leases the space in which it operates. Therefore, **real property assets** are not usually included in a sale. Also, most **financial assets**, such as cash and accounts receivable, are customarily retained by the seller. This is so for two reasons: (1) most small businesses sell their goods or services to retail customers who pay by cash, check, or credit card when a sale occurs and, therefore, have few or no accounts receivable.[22] And (2) the sellers are expected to pay off all the accounts payable at the time the closing on the sale of the business occurs so the

---

22   If businesses carry accounts receivable, as is the case in most businesses that sell products or services to another business, it is normal that the "assets" included in the sale include some cash.

new owner (the buyer) will not have a lot of outstanding bills to pay when he takes ownership.

Doozy is somewhat different from the typical business because it sells custom products, products that may be suitable for only one customer. So with every job (custom order), Doozy receives a deposit of about 50 percent of the contract price and generally receives the full balance upon delivery of the job.

If a business does carry accounts receivable for some of its customers, it may either factor its accounts receivable or have a **line of credit** (secured by its accounts receivable) to borrow against when additional short-term **working capital** is needed. The amount of "cash," or cash equivalent, that a buyer of a small business could expect to find among its assets is usually very little because little cash is needed for normal operations.

In larger businesses, let's say those with annual sales of $5 million or more, which sell most of their products or services on credit, it would be reasonable to expect the seller to include among the assets (to be sold with the business) either the accounts receivable or an amount of cash equal to one month's projected working capital. Each industry has different traditions. **The important thing is to determine what a business's short-term working capital requirements are.**

The following analyses assume that we are discussing a business that has and will sell only the following four classes of assets (some of these terms are defined in more detail in the Glossary). In a purchase agreement, each class of assets is assigned a specific value (see Chapter 6 for details). The sum of these values equals the purchase price. A related question (which will be dealt with later) is how much of each class of asset to buy. Some businesses keep far too many assets on hand. Others might have too few.

1. **Inventories**—these include raw materials, parts, work-in-process (or work-in-progress), finished goods, goods held for resale in wholesale and retail businesses, and inventories of rental equipment

2. **Fixed or "tangible" assets**—rolling stock, furniture, fixtures, and shop and office equipment and tools of all descriptions. Leasehold improvements are also often included. These are referred to as the FF&E.

3. **Goodwill**—goodwill includes many types of assets such as business records, customer lists, customer orders, forms, logos, drawings, trade names, and other "intangible" or "off-balance sheet" assets that are

vital to the smooth operation of a business. The goodwill portion of the purchase price of a business may also include the seller's management transition assistance and his or her agreement not to compete with the buyer.[23] See the allocation of purchase price in an offer for Doozy in Table 14.

4. **Supplies**—these include assets such as the shop, shipping and cleaning supplies; catalogues and advertising materials; most software and office supplies (such as stationary, business cards, copier paper and postage stamps); and other consumable items.

It is assumed that the assets that will be included in the sale of a business will be in quantities necessary to operate the business in the "normal fashion" and will be

(1)   free and clear of any debts or liens,
(2)   in good working order, and
(3)   fully insured for their fair market values.

Hidden Assets

We might add a fifth class of assets: hidden assets—that is, assets that do not appear on a company's balance sheet or depreciation schedule. It is not unusual to find hidden inventory. This results from the fact that some small businesses do not count their inventories for several years in a row. For these owners, it is a time-consuming nuisance to keep track of inventory levels. And some owners fear tracking inventory may result in having to pay more income taxes. Some manufacturing companies estimate the cost of materials that go into their finished products and "write off" these items when they are purchased. Over a period of years, valuable unrecorded inventory accumulates. Let me give other examples of hidden assets:

---

[23]   These last two items are discussed more fully in Chapter 6: "How to Structure a Purchase Agreement."

Case History – HIDDEN ASSETS

In the profile of a ceramic supply company, the broker listed (1) catalogues—$15,000, (2) conveyor system—$40,000, and (3) goods in transit—$60,000. The buyer felt he should not pay for these items because he couldn't find them on the balance sheet. Also, he found no expense on the P&L to indicate that the company had purchased so many catalogues. In this case, however, the company had its own print shop and had just run off five thousand new catalogues ready to ship to customers. There were overhead conveyors attached to the ceiling of the plant. The buyer assumed that they were property of the landlord, but they had been installed by the business owner and were moveable. So the conveyors were part of an often-overlooked class of asset called leasehold improvements. The goods-in-transit were not counted with the inventory because these goods were on trucks in transit to customers who had bought them. After some discussion, the buyer agreed that these hidden assets were very real and had value.

Moral – there are almost always hidden assets.

When looking for "assets," it is wise not to rely solely on the list or description of assets provided by the business owner or his broker. While I was working as a broker, my preference was to walk through each room in a facility, with the owner if possible, and jot down a brief description of every piece of equipment that I found and my estimate of its current value. When stumped, I would ask the owner, "What is this? What's it for? Where did it come from? Is it still used in the business, and what did you pay for it?" I found that owners usually remembered quite distinctly how their assets were acquired and what they cost.

Then I would do the same thing outside, walking through the yard and parking areas, examining the signage and any other (movable) items of potential value. This practice also helped me spot areas of concern, such as environmental hazards. During this tour, I normally found several useful (and sometimes quite valuable) assets that did not appear on the company balance sheet or on the schedule of FF&E. For example, the signage alone (i.e. neon lighting, pole lighting) could easily have cost $20,000, even in a relatively small business.

One reason to pay particular attention to the type and quantity of assets on hand is to learn how a business is organized. Another involves collateral. If a buyer intends to borrow money to assist with the purchase, lenders always want to see a lot of collateral, that is, assets against which they can file liens to help secure their loans. Every buyer should want to learn at some point during the process of buying a business what assets he is taking title to. The hidden assets mentioned above are things that can be touched and seen. Some of the more often overlooked assets are the intangibles. Two that I look for are (1) excess capacity, the capacity of a business or plant to handle more sales without having to move or to buy additional expensive equipment, and (2) the knowledge and experience of the employees—many of whom have solid ideas about how a business can grow and become more profitable.

The Question of Excess Assets or Inventory

Businesses that have more assets (than would be necessary to operate "in the normal manner") may sell for higher prices than the following analyses suggest. The presence of "excess" assets, or "excess" inventory, may also help explain the difference between a seller's opinion of value and the value calculated by a buyer. The two most frequently encountered classes of "excess" are vehicles and inventory. The buyer may not have to purchase the excess, but first, the buyer must know how much is normal.

Since no two businesses are exactly alike, it is best to think in terms of adjusting information regarding any given business to what is the norm in its market area or industry. If, for example, the value of inventories "on hand" is $100,000 and the norm for such a business to "operate in the normal fashion" is only $50,000, the estimated $50,000 surplus might either be (1) excluded from the sale or (2) be included in the sale and added to the purchase price (and to the estimated "fair market value") of the business. If possible, find out from the owner, a trade association, or from a broker what the "norm" is.

If the excess inventory is in good and marketable condition, it really does not cost the buyer anything to buy it because in the course of a few months, the buyer would need to replenish this inventory. Said differently, excess inventory in good and marketable condition does not always increase the price you would pay for a business because it is often consumed after the sale in the normal course of business. If, however, there is more than several months' excess, you, as buyer, may want to include a provision in the purchase agreement that states that one of three things will occur:

1. The seller will reduce the inventory on hand to "normal" levels by the closing date on the sale of the business.
2. Excess inventory will be purchased by the buyer at closing but will be valued at less than its **replacement or original cost**, say at 75 percent of original cost.

3. Excess inventory will be purchased in the future from seller without discount on an "as needed" basis but not later than six months after the closing.

How Much Inventory Is Normal?

Businesses turn over their inventories at different rates. The ideal turnover rate depends upon the product mix, lead time needed to reorder, reorder quantities necessary to receive price discounts, and other factors. Three to four "turns" a year is pretty normal. So if a business had purchases of $400,000 a year, it would maintain an inventory of about $100,000 with four turns. This would be a three-month supply. If a business like Doozy can replenish its inventory with a week of lead time, a one-month supply (one-twelfth of annual purchases) or less may be normal. If a business has only two turns a year, (1) it probably has too much inventory or (2) some inventory is obsolete. In either event, an explanation is needed. See section titled "How Much Inventory to Buy" in Chapter 6.

The answer to what constitutes a "normal" inventory is more than simply calculating the proper amount of total inventory. A business can have different types of inventory. It may have raw materials, parts, and finished goods. Each of these inventories will have subsets. In other words, there may be too many parts of one kind and far too few of several other kinds, but the total value may seem about right. It is therefore important to have the right balance of inventories as well as the right amount. You do not want to buy a business and discover shortly thereafter that you have to shut down operations because you have run out of essential parts.

TIP: Normal inventory levels can vary throughout the year. Some businesses have seasonal fluctuations, which makes normal levels trickier to calculate. In advance of the busy season, inventories may seem too high. However, at the end of the season, inventories may seem too low, but businesses do not want to end the "season" with merchandise they cannot sell during the next season. And they would have to discount it to clear the shelves for incoming merchandise. If inventory should turn over four times, "normal" equals about two month's sales. But instead of using average sales to calculate "normal," use projected sales for the coming two months.

Not all changes in inventory levels result from seasonal fluctuations in sales and what appears at first to be unnecessary or excess inventory may actually be perfectly acceptable. Let me share another case history that illustrates this point.

Case History – EXCESS INVENTORY.

A distributor of heating and air conditioning equipment ended the year with far too much inventory for "normal" conditions. Worse, much of it was cold weather equipment. Several well-qualified buyers passed up the business because of this over-hang of winter inventory. What the buyers did not take into account was that the manufacturers wanted to clear out their inventories and had offered their distributors a discount if they reordered before the end of the year. Three months later one manufacturer had a 6% price increase. So, even if the distributor had to borrow money to buy the "excess" inventory, it saved money in the long run. If the buyers had agreed to buy the excess inventory at the seller's original cost, it would have been a bargain.

Moral – Always learn why inventories are higher than normal.

Buildings and Other Real Property Assets

Is a building an "excess" asset? If Doozy owns the building it occupies and therefore does not pay rent, how can we value the business? How can we compare Doozy to similar businesses that do not own real estate and do pay rent? To do this, the following three steps are generally recommended:

1. Exclude the value of the building (or other real property asset) from the asking price of the business.
2. Deduct an appropriate cost of "rent" from the reported earnings.
3. Add back to the reported earnings any building-related expenses (such as real estate taxes) for which the landlords would normally be responsible.

These steps facilitate the calculation of the **fair market value** of the business alone. Of course, whether you would prefer to buy Doozy's building or rent it from the Seller is discretionary and a normal subject for negotiation. You may even wish to neither rent nor buy Doozy's building but to move the company to a different location.

Suggestion—learn which assets are carried on the balance sheet of a company and which ones were "written off," or expensed, when they were purchased. Many companies expense, or write off, several classes of short-lived assets when they are purchased, so the value of assets on the balance sheet may seem discouragingly low. Hand tools, for example, are almost always expensed. Some companies, such as dental labs, may expense all of their precious metal purchases because they are not resold and are consumed fairly rapidly. Others expense the cost of assets with a longer life, such as a three-year supply of catalogues, rather than put them on the balance sheet. As we will learn later, Doozy wrote off the entire cost of a new truck rather than depreciating it over several years.

Selecting the Right Earnings Multiple

Most small businesses change hands at prices that range between two and six times their "pretax" earnings. The HVAC company profiled earlier sold for almost exactly two times (twice) its annualized pretax earnings. The multiple for established manufacturers is more likely to range between four and eight times pretax earnings. This higher "price to earnings multiple," or ratio, is a reflection of the fact that manufacturers require more assets to operate than do typical retail or service companies.

Larger publicly traded businesses are valued on the basis of their "after-tax" earnings and, in normal economic times, will trade on the stock market (or sell) at much higher earnings multiples. Look at the price to earnings (P:E) multiples listed in the "Money and Investing" section of the *Wall Street Journal*, or in other financial publications. In normal times, the average earnings multiple, or P:E ratio, may be 12:1. For some "high tech" companies, the P:E may be 50:1 or more, but these companies are growing (or anticipated to grow) very rapidly.

The U.S. Small Business Administration (SBA) in its publication "Checklist for Purchasing a Business" recommends that no small business be valued at more than four to five times annual earnings, or a P:E of 4:1 or 5:1. While this advice may be conservative, the SBA guidelines cited below can be very instructive. Review them carefully. Remember that, unlike the publicly traded stocks sold on

Wall Street, when speaking of small businesses, earnings are "pre-tax," not "after-tax" earnings.[24] There can be quite a difference.

SBA Valuation Guidelines

- **Ten Times Earnings**—old established businesses with large capital assets, excellent "goodwill," and excellent future earnings prospects. Only very few small, privately held companies fall into this category.
- **Eight Times Earnings**—old established businesses that are successful and have predictable sales and earnings growth but require considerable managerial care.
- **Seven Times Earnings**—strong, well-established businesses that are sensitive to the general economy and are vulnerable to recessions. They require considerable managerial ability but little specialized knowledge on the part of the owners.
- **Five Times Earnings**—Medium-size businesses that require comparatively small capital investment and only average managerial ability. These businesses are highly competitive, but the established "goodwill" is of distinct importance. Market value of assets should be fairly close to the purchase price.
- **Four Times Earnings**—medium-size businesses that require comparatively small capital investment and only average managerial ability. These businesses are highly competitive but have less goodwill value than a more established company with more stable sales and earnings. Market value of assets should be close to purchase price.
- **Two Times Earnings**—businesses, large or small, which depend upon the special, often unusual, skills of one or a small group of managers. They involve only a small amount of capital and have few tangible assets, such as inventory or equipment, and are highly competitive with high "mortality" rates.
- **One Times Earnings**—personal service businesses. They require little or no capital. The manager must have special skills and thorough

---

[24] The federal income tax rate for larger companies is around 35 percent. If a company has pretax income of, say, $500,000, the after-tax income is $325,000.
Calculate: $500,000 - ($500,000 × .35) = $325,000.
If this company is worth $4,000,000, the P:E for the pretax earnings is 8:1. In after-tax earnings, the P:E is 12.3:1.
Calculate: $4,000,000 ÷ 325,000 = 12.3.

knowledge of his subject. The earnings of this type of business depend upon the manager's skill rather than his "organization," or staff. The owner can sell the business, including its reputation and "plan of business," but not his skills. The earnings of these businesses are normally the Seller's "take-home" pay.

While the SBA checklist can be helpful, it did not mention one factor that can have a large bearing on the proper multiple to select—that is interest rates, or the "cost" of money. If money can be borrowed at 5 percent, a higher P:E might be used than when the cost of money is 12 percent because the ROI will be greater. Let's refer to Doozy again and calculate the effect of different interest rates on ROI.

Assume Doozy will earn $24,000 before deducting interest payments, the company sells for $160,000 of which $100,000 is borrowed, and money costs 8 percent APR. After deducting the $8,000 first year interest on a $100,000 loan, the ROI on a $60,000 down payment is $16,000 or 26.7 percent. See calculations below. Interest rates affect earnings considerably, so the value of businesses could fluctuate with changes in interest rates.

Calculate: At 5% interest, $24,000 - 5,000 = 19,000 ÷ 60,000 = 31.7% **ROI**
At 8% interest, $24,000 - 8,000 = 16,000 ÷ 60,000 = 26.7% **ROI**
At 10% interest, $24,000 - 10,000 = 14,000 ÷ 60,000 = 23.4% **ROI**
At 12% interest, $24,000 - 12,000 = 12,000 ÷ 60,000 = 20.0% **ROI**

Doozy 's Earnings Multiple

There are two separate analyses that are useful in selecting the appropriate earnings multiple: (1) reviewing the **earnings history** (what a business has earned over the past several years) and (2) calculating the **earnings capacity** (what a business could earn in the future), which will be discussed in Chapter 5. Assuming for the moment that the information provided by the Seller is accurate, what P:E ratio do we use to value Doozy? To discover this, try to match the SBA categories and the **earnings history** set out in Table 1 below.

Doozy manufactures kitchen cabinets. This is a business that does not require a great amount of managerial talent or technical skill. Therefore, goodwill may not be of much importance in this business. On the other hand, goodwill may be a more important element than is first apparent.

As shown on Table 1 below and on Table 3, three years ago Doozy reported $34,000 on sales of $340,000 but last year reported pretax earnings of $12,000 (on sales of $300,000). Why this apparent decline? The industry appears stable. Business acquaintances believe that Doozy's owner may not be spending much time at his business in recent years. If this is so, it probably isn't necessary to discount Doozy's **purchase price** for any anticipated future drop in earnings. The business may simply need the full-time attention of an owner who can bring new energy and enthusiasm. While the acquaintances may be correct, let's look further and see if we can find a fuller explanation for this apparent decline.

With the information at hand so far, Doozy looks like a "four times earnings" business with an earnings value of only $48,000 (4 × $12,000), significantly less than its estimated hard asset value of $100,000. More importantly, at a value of $48,000 there is no goodwill.[25] The **goodwill value** would, in fact, be negative. Before we conclude that a P:E of four times earnings is appropriate for Doozy, more analysis is needed.

---

[25]   This discussion of earnings multiples is too brief to cover all relevant factors. To select the appropriate multiple, there are services that many brokers subscribe to, which provide comparable market data on businesses that have been sold. Typical multiples can be calculated from them.

PART III
INCOME AVERAGING

It's hardly fair to judge a business's earnings capacity, or the value of a business, on only one year's performance. Doozy has ups and downs like most businesses. The average of several years' earnings would probably be more indicative of Doozy's true earnings and market value. A "look-back" period of three to five calendar or fiscal years is considered a good base period for the purpose of income averaging; but sometimes, the business cycle is longer, more stable, and relatively more predictable.[26] This also should be taken into account.

Doozy's reported earnings for five years are shown in Table 1 below. The $18,000 average earnings over the past five years are considerably more than last year's $12,000 reported earnings. While the difference of $6,000 between the five-year average earnings and last year's may not seem significant, it represents an apparent 50 percent increase, which is very significant.

Because earnings over the last few years appear to be trending downward, rather than relying on an earnings average, it may be fairer and more accurate to "weigh" Doozy's earnings according to their closeness to the present. One method for doing this is to multiply the earnings by a "weight" and then average the "weighted" earnings. The selection of weights varies and is quite subjective, but normally, the last year (or most recent period) is given the highest weight.

---

[26] It is important to look at the earnings since the end of the last calendar or fiscal year and to look at monthly financial statements as well as the annual statements. If timely monthly statements are not available, every business should have some form of monthly sales record available that the owner or broker can share with you.

Table 1. Weighted Earnings for Five Years

Year	Reported Earnings		Weight		Weighted Earnings
Last Year	$12,000	×	5	=	$60,000
2 Years Ago	20,000	×	4	=	80,000
3 Years Ago	34,000	×	3	=	102,000
4 Years Ago	10,000	×	2	=	20,000
5 Years Ago	14,000	×	1	=	14,000
Total	**$90,000**				**$276,000**
	÷ 5 years		15		÷ 15
Average:	**$18,000**	**Weighted Average:**			**$18,400**

This weighted average of $18,400 is higher than the five-year simple average of $18,000. In the example shown, the weighted average is only 2.2 % higher than the simple average. But it is comforting to learn that both averages are higher than last year's unimpressive earnings. For other businesses, we find that the weighted average is far different from the simple average.

If we use the **weighted average** of $18,400, it appears that the value of Doozy is around $75,000 (4 × $18,400 = $73,600). The weighted average is a better indication of value than a value derived by using only last year's reported earnings because it takes into account (1) the business cycle and (2) the growth trend of a company or industry. If, for example, last year had earned $40,000 (instead of the reported earnings of $12,000), the weighted average would jump to $27,740.

Some buyers feel that only the most recent earnings should be considered in putting a value on a business. However, generally, a weighted average is more accurate for cyclical businesses. Remember, though, that the reason we study the past is to help us anticipate the future more accurately, so the more thoughtful buyer will base his opinion of Doozy's value on what that company might be expected to earn in the future. (You can believe the owner has ideas about what future earnings will be, so ask him when it seems appropriate.)

We still have two significantly different values: the indicated **weighted earnings value** of $75,000 and the **hard asset value** of $100,000. Which value should we trust, or should we trust either one? Let's first look at a different weighting and a different analysis period. Table 2 shows the results of using only a three-year look-back period.

Table 2. Weighted Earnings for Three Years

Year	Reported Earnings		Weight		Weighted Earnings
Last Year	$12,000	×	5	=	$60,000
2 Years Ago	20,000	×	3	=	60,000
3 Years Ago	34,000	×	1	=	34,000
Total	$66,000	×	9	=	$154,000
	÷ 3 years	×		=	÷ 9
Average:	**$22,000**	**Weighted Average:**			**$17,111**

Note that "average" earnings have gone up, and the "weighted average" has gone down with the different weighting and look-back period. Both averages in Table 2 are still quite close to the averages obtained in the analysis set out in Table 1. This would normally confirm that we are on the right track since we should expect values found by using different methods of analysis to be relatively close. If they are not close, it may be because an inappropriate measure of value is used.

The average of the four averages is $18,877, slightly higher than the weighted average found in Table 1 and 57 percent higher than last year's reported earnings of $12,000. Which average should we use? In fact, we should not rely too heavily on any of these averages because the weightings only tell us about the past. It is usually more important to learn what a business is capable of earning. To learn what Doozy is capable of earning we might analyze the reported $34,000 earnings from three years ago more closely. These earnings may be more indicative.

Relationship between Sales and Earnings

How does Doozy's earnings history relate to its sales history? Annual sales have been fairly stable, while earnings appear to have fluctuated widely. Because Doozy is a custom shop (and reports sales when payment is received), this fluctuation in earnings may simply result from the timing of receipt of payments. For example, Doozy may have received a check for a large job in the first week of January even though all the "costs" were paid the preceding year. In the following analyses, we will look for explanations for these apparent fluctuations on both the "cost" side and the "sales" side.

There normally is no good reason why earnings are not a relatively consistent percent of sales. We expect rising sales to be associated with higher earnings margins—that is, earnings will be a somewhat higher percent of sales in good years and somewhat lower percent in slow years.

In Table 3 (below), we see that earnings have apparently declined sharply from 10 percent of sales three years ago to only 4 percent of sales last year. If there has been no economic recession or rise in interest rates, or other external causes of decreasing profit margins, we would expect to find some fairly obvious internal explanation. We do see in Table 3, as expected, that reported sales for the best years have the highest margins (percent of reported sales).

Doozy's five-year sales history is from a period (1) unaffected by serious swings in the overall economy and (2) during which inflation averaged about 3 percent per year.

It is reasonable to assume that, if earnings equaled 10 percent of sales three years ago, earnings could do so again.[27] If this proves so, Doozy may be worth much more than $75,000. Assuming sales of $300,000 and pretax earnings of 10 percent, we find the following suggested earnings and business value:

Calculate:

1. $300,000 × 10% = $30,000 suggested earnings
2. $30,000 × 4 = $120,000 suggested value (price)

If we assume that (1) sales should be in the $340,000 range, with an enthusiastic new owner devoting full time to the business, and (2) earnings should be in the 10 percent range (the fair market value of Doozy may be higher than $120,000). It's good to keep an open mind about this possibility.

Table 3. Profit Margin - Earnings as Percent of Sales

Year	Sales	Earnings	Profit Margin
Last year	$300,000	$12,000	4.0%
Two years ago	320,000	20,000	6.25%
Three years ago	340,000	34,000	10.0%
Four years ago	300,000	10,000	3.3%
Five years ago	264,000	14,000	5.3%
Total:	$1,524,000	$90,000	5.9%
Average:	**$304,000**	**$18,000**	**5.9%**

---

[27] Keep in mind also that the reverse could also be true; but without further analysis, it is not possible to know whether pretax earnings of 3.3 % (four years ago), or 10 % (three years ago), of sales is more accurate.

Note that the profit margin goes up as annual sales go up and declines as sales go down, but this relationship is not perfect. Four years ago, sales did rise from the prior year, but the percentage (margin) declined from 5.3 percent of sales to only 3.3 percent of sales. It appears that more analysis is indicated.

Adjusting Reported Sales

Explore whether some of Doozy's sales three years ago were actually completed in the prior year. This often occurs in businesses that report sales on the "cash basis" as Doozy does. Doozy may have received a check in the last week of the year and not deposited it until January. A look at the general ledger and bank deposits for the last several Januarys can shed light on this. Also, we should check the date on which Doozy's bank posted the year-end deposits.[28]

Of course, if actual sales three years ago (based on dates of delivery or on dates of receipt of payment) turned out to be less than $340,000, the reported earnings of $34,000 would exceed 10 percent of sales (and may exceed the 11.76 percent of sales shown later in Table 9 at the end of Chapter 4). In custom shops, one check could be $10,000 or greater, so the date a check was deposited will alter the sales reported for a month (or year) and therefore alter corresponding "averages" and profit margins.

In a typical retail business, it is more likely that a deposit would not exceed average daily sales, but some smaller retail businesses deposit their sales receipts only once a week or have no set routine for making deposits. More often, fluctuations in daily, weekly, or monthly sales are the result of the number of days that a store is open for business. Average daily sales can actually be up when the reported monthly sales are down as a result of Sunday closings and the like.

Finally, many owners are conscious of the income tax consequences of recording year-end sales because the more sales reported, the more taxes owed. As a consequence, some owners might hold up depositing some December sales. As a result, the reported December sales are lower than expected while January sales are higher. Adjusting monthly sales can be necessary to calculate correct monthly **gross profit** margins. For this reason, it is helpful to obtain (from the owner or

---

[28]   Sometimes it is not feasible to undertake this level of analysis at the early stages of buying a business. However, after submitting an offer, it is fair to ask the owner for more detailed information. As will be discussed later, an offer should give the Buyer the right to verify all financial representations made by the seller. Or an offer might simply say, "This offer is contingent upon Buyer's approval of seller's financial records." After receiving an offer, a Seller should make all financial records, including copies of bank statements, available for review by a Buyer.

broker) a summary of monthly sales. Large businesses often break down sales (or revenue) by department (i.e., rental department, service department, etc.), but for most small businesses, the summary might look like the following. Does anything appear out of line to you?

Summary of Monthly Sales
(Attachment to Business Profile)

Month	2010	2011	2012	2013	2014
January	12,304	14,586	15,201	14,121	18,526
February	9,643	9,898	12,665	12,974	14,566
March	13,334	13,998	15,531	17,765	19,334
April	15,987	17,804	19,324	20,563	24,332
May	17,545	19,987	21,348	23,334	24,977
June	18,322	19,345	22,576	27,776	32,544
July	17,654	20,337	26,688	30,768	34,494
August	18,002	18,002	24,451	33,553	39,402
September	17,655	17,655	24,998	30,566	34,429
October	15,332	15,332	19,987	19,998	26,433
November	16,302	16,117	19,030	18,112	23,302
December	18,664	19,906	22,444	21,368	21,287
Total:	**$190,744**	**$214,310**	**$244,243**	**$270,898**	**$313,626**
Percent Increase:		13%	14%	11%	16%

Remember that sometimes, sales are not recorded in "cash-basis" businesses (like the business profiled above) until the sales receipts are deposited into the bank account. This appears to be the case for the sales reported for December 2014. Note that in each of the prior years shown, the December sales exceeded the January sales by about 50 percent. However, in 2014, the December sales exceeded the January sales by only 15 percent. In fact, the reported December sales of $21,287 in 2014 were less the November sales—a very unusual situation for this type of business. December sales in the prior years exceeded November sales by about 20 percent.

If we assume that actual December 2014 sales were 50 percent above the January sales of $18,526, they would be around $27,000. If this turns out to be true, then the actual annual sales would be around $320,000, or 18 percent greater than the prior year's sales. A check of the dates of the January 2015 deposits will enable you to confirm or to disprove our assumption. Holding back some bank deposits may simply result from a busy holiday schedule, but it often seems to occur when a business is growing.

Understanding the seasonal nature of a business is always important. It is particularly important to keep in mind when making projections of the future cash flow of a business. When monthly sales are seasonally low, it may be impossible to cover all the fixed expenses from income or from cash flow: the rent, payroll, taxes, and debt obligations will have to be paid somehow. Look, for example, at the reported February sales in the **Summary of Monthly Sales** above. How much income would you have with sales of under $10,000 in February 2010 or 2011?

Suggestion—if a business has highly seasonal sales and the seller is offering some "seller financing," ask the seller if he will accept a lower monthly note payment during a predictably slow month. If monthly principal and interest is $3,000, offer the seller $1,000 or $1,500 in February. Or even better, offer the seller a note with a "skipped" month—that is, one month each year with no note payment or one payment each year of "interest only," that is, a payment without any principal.

Cash vs. Accrual Accounting

What we see on the written page is very persuasive. However, in the case of first-generation businesses in particular, we have to look beyond the written page—that is, beyond the financial statements we are handed. Sometimes, both sales and expenses are underreported. In other cases, the sales may be reported accurately and the expenses are understated. The answer to this puzzle is the timing of posting the information.[29] A business may record (post) its sales when they are made, which is "accrual" accounting. More often, sales are recorded only

---

[29] There is another answer also. Operators of many small businesses are absorbed with business operations and have little time for bookkeeping and may have little knowledge of accounting. Many do not prepare monthly financial statements or review them for accuracy. It seems irrelevant (to operating the business) until it comes time to sell. When financial statements are not available, other records may be used to confirm sales: checkbooks, bank statements, cash register receipts, and sales tax report forms that are required by many states to be filed monthly.

when payment is received, which is "cash" accounting. Learn which accounting system each business uses.

Doozy reports on the cash basis. It records sales when payment is received and records expenses (liabilities) when payment is made. Unpaid bills are therefore not recorded as expenses. Understanding the financial reporting practices is indispensable in preparing an accurate analysis and opinion of value.

Standardizing Financial Statements

Often, we observe that one business does not earn as much as another quite similar business. We instinctively assume that something is wrong with the business that earns less. If the reasons are not immediately obvious from looking at two sets of financial statements, it is helpful to "standardize" the statements. One tool for doing this is **EBIT** (earnings before interest and taxes). In calculating EBIT, we add income taxes and interest expenses to the reported after-tax income. Be careful not to add back any "business" taxes but only the "income" taxes.

If we add back depreciation and amortization expenses as well, the result is called **EBITDA**, or earnings before interest, taxes, depreciation, and amortization. A business—often a recently acquired business, like business 3, as profiled in Table 4 below—can have a lot of interest, depreciation, and amortization expenses and therefore appear not to be profitable. But such a business may have a higher EBITDA than businesses to which it is compared and in reality be more valuable. For large and small businesses alike, it has become standard practice for brokers, appraisers, bankers, and investors to convert reported earnings to EBITDA in order to

- make meaningful comparisons between businesses, and
- put a rough value on a company (whether publicly traded or privately held.

Review the illustration below. Which business is worth more? EBIT and EBITDA should be calculated separately for each year in the look-back period. Look first at net income (the "bottom line"). Most of us would say business 1 is worth more since it has a profit margin of 8.5 percent of sales and it seems to have earned three times what Business 2 earned. Business 3 had a loss, but if we look at sales (the "top line"), most of us would say Business 3 must be more valuable. If we look at the **gross profit** margin, an important element of value, it appears business 2 may be worth more. But, when the statements are standardized through the use of EBIT and, in this case, EBITDA, all three businesses look much more comparable. EBITDA as a percent of sales varies only from 11 percent to 12.5 percent while net income as a percent of sales varies from 1 percent to 8.5 percent.

Table 4. Comparison of Income, EBIT, and EBITDA

	Business 1	Business 2	Business 3
Annual sales	$300,000	$400,000	$500,000
Cost of goods sold	200,000	250,000	320,000
Gross profit	100,000	150,000	180,000
Percent gross profit	**33.3%**	**37.5%**	**36%**
Depreciation	5,000	20,000	25,000
Amortization	0	10,000	20,000
Other operating expenses	65,000	100,000	125,000
Total expenses	70,000	130,000	170,000
Income from operations	$30,000	$20,000	$10,000
Interest	0	10,000	15,000
Pretax income	$30,000	$10,000	($5,000)
Percent of sales	10%	2.5%	(1%)
Income taxes at 15%	-4,500	-1,500	-0
Net income	**$25,500**	**$8,500**	**($5,000)**
Percent of sales	8.5%	2.125%	(1%)
EBIT	**$30,000**	**$20,000**	**$10,000**
Percent of sales	10%	5%	2%
EBITDA	**$35,000**	**$50,000**	**$55,000**
Percent of sales	11.6%	12.5%	11%

Now, back to Doozy. What is she really worth? After finding and making some indicated adjustments to her financial statements, she may be worth more than it originally appeared.

CHAPTER 4

ADJUSTMENTS TO FINANCIAL STATEMENTS

PART I
ADJUSTMENTS TO INCOME

Is $75,000 a fair price to pay for a business with $18,877 in average annual earnings and a $48,000 a year salary? Or is the $120,000 suggested value a closer indication of Doozy's fair market value? These questions lead to the observation that reported earnings (the earnings shown on the financial statements and tax returns of a business) often differ significantly from actual earnings. Earnings may be more or less than reported, but the earnings of small businesses are generally more, primarily because of strategies to reduce or defer income taxes. Other logical reasons are as follows:

Understated Earnings

Reported earnings could be less than actual earnings if companies have done the following:

1. Record no depreciation or use faster depreciation write-offs for tax purposes rather than real economic depreciation[30]
2. Have paid for certain nonoperating expenses, such as wages paid to family members who did little actual work for the company
3. Have prepaid other expenses such as insurance premiums
4. Have paid for nonrecurring costs, such as expensive additions to their physical plants
5. Have (correctly or not) failed to report or record all sales
6. Have accumulated inventories worth more than the value shown on their balance sheets (see Table 10 for a fuller discussion)

Non-operating Expenses

These may include country club dues, meals for family members, unnecessary pieces of equipment, expensive furniture for the executive office, and gas and insurance for personal vehicles. The list is long. These are expenses that have nothing to do with responsibly operating a business. The **nonrecurring expenses** are lumpy (and often "big ticket") expenses that pop up only from time to time—an expensive repair, a new roof, printing a catalogue, a training seminar out of town, onetime legal or medical expenses, or an auditing fee. These expenses are best spread out over several years, or over their "useful life."

The matter of excess inventory is important not only because most small businesses have more than is carried on their balance sheets but also because it represents hidden value. If a store has over ten years accumulated a "cushion" of $100,000 worth of unrecorded inventory, we can assume that, on average, the income has been understated by $10,000 a year. With a 4:1 P:E ratio, this "inventory cushion" could increase the value of the business by $40,000.

Calculate: $100,000 ÷ 10 years = $10,000 × 4 = $40,000

---

[30] Let's say Doozy bought a new truck for $17,500. Doozy could write off the entire cost as a Section 179 expense and have a depreciation expense of $17,500. Alternatively, Doozy could elect to write the cost of the truck off over five years and only take a depreciation expense of $3,500. In the latter case, Doozy's earnings would appear to be $14,000 higher, or more than double the $12,000 earnings reported. However, this accounting change would not double the value of the company.

Overstated Earnings

Reported earnings could also exceed actual earnings for several reasons. Bills for rent or insurance premiums may not have been paid on time. There may be, for example, unusual "one-shot" items included in the reported sales, such as damage awards from a lawsuit or proceeds received by the company from a life insurance policy. It is not unusual to find from time to time that customer deposits (made for future delivery) are included among the reported "sales." From the business owner's standpoint, such "receipts" appear to be the same as any other type of receipt. They are not. Customer deposits belong to the customer until the customer's job is completed and delivered.

There may be substantial, unrecognized bad debts among the accounts receivable, or there may be severe distortions in income caused by inaccurate accounting for inventories. Some inventory items may be old or damaged and, therefore, not be saleable at their stated book values. The point is that **you should never accept financial statements of a small business as gospel.**[31] We must usually look behind the statements to discover the reality of the financial condition of a company.

Case History – OVERSTATED ASSETS

A company tendered a contract to purchase a large equipment dealership for a price of over $2 million. This price was contingent upon purchaser's ability to confirm the representations (values) shown on seller's balance sheet. Upon inspection, the buyer found that many pieces of new equipment (that were still carried on the balance sheet at their original cost) had been leased to some of the company's customers and were damaged in some fashion. Since the seller, in the purchase contract, guaranteed the inventory values on his balance sheet, the buyer obtained an appraisal of the damaged items. When the book values of the equipment were written down to values indicated in the appraisal, the price was adjusted downward and the seller received almost nothing at closing.

Moral – a buyer should always require a seller to warrant the accuracy of company's financial statements.

---

[31] A financial statement always includes two parts: an income statement and a balance sheet and often also includes a cash flow statement. The income statement is also referred to as a profit and loss statement, or P&L.

Recasting Financial Statements

If the initial price that you are considering paying for a business is based only on a "multiple" of reported or averaged earnings, you must "recast" both the income statement and the balance sheet into a standard format to help you determine if the reported earnings are under- or overstated. This is done in various ways, including utilizing these two broad types of adjustments—(1) add to the reported earnings all prepayments, overpayments, nonoperating expenses, and excessive benefits that a company paid to the owner or to family members, and then (2) deduct any unrecorded liabilities, such as past due trade accounts payable and accrued employee bonuses or profit sharing.[32] Costs that are deducted from expenses and added to earnings are called "add backs."

First Review: Review of Annual Statements

For every business you are seriously considering, look at the results for three or four years "spread out" side by side. Review the spreadsheet in the Appendix. And review again the day care spreadsheet in Chapter 1 that shows very lumpy expenses from year to year. Why, for example, is equipment rental so high in fiscal 2008? Why is rent so high in 2007? Why is insurance so high in 2006? Finding out why expenses are lumpy is often very instructive.

Putting the statements into a spreadsheet format is an easy way to spot errors in bookkeeping and potential hidden income. When you get monthly statements, put them into a spreadsheet as well with one column for each month. It can reveal a lot about how a business is managed.

Both the reported income and the reported expenses on a financial statement can be misleading. There are many reasons for this. Some financial statements are quite accurate. Nevertheless, it is wise to check out their accuracy when considering buying a business and wise to consider what adjustments you could make to normalize the statements. Keep in mind that the adjustments can be **positive** or **negative**, that is, they can add to or subtract from the reported

---

[32]   Unrecorded expenses are important enough to be the subject of a separate book. Some business owners are unaware of this potential problem. Owners let bills and invoices stack up and do not record them until they are paid. But these expenses are real and must be considered when calculating income. The key is to review the accounts payable and the balance sheet to see if there is a change in total liabilities (including accrued expenses) from period to period. If, for example, accounts payable totaled $20,000 on 12/31 and are $30,000 on 6/30, a negative adjustment to earnings of $10,000 for the first six months of the year could be indicated.

income. The goal of a buyer is to discover what the expenses and earnings would be if you were running the business.

The timing of payment of insurance premiums is one frequently observed example of a positive adjustment. If a $12,000 annual premium is paid in December and the business owner wrote off the entire premium, how should the statement be adjusted? We could recast the statement by only recognizing one month's expense ($1,000) in that year. The balance ($11,000) becomes an asset called prepaid insurance, which should be added to the business's balance sheet, and $11,000 should be added to the reported earnings. Conversely, if it were observed that the rent or insurance premiums (or other invoices) were not paid by their due dates, we may have to make negative adjustments to earnings.

Our look at Doozy's recorded annual expenses indicates there are at least five expense categories that warrant review and may result in adjustments to the income statements for the five-year look-back period. Upon completing the review, it appears that three categories require positive adjustments; one requires a negative adjustment, and one did not require an adjustment. How will this affect Doozy's earnings and its market value? Let's look at these five potential adjustments:

1. **Purchase of delivery vehicle**—Doozy bought a low mileage delivery vehicle last year for $15,000 and wrote it off as a section 179 deduction in one year. Normally, it would be written off (depreciated) over three to five years, at $3,000 to $5,000 per year. Thus, we have a positive adjustment of $10,000–12,000. See column 1 in Table 5 below. The lower adjustment of $10,000 is used.

2. **Family health insurance**—Doozy last year paid over $4,000 for family health and life insurance. Should the portion that covers nonemployee family members be included in your adjustments? Probably not, since many companies still offer family health insurance coverage, but it is reassuring to know that Doozy can afford the cost.

3. **Bad accounts receivable**—Doozy still carries two "bad" accounts receivable on its books, one from a $2,000 sale four years ago and another from a $4,000 sale five years ago. Neither debtor can be located, but the debts should be written off, thereby reducing income in the year in which the "bad" debts were incurred and reducing the net worth in each year, including the current year. Since there appear

to be no bad debts on the books from the last three years of operation, apparently, Doozy has learned not to extend unwarranted credit to its customers. This is also reassuring.

4. **Payments to owner's wife**—Doozy's owner is paying his wife $200 per week to do some bookkeeping and office work at home. This appears to be $10,400 in hidden annual earnings.

5. **Payments to remodel home office**—two years ago, Doozy paid $6,000 for new cabinets, furnishings, and remodeling a home office where the owner's wife does her part-time bookkeeping.

Regarding item 4 above, payment for bookkeeping, it seems fair to add back only the difference between salary paid to Doozy's owner's wife ($10,400) and the cost that a local bookkeeping service would charge for the same work. A few telephone calls reveals that, based upon the number of checks that Doozy writes each year, several local firms would charge about $1,500. The difference of $8,900 is pretty significant. After deliberation, it is decided to be a conservative and only "add back" two-thirds of the potential savings (roughly $6,000) to the reported earnings each year.[33]

After the appropriate adjustments are added in Table 6 below, the weighted average earnings conservatively appear to be $28,800, or 60 percent more than the $18,000 average reported earnings for the last five years ($90,000 ÷ 5) and over twice the reported earnings for last year. To determine the weighted average earnings, observe the calculations in Tables 4 and 5. Using the same 4:1 P:E, Doozy now appears to be worth slightly over $115,000!

Calculate: $28,800 × 4 = $115,200 suggested valuation

Notice that the largest adjustments were found in the last two years. If we add $16,000 for last year's adjustments to the $12,000 reported earnings, Doozy may have actually earned $28,000, or 9.3 percent, of last year's sales of $300,000. Actual earnings from two years ago would have been $32,000 (10 percent of reported sales) if all the adjustments were added. (To review reported sales and percent of sales, refer to Table 3.) It now looks as if the notion that actual earnings are a relatively fixed percent of sales is borne out by our review.

---

[33] A detailed recasting would also include adding back payroll taxes of 9.85 percent ($591).

Table 5. Summary of Earnings Adjustments

	Vehicle Depreciation	Bad Debts	Wife's Salary	Home Office	Adjustments to Earnings
Last year	+$10,000		+$6,000		$16,000
2 years ago			+ 6,000	+$6,000	12,000
3 years ago			+ 6,000		6,000
4 years ago		-2,000	+ 6,000		4,000
5 years ago	_____	-4,000	+ 6,000	_____	2,000
Total	$10,000	-$6,000	$30,000	$6,000	$40,000

TIP: Check whether a business has credit cards. Check the balances. Use of credit card for routine purchases can be a dangerous and costly practice. One "add back" I look for is interest charges included on various invoices. Often interest is charged on late accounts payable, which inflates the cost of goods. And interest is sometimes charged on credit card purchases, as in the landscape contracting company mentioned in the second case history. If you feel you can arrange to pay your bills on time, all the interest charges are hidden earnings.

Of course, the "weightings" and look-back periods would change, if change seems indicated. For example, you may feel that a look-back period of only three years is more realistic. As seen on Table 6, weighted average earnings are $28,800 for the full five-year look-back period. Doozy's weighted earnings for the past three years average are $33,000, which is 14.6 percent higher. But +14.6 percent is still significant.[34] Actual earnings (unweighted) for the most recent three years are even higher: $33,333 per year. Which "earnings" figures to use is a matter of judgment.

---

[34] To calculate $33,000, use a 3-2-1 weighting. Add ($28,000 × 3) or $84,000 + (32,000 × 2) or $64,000 + 40,000 × 1 or 40,000 = 198,000. Then, $198,000 ÷ 6 = $33,000. Other weighting may also be useful.

Table 6. Calculation of Adjusted and Weighted Earnings

	Reported Earnings	Adjustments to Earnings	Actual Earnings		Weight		Weighted Earnings
Last year	$12,000	+$16,000	$28,000	×	5	=	$140,000
2 years ago	20,000	+ 12,000	32,000	×	4	=	128,000
3 years ago	34,000	+ 6,000	40,000	×	3	=	120,000
4 years ago	10,000	+ 4,000	14,000	×	2	=	28,000
5 years ago	14,000	+ 2,000	16,000	×	1	=	16,000
	$90,000	+$40,000	$130,000		15		$432,000
							÷ 15
Weighted Average Earnings After Adjustments							**$28,800**

Suggestion—try using different weightings and look-back periods to see the effect on weighted average earnings. Try it for Doozy and for any other business you are looking at. If the three-year look-back period seems more appropriate, we could use a weighting of 5-3-1 as used in Table 2. The 5-3-1 weighting indicates weighted average earnings of $30,667, just 6.5 percent above the $28,800 shown in Table 6.

Can you feel secure in offering to buy Doozy for $115,200, the value we get after making adjustments to income? Would the Seller accept $115,200? Maybe we should use the three-year weighted average earnings of $30,667, which at 4:1 indicates a value of $122,668, or the unweighted three-year average of $33,333. Not quite yet! There is a little more work to do before we can answer that question.

First, it is wise to review the company's expenses again, particularly expenses for the past year, since it is quite important to be able to conclude with conviction what percentage of sales the actual pretax earnings are (and could be in future years). To do this, it is very helpful to review the monthly financial statements, especially for the past year. Second, as we discuss in the next section of this chapter, we must not rely solely upon the income approach to value; we must take a good look at the asset value of the business, as well.

Second Review: Review of Monthly Statements

Our second review focuses on Doozy's **monthly** expenses, whereas the initial review looked only at **annual** expenses. We reviewed employee compensation expenditures first since that is the largest single expense account. As we looked, we tried to note any large deviations from the average monthly compensation expense. We discovered that "payroll" as a percent of reported sales in December, the last month of the fiscal year, seems to have jumped. We asked the broker why payroll had jumped. He explained that Doozy paid a $3,000 bonus to the owner's wife on the thirtieth of December last year.[35]

As seen below on Table 7, employee wages for the year are $78,000, an average of $6,500 per month, or 25 percent of sales. However, in December payroll expenses are—in round numbers—$9,500, or 46 percent, above the monthly average. This deviation was the result of the $3,000 bonus—not of employee profit sharing, as originally thought. Note also the $15,000 depreciation expense shown at the bottom of Table 7. Since the "excess" depreciation of $10,000 is included in the earnings adjustments in Table 5, the depreciation expense shown on a restated income statement would be only $5,000.

To help with the monthly review, see if the broker has a spreadsheet of monthly expenses. If not, ask for copies of the monthly "financials" and create your own spreadsheet. It can help you spot other large onetime charges (possible positive adjustment) or, perhaps, unpaid bills (possible negative adjustment). If the sales, cost of goods, and expenses are posted correctly, you should expect that the bottom line, the pretax income, to be a constant (or nearly constant) percent of sales. One thing to look for on the monthly spreadsheet is any kind of expense that occurs only once or twice a year, such as depreciation or insurance. An annual insurance premium of, say, $5,000 may be paid all in one month. As a result, that month may show a very low income. Likewise, the premium could have been prepaid during the previous December. This will result in the income for the succeeding months appearing to be unrealistically high.

---

[35] Looking at the financial statement for the twelfth month of the fiscal year can be very helpful since expenses that month tend to reflect the owner's desire to pay bonuses when possible and to reduce taxable income.

Table 7. Doozy Manufacturing Company
Statement of Income and Expenses

Sales (checks received and deposited)	**$300,000**
Less—cost of materials and shop supplies at 24%	<u>72,000</u>
Gross profit	**$228,000**
Expenses	
Owner's salary	$48,000
Employee wages, including bonuses	78,000
Payroll taxes (9.85% of wages and salaries)	12,800
Rent (4,000 sq. feet at $4.50/sq. foot)	18,000
Insurance (medical, general liability, and auto)	10,000
Utilities	14,400
Telephones	4,200
Office supplies	2,400
Taxes and Licenses, including personal property and gross receipts taxes	2,600
Gasoline (two vehicles)	3,000
Advertising (including yellow pages directory)	2,600
Part-time (vacation) employees (see note 1)	4,000
All other expenses (see note 2)	<u>1,000</u>
Subtotal	**$201,000**
Depreciation (Section 179 expense of van):	15,000
Total expenses	**$216,000**
Income (pretax)	**$12,000**

Note 1—**Calculate** vacation for 4 employees × 2 weeks = 8 weeks × 40 hours = 320 hours at $12.50/hour = $4,000

Note 2—Include interest on used van purchased in June for $15,000. **Calculate:** $15,000 at 6% = $900 ÷ 2 = $450

It seems clear that this $3,000 "bonus" should be added to the $28,800 earnings previously calculated for last year (see Table 6), so the adjustments are now $19,000 and adjusted earnings appear to be $31,800.[36] A deeper look at other expense accounts may reveal additional "nonoperating expenses" that would increase actual earnings more, but none appear significant except, per-

---

[36] To be conservative in putting a final value on Doozy, it may be wise not to use the highest of the indicated estimates of pretax earnings found so far: $28,000, $28,800, $30,667, $31,800, $33,000 and $33,333.

98

haps, the $450 paid in interest on the new van. This is a nonrecurring expense that a buyer will not have. See Note 2 above at the bottom of Table 7.

With this last adjustment, the adjusted pretax income for the last year is $31,800, or 10.6 percent, of sales—well above the 4 percent calculated using the $12,000 shown on the statement of income and expenses. See Tables 3 and 7 for reference. Using the 4:1 P:E again and the estimated $31,800 earnings, we now have an indicated value for Doozy of $127,200. Keep in mind that the $31,800 is after deducting $5,000 in depreciation expenses.

Calculate: $31,800 × 4 = $127,200 estimated valuation

Perhaps with more digging, you may find additional positive adjustments! Aren't you glad you took a deeper look at Doozy? Ten other buyers had looked at Doozy and quickly lost interest because reported earnings looked too low. These buyers had failed to restate Doozy's earnings or her net worth.

Suggestion—after making adjustments to Doozy's income statement, examine the spreadsheet in the Appendix for Bigger Manufacturing Co., a cabinet manufacturer with annual sales over $4,000,000. Bigger has a large showroom and sells to the retail public as well as to contractors. What "add backs" are indicated and what would the indicated pretax income be after making adjustments? Examine each line item carefully. Bigger appears to have had a negative operating income in five of the past seven years. In three of those seven years, it wasn't even able to pay the owner a salary, yet it was appraised at over $1,000,000 and paid its owner and the owner's children combined salaries of $356,423 in the most recent year.

Owner Compensation

A logical first step in "recasting" a financial statement is to review owner compensation. No adjustment was included (in Table 5) for Doozy's owner's salary because it ($48,000) seemed in line with compensation paid at similar businesses in that year. However, if Doozy had paid its owner a base salary of $78,000 instead of $48,000 and no adjustment were made, the company would have shown a profit in only two of the last five years and would appear to be worth much less than $124,000.

Start by selecting a reasonable owner's salary (and benefit package) for the market in which the business is located and adjust reported earnings upward or downward accordingly.[37] With Bigger, for example, we might have begun the *recasting process* by inserting salaries of $40,000, $45,000, $50,000, $55,000, $60,000, $65,000, and $70,000 for the seven years shown on the spreadsheet. Since it is a larger company than Doozy, the manager/owner at Bigger should be expected to earn a salary considerably higher than the manager/owner at Doozy. Making these (or similar) adjustments would give a much more realistic picture of Bigger's actual earnings.

TIP: You can find comparable salaries by visiting useful Web sites like *salaries.com* and *cbsalary.com*. The latter, for example, says that a lathe operator/woodworking earns (in March 2009) on average $24,093 nationally and $22,951 ($11.25/hour) in Memphis. A shop manager nationally earns $51,277 and $44,455 in Macon, Georgia. In Los Angeles, shop manager salaries ranged from $42,207 to $77,750, with an average of $56,091.

Other compensation issues involve employee wages, accrued wages, vacation pay, and the timing of "making" payroll. Study the following case history.

---

[37] A caution for buyers is that sellers understandably resist buyers who pay themselves more compensation than the down payment that the sellers receive.

Case History – BIWEEKLY PAYROLL ISSUE

After submitting an offer on behalf of a buyer, the Seller gave me a copy of his latest monthly income statement that I, in turn, shared with the buyer. Earnings were almost $7,000 less than in the prior month. The buyer became anxious and asked that I withdraw his offer and return his earnest money check. I urged him to give me a chance to discover why earnings appeared to drop so sharply. He agreed. It turned out that (1) the business paid its employees every two weeks and (2) there were three pay periods in the past month. After adjustments were made, the past month's recast income actually was $20,000 and exceeded the prior month's recast income by $9,000. The buyer was pleased, and the sale went through as planned. The prior month had payroll expenses of $48,000 (rounded). The recent month had payroll expenses of $72,000 (rounded). Adjusting for the twenty-six biweekly payrolls in a year of $24,000, normalized payroll would be about $52,000 month.

Calculate: ($24,000 × 26 weeks = $624,000) ÷ 12 months = $52,000

Moral – always ask. When in doubt, check it out.

Missing Financial Statements

Some smaller businesses do not have published financial statements. Sometimes, the most recent financial statements are several years old and have not been reviewed, even by the owner, for accuracy. While this can be unsettling, particularly to a first-time buyer, other useful financial documents can be found for almost any business. These might include:

1. State sales tax report forms (almost every business must file them).
2. Copies of the business's bank statements and cancelled checks (look at the **general ledger** if checks are computerized).
3. Copies of local property tax and federal income tax forms.
4. Copies of invoices from suppliers, phone, and utility companies.
5. Copies of lease agreements with landlords and insurance policies.
6. Quarterly or monthly payroll reports showing wages, payroll taxes, and withholding and the annual W-2, W-3, and W-4 forms sent to the Internal Revenue Service.

From these documents, a fairly accurate picture of most small businesses will emerge. These documents, however, cannot be assumed to be 100 percent accurate. Instead, they give a picture of what is happening over time. If, for example, monthly purchases from suppliers are higher (in excess of price increases or general inflation) in the current year than in prior years, it can be assumed that sales are growing and, conversely, if purchases are lower, that sales are declining.

If the financial statements are missing, they cannot be recast. Instead, they are compiled from scratch from deposit slips and checks, a process that may produce a more accurate picture of the financial condition of a company than the *recasting process.* Compiling financial statements is not as time consuming as it may seem; the typical small business may write fewer than twenty checks per month and may employ a payroll service, so there is only one payroll check per pay period. While preparing the compilation, check industry data to learn typical gross profit margins, sales per employee, sales per square foot, and typical ratios. Most small businesses in similar industries will have very similar data.

TIP: Learn how the financial statements are prepared and who posts the checks to the various accounts. Some charges may not be posted to the proper account, but more importantly to you, when you review individual checks, you may discover that some accounts include some unusual entries. I have seen country club dues posted under office supplies and children's dental bills posted under medical expenses. A check-by-check review can be very instructive.

PART II.
ADJUSTMENTS TO NET WORTH[38]

These adjustments involve company balance sheets. The previous adjustments involved company income statements. Doozy is reported by its broker to have tangible assets worth $100,000. How could it be possible to buy a business for only $48,000 or $75,000, the preliminary estimates of value, when a business has assets worth $100,000? The answer is that you can't, because a prudent owner, acting in his own self-interest, could liquidate the business for the value of the assets. There is normally little incentive to sell for a price less than asset value or the value that an orderly liquidation would bring.

To reconcile a disparity between **earnings value** of a business and its **asset value**, we must adjust (or recast) the values shown on its balance sheet.[39] There are many things to analyze in Doozy's case. If Doozy's accountant had elected to take rapid depreciation, some assets (such as the delivery van) may be worth more than their present book value. On the other hand, some items of inventory may be old or obsolete and have a market or liquidation values well below their book value, the value shown on the balance sheet, or below their original cost.

A business's **adjusted asset value** would be its minimum transfer price if that value were higher than the earnings value. Any business should be worth its adjusted asset value because you or the owner should be able to liquidate the assets at close to this price. In my experience, most businesses have assets that are not fully reflected on their balance sheets and those businesses may, therefore, be worth considerably more than their net worth or, if the seller retains the liabilities, more than the book value of the assets. When speaking of a possible stock sale, the minimum transfer price would be the **adjusted net worth** (or net asset value).

Let's take a look below at Doozy's simplified balance sheet to see if we can determine what its **adjusted asset value** might be. It appears that some values are understated and that some important assets are not shown on its balance sheet

---

[38] The term *net worth* refers to the net book value of a business: its assets less its liabilities. It is shown on the balance sheet. After making adjustments, we can calculate a business's "adjusted net worth." Remember not to confuse a business's fair market value with its net worth. They may be quite different. See Glossary.

[39] The seller should consider that there are costs involved in liquidating, such as legal and sales fees and generally some ongoing operating expenses. Sellers sometimes say that they could liquidate their business for more than a buyer is offering, but often they do not consider the expenses associated with liquidation.

at all. We also find that several classes of liabilities are unreported, but the net balance sheet adjustments (the difference between the reported book value and the market value) found are close to the $40,000 in positive income adjustments found in Part I of this chapter and shown on Table 5. This confirms our feeling that Doozy has "hidden" income.

Table 8. Doozy's Simplified Balance Sheet

Type of Asset	Book Value	Market Value	Adjustment (+ or -)
Accounts receivable	$15,000	$9,000	-$6,000
Raw materials and finished goods	40,000	50,000	+10,000
Prepaid insurance	1,000	0	-1,000
Vehicles—depreciated	6,000	16,000	+10,000
Equipment less Depreciation	0	17,000	+7,000
Miscellaneous dies	0	4,000	+4,000
Miscellaneous tools	0	4,000	+4,000
Customer contracts	0	??	??
Subtotal	$62,000	$100,000	$38,000
Type of liability[40]			
Accounts payable	$12,000	$15,000	+$3,000
Accrued salaries	0	3,500	+3,500
Accrued taxes	0	1,400	+1,400
Accrued interest	0	100	+100
Note to bank	15,000	15,000	0
Subtotal	27,000	35,000	8,000
Net worth/value	**$35,000**	**$65,000**	**$30,000**

---

[40] If Doozy is holding customer deposits, they must be shown as liabilities because they will have to be repaid if the work is not performed. Also, accrued payables, such as accrued salaries and earned vacation, must be considered. It would be awkward (as well as unfair) if several employees opt to take vacation immediately after a business is sold and the seller expects the buyer to assume this expense. The normal rule is, "Expenses incurred by a business prior to closing are paid by the seller (unless a contract states otherwise)."

TIP: When attempting to value the FF&E (which may have zero value on the company balance sheet), check the insurance coverage. It is rare for a company to overinsure, or to issue a policy based on inflated asset values. Many policies include a detailed list of the specific assets that are covered in a policy.

The assets shown on the balance sheet seem to have a fair market value of $100,000, the value indicated in the brief profile that the broker prepared for prospective purchasers. A physical inspection of the plant quickly leads to the conclusion that several classes of quite valuable assets are not carried on the balance sheet at all. They were not mentioned by the broker or listed in the profile. They include the first four assets shown below and possibly the fifth:

1.   Unbilled work-in-process (or work-in-progress)
2.   Shop and office tools and supplies
3.   Display items (often found in showrooms)
4.   Customer contracts (work orders) for future delivery of goods
5.   Prepaid insurance premiums

The first category, unbilled work-in-process, is perhaps the easiest to value because this "work" is already sold. From a "walk-through" inspection, it is obvious that the shop is full of partially completed cabinets, part of several rather large jobs for which Doozy has firm, written contracts. Some cabinets are complete except for the doors; others are complete except for painting or other finish. Still others are in an initial stage of fabrication. Work-in-process is easy to value for Doozy. It may be more difficult to value in a noncontract manufacturing business.

After reviewing the jobs in the shop, the owner discloses that they have a combined contract price/value of $30,000 and are 75 percent complete, a value of $22,500. We cannot assign the entire $22,500 to this asset because Doozy, like all companies, must earn a profit. After some thought, it is concluded that a fair market value would be 70 percent of the contract (or completion value), or $15,750.[41]

---

[41]   Normally, these calculations cannot be made very accurately at this stage in conversations with a seller. Sellers are reluctant to reveal this much detail or to take the time to make these calculations with every potential buyer. Instead, when a purchase contract is prepared, the contract will include language such as the following: "This contract is contingent upon there being on hand at time of closing unbilled

The shop and office supplies take somewhat longer to value since there are many different categories to count or inspect. The broker, based upon his experience with other companies of a similar size, feels that a value of $10,000 will be quite conservative. The broker adds, helpfully, that the buyer can always reserve the right in a formal purchase offer to count and value each class of "on-balance sheet" and "off-balance sheet" assets.[42] In this manner, the final sale price of the business will be adjusted if any of the assets have been sold or removed from the business prior to the completion of a sale.

The displays in the Doozy showroom are quite minimal and would be difficult to sell. In larger business, the displays are often quite expensive to build and install. The point to remember is that the seller paid for the displays from the cash flow of the business. If the seller had not purchased (or built) the displays, a buyer might have to, but in the case of Doozy, assigning no extra value seems OK.

The fourth class of "missing" assets is customer contracts. Many businesses, especially retail businesses, do not have customer contracts. In contrast, service companies may do all their business by contract. Since Doozy is a custom manufacturer, it does all of its business by contract. Contracts describe the job to be done and set out a price and terms of payment, a date for completion or delivery of the finished products, and perhaps a penalty for late delivery. They may also require a deposit due when the order is placed.

Doozy has $80,000 worth of written work orders on the books (a ninety-day backlog based on annual sales of $320,000) in addition to the work-in-progress. In some businesses, contracts (such as contracts for janitorial services or cell phone service) are billed monthly and may be cancelled at almost any time. Their value depends largely upon the terms of cancellation. By contrast, Doozy's contracts (work orders) are onetime contracts and are noncancelable. So if they were negotiated at a price that includes a reasonable profit, they have value.

Since Doozy's **profit margin** (pretax) is around 10 percent, we can assume that the orders "on the books" will also produce a 10 % profit, or about $8,000. If this future profit is valued at a P:E of 4:1, it could be worth $32,000.[43] The

---

work-in-process of $15,750, valued at 70 percent of seller's contract price." The seller may feel that 80 percent is fairer, so this becomes a point of negotiation.

[42] Many brokers, particularly in the case of somewhat larger businesses, include in their profile or other offering document a detailed listing of all assets in a business with market values or replacement costs.

[43] The amount $32,000 may seem like a high price to pay for contracts. Yet in many industries, contacts are sold to other firms (that may need to fill in some work). Also, these contracts have been negotiated and sales commissions paid, saving a buyer these costs. In the case of Doozy, the $32,000 is part of the goodwill that the buyer of the company will receive.

method for valuing contracts differs by industry. For example, in the security alarm industry, the rule of thumb is to use a percent of annual or monthly billing. The key is to verify that the contracts were not accepted at too low a price to produce a profit for the buyer.

TIP: Sometimes, but rarely, business owners are anxious to demonstrate that their businesses are healthy and take on new contracts at very low prices, prices that have no profit. If the backlog of orders appears to have spiked recently, some form of additional analysis may be in order before setting a value on contracts for new work. If at the same time the balance of accounts receivable outstanding in the sixty-day or ninety-day column has increased more rapidly than sales, it is possible that these "new" sales have been made to less than creditworthy customers. This could certainly be a red flag.

The value of Doozy's assets (including accounts receivable but excluding cash) may now be roughly summarized as follows:

Fair Market Value of Assets on Books	**$100,000**
Value of assets not on books	
1. Value of work-in-progress	15,750
2. Value of supplies-estimate	10,000
3. Value of unperformed contracts-estimate	32,000
Estimated Total Asset Value	**$157,750**

Suggestion—after reviewing the balance sheet of any business and compiling a rough list of assets that may be included in a sale, ask the seller (or ask your broker to ask the seller) two important questions:

1. Are there any assets used in the business that you (the seller) intend to keep?
2. Are there any assets used in the business that you own outside of the business, that is, assets that were never put on the company balance sheet? A truck, for example, that is titled in your (the owner's) name.

The answers are often very revealing. Many owners want to exclude a company vehicle (if they do not own a personal car), computer, desk, clock, or memorabilia. It is difficult to know the right time to ask these questions, but they should be asked long before the closing. Let me share another story.

Case History – REMOVING ASSETS (WITHOUT INFORMING BUYER)

After a contract had been signed and the closing date set, the buyer walked through the plant with a list of FF&E that seller had provided. The buyer wanted to learn if the assets were still "in use," and he proceeded to check off on the list each asset that he found. When he got to the seller's office, he checked off the executive desk. The seller said that the desk was not included in the sale; it had been his father's. The buyer said okay and proceeded down the list. He asked if the clock on the wall was included. Again, the seller said no. And, then he asked about the computer. The seller said no a third time. At this point, the buyer thanked the seller for his time and went home. The next day, he called and said he no longer wanted to buy the business because the seller had misrepresented several things. He added, "If there are this many "misrepresentations," there are probably others as well."

Lesson for Buyers: It is difficult for some sellers to part with "personal" items that are used or housed at the business. Removing them does not greatly affect or diminish the value of a business, so ask for a replacement allowance.

The three preceding balance sheet adjustments for unrecorded assets are not intended to constitute a complete valuation or appraisal. They are simply intended to assist buyers in making a preliminary estimate of the kinds and quantities of assets that would be conveyed in a sale of a business. This information is rarely obvious from looking at the Balance Sheet or other business records. Of course, the kinds, quantities, and mix of assets vary from business to business and industry to industry, but the quantities and values discussed for Doozy are realistic.

In the balance sheet review, no adjustments were made for unrecorded liabilities because only the assets are being offered for purchase. In other situations, a detailed review of the liability side of the Balance Sheet would be in order, especially when a buyer is considering a stock purchase. Also, no adjustment was made for prepaid insurance because the total premiums of $10,000 paid in the past year (refer back to Table 7) seem in line with costs. Often, however, some portion of the premiums are prepaid and should appear on the asset side of the recast balance sheet. If Doozy's insurance expenses had been, say, $20,000 instead of $10,000, further review would be indicated.

TIP: There may be attachments to a set of financial statements that no one has mentioned. At some point during your review, ask if there are any schedules, accountant's notes, or an opinion letter accompanying (and therefore an integral part of) the statements. These can be very instructive. Sometimes, the person preparing copies is simply in a hurry and only makes copies of the income statements. There should always be a balance sheet and cash flow statement.

PART III
SELECTION OF INDICATED EARNINGS
MULTIPLE FOR DOOZY

Using the SBA guideline of four times restated earnings, Doozy may be worth $115,000 to $125,000—depending upon the look-back period selected and other factors discussed in Part I or Part II above. It now appears, however, that we could use a valuation guideline (earnings multiple) of five times earnings because the restated earnings are much more stable and predictable than the reported earnings originally appeared. The asset value we have uncovered so far seems to support a higher valuation for the business as well.

It appears that Doozy's earnings are, in actuality, growing (as a percent of sales). This is a key indicator of value since it may indicate that the company is operating more efficiently or that its products are of such a quality that they command a higher price in the marketplace. Growing businesses, whether the growth is in profit margins or in "top line" sales, quite logically should sell at a higher multiple of earnings, or P:E, than businesses that show no growth. Why? Because future earnings will probably exceed the historic earnings.

Doozy's adjusted earnings of $31,000 ($28,000 plus bonus) for last year are almost double the adjusted earnings ($16,000) from five years ago. And earnings for the last three years now appear to average almost 11 percent of sales, even though reported annual sales have declined from their peak three years ago. This is quite an improvement from the **profit margins** shown on Table 3 and from the 4–6 percent margins shown below for the two oldest years. With this promising picture, a P:E ratio greater than 4:1 may be in order.

Table 9. Adjusted Earnings (Unweighted) as Percent of Sales

	Adjusted Earnings	Reported Sales	Percent of Sales
Last year	$31,000	$300,000	10.33%
Two years ago	32,000	320,000	10.00%
Three years ago	40,000	340,000	11.76%
Four years ago	14,000	300,000	4.67%
Five years ago	16,000	264,000	6.00%
	$133,000	**$1,524,000**	**8.72%**

Adjusted earnings in recent years look quite stable as a percent of sales. Perhaps the owner has learned some important lessons. We can therefore assume with a relatively high degree of comfort that future earnings will be 10 percent of sales or more. It is also comforting to learn that Doozy can achieve 10 percent of sales even when the owner has apparently spent some time away from the business. Perhaps, if the new owner were to spend more time at the business (than the present owner), sales would begin to increase again.[44]

The average margin of earnings (see Percent of Sales) is considerably higher for the three-year look-back period (10.73 %) than it is for the five-year look-back period (8.72 %). While the difference between 10.73 % and 8.72 % seems to be only 2 %, remember that 10.73 % is actually 23 % greater than 8.72. And the 10.33 % achieved last year is 76 % higher than 6.0 % achieved five years ago. These are highly significant differences. The following calculations use data from Table 9.

Calculate: Adjusted Earnings divided by total sales for five years:
$$\$133,000 \div \$1,524,000 = 8.72\% \text{ of sales}$$

Calculate: Adjusted Earnings divided by total sales for three years:
$$\$103,000 \div \$960,000 = 10.73\% \text{ of sales}$$

If a 5:1 P:E ratio now seems warranted, the income value of Doozy is in the range of $150,000 to $170,000, much more than the $100,000 estimated market value of the tangible assets and close to the estimated $157,750 asset value.[45] Both estimates of value are in the range of the asking price of $160,000. We can calculate these values in several ways: (1) multiplying last year's restated earnings of $31,000 by five to suggest a value of $153,000 or (2) multiplying the $34,333, average actual earnings for the last three years ($103,000 ÷ 3), by five to suggest a value of $171,666.

---

[44] A word of caution about time spent on the job—a current owner can make the operation of a business seem almost effortless because the products, markets served, and operating procedures are so familiar. Even the simplest task may take a new owner much longer. Every buyer seems to start with the assumption that he or she can "do a better job" than the previous owner. It is easy to see what the owner has done wrong. It is sometimes difficult to see what he has done right.

[45] A word of caution about which earnings multiple to use—when interest rates go down, the multiple tends higher, and when rates go up, the multiple tends lower. Example, at a price of $150,000, assuming all the money was borrowed, 10 percent interest would be $15,000, almost half of Doozy's restated earnings. At 5 percent, interest would be only $7,500.

Here, we have two income values: (1) $153,000 and (2) $171,666. Should we rely on the one derived from last year's earnings alone, or the one representing an average of several years? Should these values be given different weights? Arguments could be made both ways, so in this case, a simple average of the two income values seems indicated.

Average of Income Values for Three- and Five-Year Periods

Calculate: $153,000 + 171,666 = $324,666 ÷ 2 = $162,333

With the higher valuation now indicated, there is a goodwill value of $50–60,000, which is about one third of Doozy's indicated fair market value. This seems in line with the spread between the present market value of the tangible assets (equipment, inventory, supplies, and financial assets) and the intangible assets (goodwill) found in other small but well-established cabinet manufacturers.

Since the values indicated seem to support each other, it is probably not necessary to do other value analyses. However, an experienced broker or industry group can provide information regarding the third basic valuation method: the market approach to value or **comparable sales method**—i.e. prices at which similar companies have recently sold. Such information is always helpful if available. But remember, because each business is unique, the user of such "comparable" sales data must be alert to the need to adjust the data of a comparable business to the subject business (in this case, Doozy) before drawing any conclusion about value.

The market approach is used extensively in valuing real estate but is used less in valuing businesses. In most real estate markets, we have at hand information that lets us test the validity of market data. We can determine the location and the square footage of a house. So we know that two houses on the same street should sell for about the same price if they are about the same size (square footage) and in comparable physical condition. If one house is offered for a substantially higher price, it probably has more square footage. But if, for example, two coin-op laundries are for sale (one for $100,000 and another for $200,000), we do not know how to explain the difference in values so easily.

Suggestion—if you like a business and the owner insists that it has been profitable but you cannot confirm a positive earnings history, ask the seller for his personal net worth statement. If the seller has owned his company for a long time and says that he has made a lot of money, these "earnings" should show up in a robust personal net worth. Simply observing the size of house the seller lives in and the cars his family drives will not indicate net worth because it will not indicate the level of debt the seller has. This suggestion should be undertaken cautiously and at the right time, probably after your original offer to purchase has been declined.

The process of adjusting earnings and net worth can seem almost endless to first-time buyers. For other buyers, the process is quite quick; they may already have certain yardsticks (purchase criteria) in mind. They want a small manufacturing business with at least a ten-year track record and with excess capacity that they can buy for no more than 35 percent of annual sales. And they want an annual return on their investment (ROI) of at least 30 percent after all expenses, including taxes. What yardsticks would define an attractive business for you?

If different values have been found through the use of different methods, it is always useful to find some way to rank or weight the different values. Should some values be discarded? Should some be weighted more highly than others? The process of reconciling values can be very useful, particularly if the values differ substantially. Remember, though, that value is based far more on future earnings than on the historic earnings.

PART IV
ACCURACY OF FINANCIAL STATEMENTS

The prime objective of analyzing financial statements is to determine their accuracy and, ultimately, their reliability. Let's face it: the financial statements of many small businesses, as stated earlier in Chapter 1, are not very accurate. Little time and attention goes into their preparation except for purposes of reporting income to the federal government. However, the statements may be very reliable—that is to say, we can figure them out with a little effort. A lot of people beside yourself will need to rely upon them: your bank or other lender and your suppliers, that is, the people that you want to extend credit to you. One key to reliability is to see if statements are prepared in a "consistent" manner year over year and month over month.

Another important objective of the *review process* is to get a feeling for what a business is really doing and to see if it can meet your goals. Are costs under control? Have costs risen more rapidly than revenue? Is revenue growing? Is the business making money? And does it have a positive cash flow? Are there changes that could be made that would increase earnings or cash flow in the future? These are all important questions but have little to do with accuracy.

What is meant by *consistent*? This term is often heard but rarely explained. I look for several things, such as the following nine. Apply them to any business you are looking at. How many "yeses" and how many "nos" would you count? A lot of "nos" will make it difficult to determine profitability.

1. Are the statements for different years prepared in the same manner? Are the monthly statements prepared in the same manner as the annual statements?

2. Did the same person prepare the statements for each of the periods reviewed? Did the person who prepared the internal statements also prepare the year-end federal tax returns?

3. If statements (or tax returns) were prepared by a CPA, ask if company has used the same CPA for several years. Has the company frequently changed CPAs?

4. Do figures on the annual federal tax return match figures on the company's income statement and balance sheet? Are there obvious reasons for any discrepancies?

5. Do the financial statements match the company's bank statements? If not, are the reasons obvious?

6. Do the "retained earnings" shown on the most recent balance sheet equal the sum of the equity on the prior balance sheet plus the pretax earnings on the current income statement?

7. Does the cost of goods on the income statement reflect changes in the value (amount) of inventory? Sometimes inventory is only valued at the end of the year for tax reporting purposes, so new inventory is not put on the internal monthly financial statements.

8. Is the depreciation account posted in a consistent manner from period to period? Sometimes depreciation is only taken at the end of the year, making it difficult to compare financial results from different periods.

9. If a certain expense item is accrued on one income statement, is it also accrued on other statements?

All of these are good questions to keep in mind, but be wary of getting bogged down in too much detail. Too much analysis can lead to paralysis, as has been said many times. Try to stay focused on what you are trying to learn—that is, will the business, in your opinion, in the future earn enough to meet your financial objectives?

In Doozy's case, the net effect of the *review process* was positive: **adjusted earnings** exceeded **reported earnings**. It was relatively easy to make the adjustments necessary to "recast" the year-over-year earnings into a consistent format because the financial statements are essentially accurate. But in many businesses, this is not so. Review the case histories below. Adjusted earnings may be much less than reported earnings. Looking, for example, at Case number 1, if the equipment used in the rental fleet were written down (depreciated), as it should be, adjusted earnings would be much less than the reported earnings.

CASE HISTORIES: OVERSTATED EARNINGS

Case No. 1 Heavy Equipment Sales and Rentals

A heavy equipment sales and rental company reported over $500,000 in pretax income on its most recent year-to-date financial statement and over $700,000 for the last full year. This seemed a most attractive trend to a group of potential buyers. It turned out, however, that the reported numbers were misleading because the owner had not written down (or depreciated) the book values of some of the new equipment that he had been using in his rental fleet. After deducting appropriate depreciation charges, it was determined that the income, at best, was a breakeven.

Moral – check (1) whether depreciation has been taken in the current year and (2) whether book values of rental equipment and other depreciable assets have been written down.

Case No. 2 Small Retail Shop

The owner of a small retail business proudly handed me his latest year-to-date financial statement. It showed a significant increase in profit. After scanning the statement, it became clear that rent for the last month had not been paid and payroll for the last week had not been posted. Instead of the $10,000 profit shown, true monthly profit was closer to average monthly earnings of $5,000.

Moral – check obvious expenses on monthly statements. Often they have not been posted (through no intent by the owner to misrepresent company earnings).

TIP: a buyer's adjustment process is for his edification, not for the seller's. While it is intended to confirm the representations that a seller has made concerning his business, it is not intended to educate the seller, that is, to show the seller that his business has in reality earned more than he thought it had earned or may be worth more to you than he is willing to sell it for.

The next three case histories involving embezzlement illustrate this point. Of course, embezzlement is the product of lack of adequate financial controls or oversight by the owner. It bears repeating that keeping accurate books and records is not instinctive to most first-generation owners; they are focused on running and growing their businesses. Only later do they find that their lack of oversight became obvious to employees, some of whom found ways to take advantage of the situations.

CASE HISTORIES: UNDERSTATED EARNINGS

Case No. 1 Liquor Store

While the owner was attempting to sell his store, we asked why the reported gross profit margins seemed so low. Since he used industry standard "markups," the gross profit margin should have been considerably higher than the reported margin. The owner was at a loss to explain this. We thought some of the money was being spent for nonoperating expenses or, perhaps, for bottles given away as promotional items. With low margins month after month, we were unable to sell the store. Some months later, the owner called to tell me that my questions had spurred him to look more closely at the daily sales reports. There, he found the obvious answer: a longtime employee was not ringing up all the sales. Instead of putting the sales proceeds into the cash register, the employee was putting the proceeds of the unrecorded sales into his pocket.

Lesson for buyers—a business showing little profit on paper may, in fact, be quite profitable.

Case No. 2 Restaurant and Bar

This bar was located near a university and was constantly packed but showed no profit. The cost of goods seemed much too high. In fact, one month COGS reached almost 90 percent. (COGS should have ranged between 25–35 percent.) The owner seemed at a loss to explain this so I invited a restaurant man to join me for drinks at the bar one evening. This is what we found: the place was crowded as usual. Everyone was having trouble getting service. Students kept coming in to "work" the evening shift and, we soon discovered, kept leaving shortly thereafter. They simply had gone back to the kitchen, eaten a free meal, and soon left for their evening classes. No wonder service was slow and the cost of goods so high.

Moral – financial statements do not have the last word when determining if a business is viable or attractive.

Case No. 3 Forklift Distributor

The owner of this well-established, growing business wanted to retire. The financial statements, month after month, showed reasonable earnings, but the cash balances in various accounts were declining. The owner was convinced that the statements were being properly prepared. Operating expenses seemed in line. Purchases seemed in line also. Finally, I asked the bookkeeper to run a cash flow statement. For many months, she declined to do so. It turned out that she was reversing the depreciation charges on older trucks in the rental fleet, thereby creating fictional profits. It appeared to me that she had taken the cash.

Moral – financial statements should have three components: the P&L, the balance sheet, and the cash flow statement. Ask to see all three and review them. They should be in agreement.

Business owners are often unaware of misstated earnings. For many owners, it made little difference what the statements showed until time to prepare the annual tax returns or to offer the business for sale. Some misstatements are from recent reporting periods, but many have "been on the books" for a long time. Doozy, for example, carried several bad (uncollectible) accounts receivable on its books for several years. Some companies carry hundreds of thousands of dollars of uncollectible accounts on their balance sheets. Some carry inventories that are widely under- or overstated.

Sometimes, if financial statements seem to contain many inconsistencies, the best way to proceed is to ignore prior years and concentrate instead on the current year. Simply reconstruct the books for the current year check by check and account by account. This is not as onerous as it might seem. Expenses for many accounts can be "reconstructed" from source data like leases, utility and phone bills, and insurance policies. Accountants call this process of reconstructing financial records "forensic accounting."[46] They don't seem to like to do it, preferring, in my experience, to rely largely on "published" reports.

The more obvious reasons for misstated earnings are listed below. Some produce negative adjustments and others positive adjustments to earnings.

1. **Pilferage** of cash, supplies, or inventory (by owners, employees, or customers) *positive*

---

[46] Forensic accounting is a little like archeology; the archeologist has to guess the shape of a pot from the pieces he can find. Accountants have to "reconstruct" financial statements from what they can find or surmise.

2. **Embezzlement** of cash or equivalent—*positive.*

3. **Inventory issues**—inventories may not have been fully or accurately counted in years: *positive or negative.*

4. **Unpaid bills**—lags in posting accounts payable or checks. Sometimes checks have been written but not mailed, and bank balances appear favorable: *negative.*

5. **Employee benefits**—mandatory bonuses, vacation pay, and retirement plan contributions are not booked as expenses. Few small businesses audit these accounts consistently: *negative.*

6. **Prepayment of expenses**—many businesses do this at the end of the year to reduce taxable income: *positive.*

7. **Payment of personal and family expenses**—this is the matter of nonoperating expenses. Always ask the owner (or broker) to list them; they can add up: *positive.*

8. **Lags in booking sales or purchases** of new items of inventory—this makes the reported inventory appear lower than it really is: *positive.*

9. **Extravagant or unnecessary purchases** by owners—one owner of a modest business spent $6,000 for the "executive" desk in his office: *positive.*

10. **Bookkeeping errors**—expenses for similar items are posted to different (incorrect) accounts over many months: *neutral.*

11. **Inventory accounting practices**—use of LIFO accounting (during periods of increasing prices) could understate the value of inventory greatly and therefore understate earnings: *positive.* (See following discussion).

Inventory: Issues and Opportunity

Since the inventory is the most expensive asset included in most acquisitions, it warrants additional mention. Correctly or incorrectly, some companies write off (expense) the cost of their inventories when they are purchased, so their value is never shown on the balance sheet. When inventories are shown on the balance sheet, it is not clear how they were valued unless the financial statement contains footnotes telling us how. Even then, there may be some discrepancy between the explanation in the footnotes and reality, unless statements have been audited. In that case, the counting and valuing has been monitored and the values shown can be relied upon.

Case History – UNRECORDED INVENTORY

A dental lab that made crowns and implants had a lot of precious metals (gold, silver, and platinum) in its inventory; none of which showed on its balance sheet. During the year preceding the proprietor's divorce, purchases of these precious metals seemed to rise substantially while gross profit (and the bottom line) appeared to decline. On paper, earnings were dismal. When the inventory was counted, it turned out that the opposite was true: inventory had increased substantially, and the lab had in fact been quite profitable.

Moral – when purchases increase, see if book value of inventory has changed. If it hasn't, this may be concealing profits.

Many companies carry their inventory on the books at "original cost." This "cost" may be well below current "replacement cost." When an item of inventory is sold, it may be difficult to determine if the book value of the inventory is reduced by the original cost or by the current replacement cost, unless inventories are computerized. Even then, the values shown on the books are often not accurate because of shrinkage, breakage, or obsolescence.[47]

Sometimes, this "exchange" of old and new items of inventory produces an artificial profit and sometimes a loss. So over a period of years, the book value of the inventory can become much less than or can exceed its current value.

If the inventory is not computerized, owners have a choice of what values to use when they "take inventory" at the end of the year. Let's say that a store counts the 1.75 liter bottles of Makers Mark Kentucky bourbon and then "extends" the count at some cost per bottle. The oldest bottle in inventory cost $21.00 and the most recent cost $22.00. Which "cost" should be used? Using the lower cost will appear to reduce profit, while using the higher cost increases profit, if the store properly records its cost of goods on its income statement. To avoid this quandary, some businesses use a blended or average cost.

If a store makes no effort to adjust the cost of goods to reflect changes in inventory, the resulting gross profit and gross profit margin cannot be fully relied upon. See Table 10 below. It can appear "on paper" that a store is making money and that purchases have not increased, while the inventory and the gross profit margin are actually declining. Let's say that a "good" liquor store or other retail

---

47 It is useful to learn the difference between LIFO (last in, first out) and FIFO (first in, first out) inventory valuation methods. LIFO tends to understate earnings, particularly if replacement costs have been rising.

store should have at least a 25 percent gross profit (or a cost of goods sold no greater than 75 percent), and Store 1 appears to meet this criterion. But as illustrated below, if the inventory had in fact declined, the actual gross profit may be much less. If purchases are pretty level as shown below, when inventory increases, margins (and profits) go up, and when inventory declines margins go down. Determining the Cost of Goods Sold accurately is vital to deciding what value to assign to a business and to forecasting accurately future earnings and cash flow.

Table 10. Cost of Goods Sold Calculation

	Store 1	Store 2	Store 3
Reported sales	$400,000	$400,000	$400,000
Beginning inventory	?	120,000	150,000
+ Purchases	300,000	+ 300,000	+ 300,000
- Ending inventory	?	- 150,000	- 120,000
= Cost of goods sold	300,000	270,000	330,000
Gross profit	$100,000	$130,000	$70,000
Gross profit margin	25%	32.5%	17.5%

TIP: Determining the gross profit (as a percent of sales) is always important to analyzing a business correctly. Has it gone up or down recently? Has the gross profit margin (percent) fluctuated significantly? If purchases have gone up, it at first appears that the gross profit margin has gone down. But without knowing if the value of inventory has changed, it is not possible to tell. The key is to understand how to calculate the cost of goods sold (see Table 10) and to use that calculation instead of relying simply on the amount of purchases (or the cost of items purchased). Some businesses "expense" all their purchases and show no inventory on their balance sheets. It is important to remember that accurate projections of future earnings are not possible without an accurate COGS.

It is tempting to rely upon financial statements exactly as they have been prepared, but as we have seen, they often do not tell enough about a business to give a buyer confidence. Many wonderful businesses can be found and purchased at fair prices if we look a little deeper and learn through some basic analysis what a business has really been doing.

SUMMARY

For every business that a buyer seriously examines or considers purchasing, he should perform these steps or calculations before attempting to select an earnings multiple or conclude what a business is worth.

1. Confirm the top line results, i.e. the reported sales, and make necessary adjustments.
2. Prepare five-year spreadsheet of sales and expenses.
3. When appropriate split expense accounts like taxes and insurance into smaller and more meaningful groupings. For example, put Payroll Taxes and Business Taxes on separate lines
4. Adjust or recalculate the gross profit (and gross profit margin) to take into consideration changes in inventory levels if purchases (instead of cost of goods sold) are used on the seller's income statement.
5. Make year-over-year adjustments (both negative and positive adjustments) where lumpy expenses are out of line or where any expenses appear not to have been paid when due.
6. Delete any nonoperating expenses where appropriate.
7. Make adjustments for large onetime, or nonrecurring, expenses.
8. If all expenses (such as employee vacations and bonuses) are not fully accrued, add them to the adjusted income statement.
9. Find or calculate appropriate owner compensation, adding back to income any excess compensation or benefits (adjust to market).
10. Make adjustments to balance sheet to reflect necessary changes, such as in the case of overstated or understated assets or liabilities.
11. Select indicated P:E or earnings multiple.

TIP: Look at the balance sheet again. Has the original cost of the fixed assets changed from year to year? Has the amount of the depreciation expense changed from year to year? If depreciation expenses are declining, the owner may not have invested in new equipment. This could suggest that income in recent years has been overstated a little. It could also mean that a new business owner will have to make a considerable capital investment in the near future.

An excellent source to learn more about analyzing financial statements is "Fire Your Stock Analyst," by Harry Domash. Mr. Domash discusses in much greater detail some of the topics discussed above: valuation ratios, cash flow, historical sales, earnings growth, and much more. His perspective is analyzing publicly traded stocks, but most of the analysis is equally applicable to smaller privately held companies.

CHAPTER 5

EARNINGS CAPACITY AND OTHER VALUATION FACTORS

EARNINGS CAPACITY

In the last chapter, we analyzed what Doozy's earnings history has been. The question now is, "What could Doozy earn in the future"? Does Doozy have the "capacity" to grow, and if so, can we determine how what will that growth cost? And do you have the skills to support and manage that growth? There are many items to think about when trying to determine the **earnings capacity** of a business. Let's look at some:

- **Market characteristics**—is the market or trade area strong enough to absorb additional sales of the products or services a company makes or sells? Can it absorb more custom cabinets each year? What kind? Perhaps a competitor has recently gone out of business or a new well-financed competitor has recently entered the market with high efficiency equipment. If a retail business, are there changes planned to the street system, such as new stoplights or new interstate highway exit ramps?
- **Plant capacity**—is the physical plant adequate to produce more cabinets (handle more sales) without leasing additional space or purchasing new equipment? This seems to be the case with Doozy, but not all businesses have excess physical or plant capacity. Check to be sure

the present equipment is in good repair and working properly. Or better yet, have someone with specific industry knowledge check the equipment for you.[48]

- **Capital requirements**—does the business need immediate capital for operations or for its plant and equipment? Does the business have a delivery truck? Does it have a reasonably new computer system? Are some assets missing? Do the assets in place at the business seem to match the assets listed in the profile or on the balance sheet? I have seen businesses where aging owners reduced inventories and deferred maintenance during the years or months preceding a sale. If this has occurred, you may have to assume the cost of replacing some inventory or upgrading some equipment (a hidden cost) immediately after buying the business. See case history below.

Case History – MISSING INVENTORY

A buyer offered to purchase a business for $240,000. The listing price included inventory of $100,000. The terms of purchase were $100,000 down payment and a note for the balance, said note to be adjusted for any change in inventory between the time the offer was accepted and the day of closing on the sale. The owner, realizing that change in inventory values would not change the down payment, reduced the inventory by $50,000 during the month before the closing. By so doing he put an extra $50,000 in his pocket, but the buyer did not have sufficient inventory to operate. The $100,000 down payment was all he could squeeze together, so he had to borrow money from family to replace this missing (and badly needed) inventory.

Moral – always state a minimum inventory value in your contract.

- **Employee productivity**—can the present employees at Doozy be expected to handle more work without reducing the quality of that work? Ask the owner or check with industry sources to discover what "output per man-hour" should be. Output pertains to office and sales employees as well as to warehouse and shop workers.

---

[48] Checking the equipment can sometimes be a delicate matter to business owners since they quite properly regard as future competitors that may open a similar business somewhere in their market area. Again, this matter can be handled as a contingency in the eventual purchase contract.

- **Employee retention**—will key employees stay with the business after it is sold, and can employees easily be replaced at or near their current level of compensation? It would seriously impact future earnings if the new owner could not quickly replace key employees at or near their current salaries.

- **Efficiency**—are there more efficient ways by which Doozy can operate or by which Doozy can manufacture or market its products? What will it cost, if anything, to increase production or sales efficiency? Often, older businesses have not invested in the newer, more efficient equipment that is readily available, while newer competitors have. Can the shop or business be laid out so that materials can be handled more efficiently or so there is less waste?

Answering these questions will help you to forecast your sales and expenses and to prepare a budget. Both of these steps should be completed before submitting an offer to buy a business. Your broker, as well as friends in the industry, can assist you.[49]

Forecasting

It is important to forecast both sales and expenses. To do this requires making a few assumptions. Let us first assume for the moment that you are comfortable forecasting 12 percent growth each year for the next five years. At this rate, after five years, Doozy's annual sales will have grown to $528,700—a 76 percent increase over last year's sales of $300,000. To accommodate this growth, will Doozy need more space? Need to hire more employees? Purchase additional equipment? If the answer is yes, any additional costs must be included in your projected expenses and in your monthly budget.

In smaller manufacturing plants, there is often excess capacity. The buildings are large enough and the equipment adequate to handle more sales than the plant currently produces. This seems to be so with Doozy since it reported sales three years ago of $340,000. Calculating excess capacity is always wise.

Let's now assume that there has been 5 percent inflation in each of the last two years.[50] If that is so, $340,000 three years ago would represent sales of

---

[49]   Remember, while talking to friends, that all information about a business opportunity must be treated confidentially, including the fact that a business may be available for purchase.

[50]   While 5 percent inflation is used below, current (2016) inflation is unusually low—about 1 percent. Be careful when calculating inflation. Actual rates for many regions and cities are compiled by the Department of Labor, Bureau of Labor Statistics.

$374,850 last year—an increase of 11 percent over the $340,000 and 25 percent over the $300,000 in recorded sales last year. So if inflation has in fact risen by 5 percent a year, we know that Doozy has at least 25 percent excess capacity, that is, the capacity to increase sales by 25 percent without having to increase its physical plant or equipment. This is reassuring to know.

Calculate: $340,000 × 1.05 = 357,000 × 1.05 = $374,850

Doozy's owner suggests that the plant could easily have handled sales well in excess of $340,000 three years ago. To back that up, he provided a breakdown of monthly sales showing three different months when the plant sold over $35,000 worth of goods that year. With monthly sales of $35,000, what would the plant "capacity" be next year?

Potential Annual Sales: $35,000 × 12 months = $420,000 two years ago

Inflation Adjusted Potential Annual Sales:
     $420,000 × 1.05% × 1.05 × 1.05 = $486,000 next year

These historic monthly sales numbers suggest that the plant may have the capacity to produce 50 percent more than last year's reported sales of $300,000. For the actual buyer's complete first year forecast of income and expenses, see Table 16 in Chapter 8. This **excess capacity** is another hidden asset because it appears that Doozy could produce sales of almost $500,000 without requiring more equipment or renting additional space. But be careful. Because Doozy achieved monthly sales of over $35,000 in three different months does not mean that Doozy could achieve sales of $35,000 for twelve consecutive months. Remember that the reported sales are based on "date of receipt of payment" and not on when the work was actually performed.

One key to forecasting income accurately is to separate business expenses into Fixed Costs and Variable Costs. The worksheet in the Appendix shows the positive effect on Income for a business about the same size as Doozy if Fixed Expenses are just $40,000 out of Total Expenses of $190,000. In the current year, the Pretax Income of $10,000 is just 3.3% of the $300,000 in Revenue. Five years later, forecast pretax income is $41,000 or 8.5% of forecast revenue, an increase of 410%. During the same period, Revenue is forecast to grow at just 61% or an annual rate of increase of 10%.

If the Fixed Expenses were greater than $40,000 (21% of Total Expenses), the positive effect on income would be greater. The largest fixed expenses generally are Rent and Debt Service (the sum of principle and interest payments). Note that Depreciation is not included as an expense in this calculation. Refer to Table 7 and Table 16 for Doozy's current and projected revenue and expenses.

Forecasting revenue is beyond the scope of this book. In some cases, it is advisable to conduct a market study. In other cases, using the "straight line" method should be adequate. This is what is shown on the worksheet in the Appendix—revenue is projected to grow at 10% each year which would appear as a "straight line" if plotted on a graph. Every buyer should be aware; however, that many factors can influence future revenues including inflation, general economic conditions and where the economy is in its current business cycle.

As you know by now, **forecasting** is very important. In the final analysis, it is future revenue and earnings that should determine how much you are comfortable offering for a business. Forecasts are based upon a set of assumptions that are probably unique to each business acquisition. So another suggestion:

Suggestion—forecast future revenue and earnings several different times, each time using different sets of assumptions. Prepare a low forecast, a "worst-case" scenario, as well as a high forecast, the "best-case" scenario. Then forecast cash flow using each different set of assumptions. This is not done so much to determine the value of a business as it is to help you be sure you will have adequate working capital to fund the business as it grows.

Reconciliation of Values Found

The question now is how to reconcile the different values indicated. Remember that in Chapter 4, we discussed three methods of valuation and concluded:

- Income method suggests $150,000–$172,000 value range
- Asset method suggests $157,750 value
- Comparative method suggests value unknown

To reconcile our values, we might first see if there are any other applicable valuation methods. Then we must look for external factors that impact Doozy or may impact Doozy in the future. Some of these may indicate a discount in value while some may indicate a premium. Remember that the consistency of earnings found after making adjustments indicated replacing the initial 4:1 earnings multiple with a 5:1 multiple.

Other Valuation Methods

There are a few other valuation methods, or approaches, that knowledgeable buyers and analysts use, including (1) **replacement value,** (2) **discounted cash flow value,** and (3) **percent of sales.** In the first method, we must determine the cost of replacing, or "duplicating," the business in its present form. Surely, we would not pay more for a business than it would cost to build it from scratch.[51]

To determine **replacement value,** we must determine the cost to (1) duplicate the physical facilities and tangible assets in their present (not new) condition and (2) duplicate the income stream. Thus, we would estimate how much it would cost, in addition to replacing the hard assets, to build up sales to the $300,000 range (in Doozy's case) and, thereby, replace the income stream.

The **discounted cash flow** method requires (1) forecasting Doozy's future earnings and cash flow and then (2) discounting the future cash flow to its **present value.** For example, if next year's cash flow is projected to be $100,000, we discount this amount by the current cost of money (or more if the business appears unstable). Assuming a cost of money of 10 percent, the present value of the $100,000 projected cash flow is $90,000.

Now, turning to Doozy, assume for purposes of this calculation that the $31,000 pretax income will grow at 10 percent per year for the next five years. The present value of Doozy's future cash flow stream may be calculated as shown below in Table 11. To get first year cash flow, we add the projected ten percent increase in income ($3,100) and any noncash expenses, such as the $5,000 depreciation (the restated depreciation for last year), to the base income. We

---

51 One interesting method not mentioned is the excess earnings method. It has been used by the U.S. Treasury Department since the days of prohibition. Essentially, the appraiser uses this method to calculate the value of the intangible assets. To do so, he calculates a return on the tangible assets (which are known) and subtracts that return from the total return (earnings). The "balance" of the earnings is then assigned to the intangible assets, using a rate of return that reflects the estimated risk involved-generally 20–25 percent. The goodwill portion of a company's value is thus estimated to be four to five times the "balance" of the earnings. In the view of the IRS, this method proves the existence of goodwill value, even when owners argue there is no goodwill. See Pratt, page 285.

deduct no debt service payments that a buyer may have in the future. We look only at Doozy as it is today.

In most cases, a buyer will have less taxable income and more depreciation than the seller had—since the buyer, when calculating future depreciation, will use the higher market value (or purchase price) of the depreciable assets instead of the lower book value of the assets carried on the seller's balance sheet.[52] Of course, the amount of annual depreciation expenses will increase if new equipment is purchased during the five-year "look-forward" period.

Next, multiply the cash flow by the indicated discount of 10 percent: the first year, multiply $39,100 by .90. The second year, multiply $42,510 by .81 (.90 × .90), and so on, and then add the sums derived—giving an estimated **present value** for Doozy of $168,854 using the **discounted cash flow method** of valuation (if our assumptions are valid).

Look again at the **present value of future cash flow** in Table 11. Would you pay $32,406 (the present value) for a **projected cash flow** five years from now of $54,926? If not, maybe a discount rate greater than 10 percent is appropriate (maybe 12 percent or even 15 percent). There are no guarantees when it comes to projecting earnings or cash flows, so caution is always advised.

Table 11. Calculation of Present Value of Projected Income and Cash Flow[53]

	Base Income		Add 10%		Depre- ciation		Cash Flow	Discount at 10%
First year	$31,000	+	$3,100	+	$5,000	=	$39,100	90%
Second year	34,100	+	3,410	+	5,000	=	42,510	.9×.9
Third year	37,510	+	3,751	+	5,000	=	46,261	.9×.9×.9
Fourth year	41,261	+	4,126	+	5,000	=	50,387	.9×.9×.9×.9
Fifth year	45,387	+	4,539	+	5,000	=	54,926	.9×.9×.9×.9×.9

---

[52]   All of Doozy's equipment has been fully depreciated, including the truck. In making adjustments, we elected to "add back" $10,000, leaving $5,000 in depreciation. This assumes the cost of the truck will be depreciated over three years ($15,000 ÷ 3 = $5,000). The buyer of Doozy valued fixed assets at $45,000 and took $9,000 annual depreciation. See tables 14 and 15.

[53]   The actual discount is 100% to 90%, or 10%, roughly the cost of borrowing. If the cost of borrowing is less, a lower discount rate might be used. This discount can change year over year as economic and business conditions change. The future cash flow is then multiplied by the discount to bring it back to a present value. Thus, next year's projected cash flow will be $35,190 in present dollars. Calculate, $39,100 × .90 = $35,190.

Present Value of Future Cash Flow

	Cash Flow				Present Value
First year	$39,100	×	.90	=	$35,190
Second year	42,510	×	.81	=	34,433
Third year	46,261	×	.73	=	33,771
Fourth year	50,387	×	.656	=	33,054
Fifth year	54,926	×	.59	=	32,406
Estimated Present Value					**$168,854**

The third method, **percent of sales method**, is the simplest. Many similar businesses in many different markets sell at or near the same percentage of annual sales—30 percent, 40 percent, 50 percent of annual sales, or more in some industries. Percentages may not vary much from one community to another because similar types of business in many industries must purchase and maintain approximately the same complements of equipment and inventory. This is particularly true of franchised businesses such as a UPS Store, Jiffy Lube, or Subway Shop.

For example, in some markets, laundromats are priced close to 90 percent of annual sales. Thus, if sales are $100,000, a laundromat might sell for $90,000, all things being equal. A typical retail shop may sell for 35–40 percent of the past year's sales. Subway sandwich shop prices average around 45 percent of annual sales in markets I know. Check with local sources, including your broker, to see what percent (or range) should apply to the type of business you are considering.

After learning the usual percentage in your area, be sure to make any upward or downward adjustments that seem appropriate. For example, Laundromats with new equipment should be worth more than ones with ten-year old equipment because future maintenance and utility costs may be less. These "percentages" are certainly not guaranteed and should be used cautiously. They are only rules of thumb. Each business is different, but within certain industries, sales data on comparable businesses indicate that the sales prices tend to cluster around a certain percent of annual sales.

For better or worse, excluding certain popular franchises, similar businesses within the same market area cannot always be found, so industry standards (such as the **percent of sales** method) are only useful starting places on valuing a business. However, if "comparables" can be found, it is important to make all appropriate adjustments, and use EBIT and EBITDA before drawing conclusions.

After various suggested values for a business have been found, we should "reconcile" them. Some values may be of dubious validity because of limited backup data. Other values may not appear applicable to the subject. You must rely more on the values that appear appropriate. In other words, the process of reconciling disparate values is as much an art as it is an exact science. It is in attempting to reconcile values derived by different methods, and in determining how much weight to give each method, that previously overlooked or critical valuation factors are brought to light.

OTHER VALUATION FACTORS

There are many factors not found in financial statements that can impact the value of a business. Try to develop your own list of factors and consider them carefully. My short list includes the following ten. Experience has shown that in virtually every valuation, these ten factors play a role. Although there may be some change in the importance or weight assigned to each factor, they (and the foregoing discussion about methods of analysis) are as applicable to the success of small neighborhood businesses as to businesses with annual sales of $10,000,000 or more. Analysis is not limited to financial analyses. Let's look briefly at these "other" factors.

1. **Competition**
   How much competition is there? Who are Doozy's competitors? What effect if any do they have on how Doozy conducts its business and prices its products?

2. **State of the Economy**
   Where is the economy within the business cycle? Is the overall economy still expanding? Is a slowdown in the economy anticipated? How would it affect business? What's the state of the economy in general?

3. **Trade Area**
   What is the business's market or trade area? Can it be expanded? Is it contracting? What will it cost to expand into other trade areas?

4. **Stability of Market**
   Is the market (for custom cabinets like those in Doozy's product line) stable? Growing? How fast? Are Doozy's sales growing at the same rate as the market? Should Doozy's growth rate match the rate of growth in

its market area? If it has not kept up with the market, have you found reasons why it hasn't?

5. **Key Employees**

Are there management or technically skilled people who will stay with the business after it is sold? Can you readily find people with the necessary skills to operate the business if some of them leave?

6. **Position/Reputation of Company**

How well established is the company in its market? When was it started? What is its reputation within the community and within its particular market? Is it getting referrals from satisfied customers? Ask the owner how he gets new business.

7. **Financial Condition**

What is the company's financial condition? Does it need more working capital to fund present or anticipated growth? Can it qualify for a line of credit? Are the assets in the business managed well? If there are accounts receivable, are many of them old? Are the inventories overstocked or understocked?

8. **Stability of Profit Margins**

How stable has the gross profit margin been over the last few years? What should it be? Are there any obvious explanations for deviations in the reported **gross profit margins**?

9. **Reason(s) for Selling Business**

What are the Seller's motives for selling, and what are his future plans? Does he, perhaps, intend to open a competing business?

10. **Location of Business**

Will the location be desirable in five years? If not, can you get out of the lease by then? Location is related to the size of the trade area. Thus, location may be a much more important factor for smaller neighborhood businesses.

Suggestion – Whether starting a new business or buyhing an existing business, it is advisable to prepare a Business Plan. Every potential lender you contact will expect you to have a carefully thought out plan that demonstrates in both text and in your Cash Flow projections that your venture is viable and will generate sufficient ROI. Many on-line resources including Score.org and SBA.gov have templates for a business plan. The ten Valuation Factors listed above are standard components in most plans.

Remember, what will happen in the future under your direction is far more important than what occurred in the past under the previous ownership. Can the business be improved in any critical areas under you leadership? If your answer is a resounding *yes*, try to identify the specific areas in which improvement seems attainable.

Ask yourself questions like, Can the **inventory turnover** be improved? Can output per man-hour be increased? If the inventory levels were decreased, how much would the **ROA** and **cash flow** increase? Would a new compensation plan encourage the employees to take a stronger interest in the business? What can you realistically do to make the business more competitive and profitable? You cannot find the answers to these questions by relying solely upon reviewing financial statements. You must try to understand the business.

In the final analysis, you must weigh the values indicated by the different valuation methods. **Replacement value** may be indicated for a given laundromat. The **percent of sales value** may be a more appropriate yardstick for a dry-cleaners, since its value is influenced by the sale prices of comparable businesses in neighboring areas. Where few comparable businesses exist, **earnings value** may be the most reliable measure of all.

How Much Is a Fair Price?

Whatever value you assign to a business and whatever price you are able to buy it for, keep in mind that whatever the business earns, cash flow must be adequate to accomplish four critical things: (1) pay your salary, (2) pay your debt service, (3) pay the operating expenses of the business, and (3) provide for any working capital requirements. Let me share a short story about cash flow.

Case History – UNDERSTANDING CASH FLOW

A buyer called me six months after buying his business and said, "You told me that the business was earning about $10,000 a month, and I relied on that. I have paid myself $10,000 each month, and now I can't pay my bills." The buyer didn't tell me was that sales had increased substantially and he therefore had to increase his inventory, which soaked up much of the cash flow. He learned that growth is often hard to manage and that growth is expensive.

Moral – learn the difference between earnings and cash flow. Even when a business is making money, growth can soak up cash flow and leave you struggling.

My experience indicates that no more than two-thirds of projected cash flow should go toward debt service. So in the case of Doozy, with a projected cash flow of $39,000 (see Table 17 for details) over the twelve months after a sale, debt service (the sum of the principal and interest payments, or P&I) should not exceed $26,020.

Calculate: $39,000 × .667 = $26,020.

Using this guideline, let's calculate how much a buyer can afford to pay for Doozy by looking at five offers using different *prices*, *terms*, and *interest rates*.

Table 12. Debt Service as Percent of Cash Flow

	Offer 1	Offer 2	Offer 3	Offer 4	Offer 5
Purchase Price	$150,000	$150,000	$160,000	$170,000	$170,000
Down Payment	50,000	60,000	60,000	60–,000	60,000
Balance Due	100,000	90,000	100,000	110,000	110,000
Interest Rate	7%	8%	9%	9%	7%
Term of Note	4 years	4 years	5 years	5 years	5 years
Monthly P&I	2,395	2,197	2,076	2,283	2,178
Annual Payments	$28,735	$26,367	$24,910	$27,401	$26,137
Percent of Cash Flow	73.7%	67.6%	63.9%	70.3%	67.0%

The conclusion appears to be that a buyer can comfortably buy Doozy at the asking price of $160,000 with a down payment of $60,000 if the seller will accept a note for $100,000 with a term of at least five years and interest of 9 percent APR or less. The key variable seems to be the five-year payout. Perhaps the best initial offer would be $150,000 with a $50,000 down payment and a 7 percent note paid over five years.

With rapidly growing businesses, buyers can sometimes safely pay a price that might require debt service of almost 100 percent of forecast cash flow (more than 100 percent of forecast pretax income!). With traditional "bread and butter" businesses, however, businesses that are affected by the ups and downs of the economy, two-thirds of projected cash flow is a good yardstick to keep in mind.

Misrepresentations and Their Effect on Value

Sometimes, sellers do misrepresent things concerning their businesses. They might do this in offhand verbal representations as well as in the representations shown on their financial statements. And their agents often repeat the misrepresentations to buyers. Most of the "misrepresentations" are unintentional and not intended to take advantage of an unsuspecting buyer. Some misrepresentations are, in fact, favorable to the buyer. But since it may not be possible to spot every misrepresentation, a well-thought-out and carefully drafted purchase contract (which is discussed in detail in the next chapter) is always the best defense.

The most common misrepresentations involve inventory, which is usually the most expensive "asset" included in a business sale. Whether inventory values are overstated or understated, this fact will come to light during the *due diligence process* (see Chapter 7), and with a well-drafted contract, the purchase price will be adjusted accordingly at the closing on the sale. Actually, understated inventory values may in fact be a positive sign for a buyer instead of a red flag. Normal business practices differ, but some types of inventory in some businesses may be written when it is purchased. Sometimes, inventory values are written down in value at the end of the fiscal year. Frequently, understated inventory turns out, in fact, to be understated profit. This difference between actual and reported inventory values is often referred to as the "inventory cushion."

When a seller says something as an inducement to a buyer, such as, "I know the balance sheet only shows an inventory of $100,000, but I am sure that there must be $200,000 worth out in the warehouse," take the seller up on that representation. The seller's statement is not intended to defraud, even if $200,000 turns out to be somewhat exaggerated. Put in your purchase contract some wording like,

"This price includes current inventory items with a value (or original cost) of $200,000."

Try to determine when the cushion was created. In some cases, owners have not changed the inventory values on the books for five years. If, as in the example above, a business actually has a $100,000 cushion consisting of salable merchandise in good condition, the business's earnings have been underreported by $100,000 or $20,000 per year. Of course, if inventory values (or other asset values) are overstated, the reported earnings likely are overstated.

What is more common than a pattern of repeated misrepresentations is some onetime event in the past (perhaps the result of an owner's effort to reduce taxable income or a bookkeeping error or omission) that might mislead or concern a buyer. Often, for example, bookkeepers do not add depreciation charges to monthly P&Ls. Some owners, however, have intentionally misrepresented something to the detriment of a customer, an employee, a supplier, a bank, or to some taxing authority. Again, in my experience, the occurrence of such events is limited. Nevertheless, many buyers tend, understandably, to shy away from a business after a red flag regarding misrepresentation comes to light. The valuation techniques set out in the preceding chapters, especially the *recasting process*, should enable a buyer to put those concerns to rest (in most cases).

Misrepresentations can involve every aspect of a business: the sales, the value of certain assets shown on the balance sheet, the physical condition of certain assets, the stability of the workforce, and of course, the business's growth and income potential. What is the prudent buyer to do in the face of misrepresentations? Almost always, the best advice to a buyer to avoid paying too much "blue sky," or purchasing nonexistent assets, is "**Let your contract do the talking.**"

Be sure to obtain a properly drafted purchase contract before committing to buy a business. Of course, even with a proper contract, it can be dangerous to buy when the misrepresentations cannot be resolved or when it seems clear after careful review and analysis that a business will not meet your expectations. As stated in Chapter 1, some businesses are bad businesses and are not saleable.

As you wind up your *valuation process*, review again the **cardinal rule**, to wit.

At the valuation you feel is appropriate, do you believe the business, under your leadership, will generate enough cash flow in the future to

- pay you an adequate salary,
- pay the projected operating costs of the business,
- provide some reserve cash for future working capital, and

- pay the interest and principal on the debt you will incur when you buy the business?

If your answer is *no*, you are probably paying or offering too much.

CHAPTER 6

HOW TO STRUCTURE A PURCHASE AGREEMENT

PART I
TERMS OF PURCHASE

This chapter deals with the *contract preparation process*. When you have decided to prepare an **offer to purchase** a business and have decided what you feel is a fair price, there are some other important decisions (choices) to make before submitting an offer to the seller. These include the following:

1. Choosing whether to structure the purchase (and sale) as an "asset sale," or as a "stock sale."
2. Determining which assets to include in your "offer to purchase" (see Which Assets to Purchase section below) or to buy the assets as offered for sale in the profile or other offering document?
3. Deciding how much of each class of assets to offer to buy: How much raw material? How much inventory of resale merchandise? How many vehicles?

4. Deciding whether to pay "cash" for the business or ask the seller to accept payment over some time period, that is, to accept "terms" (see To Pay Cash or Terms section below).

5. Choosing which "contingencies" to include in your "offer to purchase" (see Contingent Nature of Contracts in Part II).

6. Determining how to allocate the purchase price among the assets to be purchased (see Allocation of Purchase Price in Part II).

7. Determining how (in what form) to "take title" to the business (see Taking Title in Part II).

Asset Sale or Stock Sale

There are two basic methods used to purchase a business: buy the stock of the corporation from the shareholders or buy the specific assets (including, of course, the goodwill) from the corporation or directly from the owner if the business is not incorporated. This decision is easy if the business is not incorporated because no stock has been issued.[54] Sometimes, the form of sale is a combination of the two methods. In such a case, the buyer will purchase the corporate stock and also purchase some assets, such as noncompete agreements, from individual shareholders directly. Normally, a noncompete agreement is between the buyer and the majority shareholder. However, sometimes, if several shareholders have been active in the management of the business, it is prudent to have agreements with more than one shareholder.

If a stock purchase is contemplated, a buyer may also choose not to purchase all the outstanding stock. He may want only to buy a controlling interest, which may be 51 percent of the issued and outstanding stock or, in some cases, even less that 51 percent. This alternative, however, is seldom used in buying a small business for several reasons: (1) there may be state laws that protect minority stockholders in closely held corporations, and (2) the stockholders may have entered into buy/sell agreements with each other that prevent any sale of shares of stock unless all stockholders consent to the sale and all the outstanding shares of stock are sold.

Even if the business is incorporated, it's usually best to buy the "assets and goodwill" rather than the "stock." This is so because when you buy stock, you buy the whole corporate structure and, thereby, inherit whatever undisclosed lia-

---

[54] There are several types of corporations: C corps, S corps, and LLCs. It is advisable to become familiar with the characteristics of each. Usually, the best place to begin is with your accountant.

bilities or skeletons there may be lurking in the corporate closet—like latent tax deficiencies, unfavorable leases, lawsuits, or other old claims that haven't settled. Even if the seller agrees to "hold you harmless" from any undisclosed liabilities, there could be many unforeseen problems (or financial liability) arising from obligations that were incurred by the corporation prior to the date of your purchase. If you buy stock, these obligations could become your obligations.

Let me give two examples of the kind of things that could happen. In the first example, a former employee brings a lawsuit against the corporation after you buy it. He alleges that he was wrongfully dismissed (by the former owner) and sues the corporation for back wages and damages of $100,000. While neither you nor the former owner believes the suit has merit, you end up spending $25,000 in legal fees, take a lot of time away from the business, and incur many sleepless nights.

In the next example, let's assume that, at the time you bought the corporation, it owed $20,000 to a supplier of one of its main lines of goods. The **payment terms** that the supplier has extended to the corporation for many years are "net thirty days" with 2 percent discount for payments made within ten days. The $20,000 invoice was not paid within these terms, perhaps because both you and the seller were preoccupied with matters relating to the closing on the sale of the business, and as a result, the supplier cancels the line and gives it to a competitor. It may have been a very important line, a line that you liked and one of the reasons you bought the company.

If you had purchased the assets instead of stock, you would have requested from this supplier before the closing a letter giving you the right (perhaps exclusive rights) to handle this line of merchandise in your market area. You would have also requested in your purchase contract that the balance due all suppliers be paid by the seller before the closing or paid from closing funds. These are prudent safeguards.

In some cases, buying "stock" is perfectly OK, particularly if the corporation can meet the following conditions.

1. The selling corporation has carried appropriate insurance coverage.
2. The financial records will pass an independent audit.
3. The shareholders personally will "indemnify" you from possible future losses resulting from events that occurred during their period of ownership.

4. The shareholders will permit you to defer (or hold back) a substantial amount of the purchase price until all their contractual commitments (the commitments set out in the purchase contract) have been satisfied.

5. Corporation has sufficient cash to meet its obligations.

The chief advantage to buying the outstanding stock (instead of the assets and goodwill) is that everything is "in place." You normally won't need new licenses, new bank accounts, new leases, new employment agreements, and the like before taking over. And you might be able to assume existing dealership or supplier agreements without having to qualify for them in your own name (and credit situation), a sometime lengthy process.

If the decision is made to purchase corporate stock, it may still be prudent to buy other assets "outside of the corporation" as well. This is appropriate when some assets are owned individually by a stockholder (or by another person involved in the sale) rather than by the corporation. An example is a "noncompete" agreement with the owner or majority stockholder. Most buyers expect a former owner not to compete with him (her) after the sale and, therefore, purchase a **noncompete agreement.** This "asset" is not owned by the business. The business (whether it is a sole proprietorship, partnership, or corporation) and therefore is not responsible for the fulfillment of the agreement; the individual owners or stockholders are.

Lease Purchase or Option Purchase.

A third method used to buy a business is to lease it from the owner with an option to purchase it later at an agreed-upon price. This mechanism is not often used but should be part of a buyer's tool kit. A seller is very unlikely to agree to simply lease his business (as in leasing a building) because a seller wants or needs some cash at the closing. Often, the seller has bills to pay off as well as certain closing costs and a brokerage fee. The way to resolve the lack of down payment in a lease/purchase is to lease with an option to purchase. Instead of selling the business outright at closing, the seller sells an option. The option price becomes the down payment. From the buyer's point of view, he gains time to decide if a certain business will help him reach his goals.

Buyer and seller still negotiate a price for the business. Parties enter into an option agreement to buy the business within the option period (typically a year or two) at the negotiated price. The price for the option might be as little as $2,000–3,000, or it might be $20,000–30,000. The option price represents the money the seller will lose or forego by not getting paid for a year or two, including interest he would not earn from a larger down payment. If he received all cash, the agreed-upon price for the business were $300,000 and interest rates were 6 percent, the seller would "lose" $18,000 a year, or $36,000 over two years. The option price is paid to seller at closing. Sometimes, part of the option price is credited toward the price of the business, but what the option really does is hold or guarantees the price of the business for a certain period. For that, a seller is entitled to compensation.

The parties to a lease purchase agreement also must agree to a lease payment (usually the monthly lease payment). Let's assume the lease payment on a $300,000 acquisition is $4,000. A portion of this payment is credited against the purchase price. In other words, the lease payment is treated as a partial payment of principal and interest. If, for example, fifty percent of the monthly lease payment of $4,000 is credited toward the purchase price, the price will be reduced by $2,000 each month. If the buyer exercises his "option to buy" at the end of two years, then the price is effectively reduced by $48,000.

In a lease purchase agreement, there would normally be additional covenants between the parties to cover the operation of the business while it is under option (see discussion of buyer and seller Warranties in Part II of this chapter). In other words, the seller would have to protect himself against the possibility that a buyer could harm or destroy his business if it were not properly managed. Obviously, if a seller (lessor) has to take over management of his business, he should expect the business to be in the same condition it was in when the lease began. Three typical covenants would be the following:

1. A limit on the compensation a buyer could pay himself
2. A requirement that buyer pays company bills and other financial obligations on time
3. A requirement that buyer gives the seller timely financial reports

At the end of the option period, the buyer would have the "option" whether to proceed with the actual purchase or not. If the buyer does not exercise his option, the seller would then be free to sell his business to someone else.

Which Assets to Purchase

The concept of which assets to purchase does not occur to all buyers, but making the right decisions about assets can impact your future success. Most businesses have some nonoperating assets—that is, assets that are not used in the business and are, therefore, not essential to its present or future operations. Sellers feel that a business cannot be broken up and, at the beginning of the *negotiating process,* expect the buyer to buy "everything on the books," or "everything you see here." If you determine that a business has too many (or some unnecessarily expensive) assets, it may be wise to exclude some in your initial offer.

If, for example, the owner or other family members are driving large new pickup trucks with all the bells and whistles while more modest vehicles would be adequate, do not hesitate to suggest that these assets be excluded. Often, there is unused equipment in storage or sitting idle. Sometimes, the furnishings in the executive office are far more extravagant than necessary.

In most business transactions, inventory is the most expensive asset, so it merits your most careful attention. Let's look at a retail furniture store. How much inventory should the business have? A sixty-day supply, a ninety-day supply, or more? Normally, thirty or more days elapse between acceptance of an offer and the closing, so sellers will have time to sell any excess or unwanted inventory as well as any other assets you may elect not to buy. In regard to inventory, it is wise to include in your purchase contract a clause that limits the amount of inventory you agree to buy. See discussion below on "How Much Inventory to Buy."

Other sellers will instinctively want to exclude from a sale all financial assets, such as cash and accounts receivable. However, it may be appropriate for the seller to leave in the business enough cash to provide you, the buyer, with a level of working capital necessary to operate the business. This is particularly true with businesses that sell their products on credit as opposed to the typical retail business in which customers pay for their purchases at the time of each sale. **If the needed working capital is not included among the assets purchased, the buyer will have to provide it from other sources.**

How to Treat Customer Deposits

In the case of Doozy, the seller will give you (not sell) all or part of the deposits the customers made when their orders were placed. Legally, **customer deposits** are not assets of a business, even though they may be recorded (incorrectly) as cash under assets on the seller's balance sheet. If a customer's deposit is shown under assets, the same amount should be included under liabilities because deposits must be returned if an order is not filled. Often, deposits are prorated between buyer and seller based on some formula, generally a formula relating to the percentage of completion of each order at the time of the sale. If an order has not been started, the full deposit would be given to the buyer. In some cases, it might be fair for the seller to give the buyer the full deposit less the cost of marketing and other costs that the seller has already absorbed.

When a business (or its owner individually) owns its business premises, buyers face the "asset" decision of whether to purchase the real estate or simply to lease it from the seller. It generally seems wise not to be burdened by the additional debt associated with buying the real estate, unless the buyer is convinced that the location is desirable and the price is attractive. Sometimes, it may be prudent to move the business to another location, in which case the buyer will neither buy nor lease the real estate. In other cases, a seller may make a buyer an attractive deal if the buyer does agree to buy his business and associated real estate.

How Much Inventory to Buy

Another decision is to decide how much of each asset, or class of assets, to purchase. This decision most often impacts inventory. If the inventory on hand appears too low to permit the business to operate efficiently, the buyer might require the seller to increase his inventories. The buyer may also stipulate that as of the date of closing, there are on hand inventories of raw materials valued—say, at not less than $100,000. Likewise, inventory might be too high, so the buyer may decide to cap the value of raw material inventories that he will purchase at, say, $50,000 and cap total inventories at $125,000.

The seller will probably resist excluding or discounting any part of the inventory, but a prudent buyer should be careful. If the amount of inventory on hand appears to be far above necessary levels, a buyer might put one or more clauses in the purchase contract, such as,

> *"Excess inventory will be valued at its Book Value or replacement cost, whichever is the lesser, less a 10 percent discount" or "Any inventory in excess of $100,000, valued at Seller's original cost, will be discounted by 20 percent. If inventory value exceeds $200,000, the excess will be excluded from the sale."*

Of course, the proper discount could be greater than 20 percent, depending upon the age and condition of the inventory in question. The buyer could also offer to purchase the excess inventory from seller on an as-needed basis. There are many ways to handle excess inventory. If a seller has not conducted a complete count of the inventory for many years, he may be quite surprised by how much is on hand. Since any "excess" inventory will increase the sale price of the business, a seller should be willing to give the buyer favorable terms as an inducement to take all the inventory on hand at the time of closing.

To Pay Cash or Terms

There are essentially two ways to pay for a business: (1) pay cash or (2) pay on terms. Most small businesses are sold on terms—that is, the buyer makes a cash down payment at time of closing, and the seller accepts a **promissory note** (see sample notes in Appendix) for the balance of the purchase price. There is a third payment option called **assumption of debt**. Often, the final terms of sale are a combination of cash, note, and assumption of debt. Let me illustrate with summaries of three possible terms of sale.

Hypothetical Terms of Sale	Offer 1	Offer 2	Offer 3
Cash Paid at Closing	$150,000	$60,000	$25,000
Cash Paid 90 Days from Closing[56]	125,000	0	25,000
Assumption of Note on Truck	0	15,000	15,000
Assumption of Accounts Payable	0	70,000	40,000
Note to Seller, 1-Year Maturity	0	30,000	0
Note to Seller, 5-Year Maturity	0	115,000	200,000
Purchase/Selling Price	**$275,000**	**$290,000**	**$305,000**

Terms can differ considerably. However, a down payment of at least thirty percent (30%) or one-third of the selling price is generally expected. Assumption of some of a seller's debt is essentially the same as a larger down payment. Notice above that with a larger down payment, the selling price is less.

---

[55] The ninety-day deferred payment might (1) pay for management assistance, (2) protect buyer from undisclosed liabilities, (3) assure buyer of collectability of accounts receivable, or (4) cover a variety of other short-term situations. It is always wise to hold back some money.

Terms of Promissory Notes

Usually, note payments (principal and interest or **P&I**) due seller are (1) level—that is, the payments of P&I do not change during the term of the note, (2) they are paid monthly, and (3) the first payment is due thirty or forty days from closing. There are several common variations to the standard terms of promissory notes taken back by sellers. These (and other) variations could be useful during the *negotiating process*. It is highly unlikely that a bank would accept such variations, though. Parties may agree to start with lower monthly note payments and increase them over the term of the note. For example, note payments may be set at $1,200 per month for the first year and increase to $2,000 per month during succeeding years.

1. Parties may agree to start with lower monthly note payments and increase them over the term of the note. For example, note payments may be set at $1,200 per month for the first year and increase to $2,000 per month during succeeding years.

2. Parties may agree to an adjustable interest rate, with the interest rate on the note changing yearly to reflect changes in the prime rate (the rate that banks give their best customers) or some other customary rate.

3. First payment of P&I may be deferred until forty-five, sixty, or even ninety days after the closing to give the buyer a little breathing room.

4. Buyers may reserve the right to skip one or more monthly payments (of principal, not interest) during a year because of the seasonal nature of some businesses.

5. Buyers may pay interest only for the first several months.

6. There may be separate notes to pay for different parts of a business, such as a note for the value assigned to management assistance and another note for the rolling stock. One note might be paid directly to the seller, and another note paid to the corporation that owns and is selling the physical assets.

7. Notes for management assistance and noncompetition may not require interest since at time of closing, seller has not "performed" these services but sellers may resist foregoing interest payments.

The typical maturity for promissory notes is three to five years. When buying smaller, less well-established businesses, a shorter maturity is not unreasonable. For larger businesses, a longer term is common. Some buyers may also want a **balloon note**. In such cases, the seller might accept a note amortized, perhaps, over five to six years but require a balloon payment (the balance of the principal) at the end of three years. This has the advantage that (1) buyers get smaller monthly note payments during the early years of ownership and (2) sellers get paid off more quickly.

If the owner is really committed to selling, you are much more likely to buy at a favorable price and on favorable terms. Whatever the agreed-upon price and terms, most sellers will expect a personal guarantee from you (and your spouse) as well as specific collateral to back up the note. The collateral for the note is in most cases limited to the assets of the business (the assets being sold) rather than "outside" assets—that is, assets such as your personal residence. Sometimes, it is reasonable to expect the seller to release some of the collateral as the buyer pays down a note.

All notes call for penalties (late fees) if note payments are not received on time. Late fees are added to a note and accrue interest if they are not paid on time. Typically, a payment is late if received ten to twenty days after the due date. The late payments are generally not onerous but are stiff enough to encourage compliance on the part of the buyer. If there is a string of late payments, virtually, every note permits seller to foreclose on or to repossess the assets assigned to seller as collateral or even to take back the entire business. In most situations, neither buyer nor seller wants foreclosure to occur.

A note may contain a **default clause** that specifies that full payment is due upon default (nonpayment of one or more monthly payments) by buyer. In such cases, there is no "cure," and there are no late fees, simply a demand for full payment. Such a provision is not in a buyer's interest.

A seller can take back (hold) several notes as shown in Offer 2 above. The one-year note, for example, could be for payment of a noncompete agreement. This note may carry no interest since the seller will not have "performed" until after the year is complete. It is useful to think of paying for different assets over different terms, while contemplating your offers.

For a seller, the key to accepting an offer "on terms" is to feel protected—that is, to believe that the collateral is adequate to cover the deferred obligations of the buyer in case he is forced to repossess the business or has to liquidate the assets. Rightly or wrongly, the seller worries that the buyer may not be able to "keep the business together" and pay him off under the terms of the purchase agreement.

Security Agreement

When notes are secured by specific items of collateral, a security agreement is attached to the note. This agreement spells out in detail the buyer's obligations to the seller and the specific procedures the seller must follow in order to regain possession of the collateral. There is another use for security agreements that a buyer should not overlook: if properly drafted, they make the sellers feel secure accepting offers to sell on terms rather than requiring all-cash offers.

In a typical security agreement, a buyer may be required to

1. Keep all collateral at all times in good repair, adequately insured, and housed on business premises
2. Allow secured party to inspect premises and collateral after receiving reasonable notice
3. Not sell or transfer secured property without express permission of secured party
4. Provide secured party with timely monthly financial statements or other evidence that inventories are maintained at required levels

Both the note (or notes) and security agreement must follow the terms set out and agreed to in the purchase contract. See paragraph 6 under Special Stipulations in sample contract in Appendix.

All-Cash Offers

Many all-cash offers do not require a buyer to pay 100 percent of the purchase price at closing, but they do preclude any long-term seller financing, such as a note with a maturity of longer than one year. It is typical for a buyer to expect a seller to discount his asking price somewhat as the terms of sale approach an all-cash offer. The appeal of all-cash to a seller is obvious; he thereby avoids the risk and frustration (not to mention potential cost) of having to track down the buyer when (if) he has not received payments on time and, in extreme cases, suing the buyer. Even if seller requires a 100 percent cash sale, it is advisable to hold some money back for a few months to protect yourself against the risk of undisclosed liabilities and to ensure that seller has met all his promises, such as providing the transition assistance or complying with the terms of the noncompete agreement.

If a buyer assumes some of a business's debts, it is the same as paying cash since the seller will not have to pay these debts off. You could, for example, assume a car note or equipment note or some accounts payable as a method of paying part of the purchase price as in Offers 2 and 3 above.

In Table 13 below are two possible offers for the purchase of Doozy. Look at Offer 1 first. The seller would get the full $100,000 value he placed on the "hard" assets in the profile, and the deferred payments would be backed by promissory notes. Of course, this is not really an all-cash offer because some of the payments are deferred. However, a buyer who is making Offer 1 is offering to pay seller the full value ($100,000) he put on the business assets in exchange for which he is asking the seller to let him defer the balance of the purchase price.

Although Offer 1 appears to exceed seller's asking price of $160,000, it is more favorable to the buyer than it at first appears because (1) the **present value** of the deferred payments for the noncompete agreement is less than the $50,000 face value of this obligation and (2) buyer will not have to worry about meeting monthly debt service obligations as he would in Offer 2. Which would you prefer: to pay $40,000 now or pay $50,000 in two years? Which would a seller prefer: to receive $40,000 now or $50,000 in two years? Maybe the seller would agree to accept $35,000 now.

In Offer 1, the seller would receive a **consideration of sale** less than the stated purchase price of $170,000 but close to his asking price of $160,000. To calculate the **present value (PV)** of the $50,000, discount it by a rate of interest commensurate with the risk to the holder of the note, perhaps 12 percent. At 12 percent interest (or discount rate), the present value is $39,860. The "cash" discount in this case would be $50,000 less $39,860, or $10,140, making the present value of the $170,000 offer just $159,860. See calculation below.

Some sellers might accept a higher discount than 12 percent in order to receive more cash at closing on the sale of the business. If the seller insisted on all cash, the buyer might offer a little less, say $140,000 or $150,000, still deferring the $20,000 allocated to management assistance for sixty-five days.

Calculate: $50,000 \div 1.12 = $44,643 PV after one year
$44,643 \div 1.12 = $39,860 PV after two years

Table 13. Terms of Two Hypothetical Offers

Offer 1—Purchase for All Cash	Value/Price	Terms of Payment
Down Payment (buys FF&E and Inventories—the hard assets)	$100,000	Payable at closing
60-day Management Assistance Contract	20,000	Payable 65 days from closing
Two-year Non-compete Agreement	50,000	Payable two years
Purchase Price	**$170,000**	from closing

Offer 2—Purchase on Terms	
Purchase price (estimated)[57]	**$150,000**
Down Payment	50,000
Note to Seller	100,000
Interest Rate on Note	7% APR
Term of Note	Five years
Method of Payment	Equal monthly payments
Monthly Payment to Seller	$1,980

Buyer's Return on Investment and Cash Flow in Offer 2	
1st Year Income before interest or taxes	$36,000
Forecast 1st Year Cash Flow	42,000
Interest Payments 1st Year On Note	6,400
Forecast Income After-interest Payment	29,600
Estimated 1st Year Principal Payment	17,240
1st Year Cash Flow after paying principal	24,760

Which offer is better in terms of the return on your investment? Remember that your ROI is higher when the down payment/investment is lower. This will be true whether you use third party (bank) financing or seller financing. Let's use the example of Offer 2. Your investment is $50,000. Before deducting interest or additional depreciation expenses, projected pretax income is $36,000. At 7 percent APR, your interest payments the first year will be a little over $6,400. This would make forecast pretax income about $29,600, which is a 59.2 percent return on a down payment of $50,000.[57]

---

[56] In offer 2, the "allocation of the purchase price" must be changed from the allocation in offer 1. Perhaps the "price" assigned to the noncompete will be reduced to $30,000, or only $80,000 allocated to the hard assets.

[57] Earnings from "operations" are the same before and after the purchase.

Calculate: $29,600 ÷ $50,000 = .592, or 59.2% **ROI**

The principal payments due seller in offer 2 (approximately $17,240 the first year) are not deducted from earnings because they go toward reducing debt.[58] However, if a buyer pays $100,000 in cash at closing, plus $20,000 sixty-five days after closing as in Offer 1 (a down payment of $120,000), anticipated ROI is only 30 percent, or half the ROI of a buyer who pays a more typical "one-third down."[59] If any portion of the $120,000 were borrowed, the ROI would increase. With the larger down payment and an (almost) all-cash offer, the cash flow first year, however, is greater than in Offer 2.

Calculate: $36,000 ÷ $120,000 = .30, or 30% **ROI**

Suggestion—before preparing an actual offer or letter of intent, prepare several different offers (in the simplified form shown in Table 13) with different offering prices and terms of payment. Be creative. And then, for each hypothetical offer, calculate the probable future income, cash flow, and ROI. Then, try to determine the advantages of each to the seller and to you as the buyer. And finally, try to determine possible "trade-offs" that you think a prudent seller might accept. Would he accept your price if you reduced the time of the management assistance, or noncompete periods? Would you agree to a higher price if the seller would agree to extend the term of the note from five years to six years?

What Does the Word *Terms* Mean?

The *terms* of purchase can mean a lot of different things to different people. You will see the word *terms* many times in the rest of this chapter, so a clear understanding of what this word means is important. It seems instinctive, when buying a business, to assume that the word *terms* refers to the financial aspects of an offer: the price and the amount of down payment, for example. Review the "offers" in the preceding pages to see some of the more common financial

---

[58] Note that after paying both interest and principal ($23,640), there is still $12,360 left to add to working capital under the above terms of purchase.

[59] Perhaps, if the buyer offered "all cash," the seller may have accepted a price of $135,000, which would be a discount of 10 percent. In that case, the ROI would be a little lower ($35,000 ÷ $135,000 = .267, or 26.7%), but there would be no principal, interest, or other deferred payments in the future.

terms. Actually, the word *terms* can refer to any of the hundreds of "variables" that might be contained within an offer.

It is impossible to list all the possible different terms; buyers and sellers have to be creative sometimes to put a deal together. The important thing to remember is that some aspects of an offer may be appealing to a seller and some may be "turnoffs." When you begin preparing an offer, you will not know what terms will get favorable attention from the seller. But as offers and counteroffers flow back and forth between buyer and seller, you will discover which terms the seller finds appealing. In the end, it may not always be the highest price that brings the seller to the closing table. Let me give some ideas to think about:

- The buyer agrees to close on the sale within thirty days of seller's acceptance of his offer (because he doesn't have to wait for a bank to approve a loan request).
- The offer is clearly spelled out in only two or three pages instead of a forty-page contract filled with unfamiliar legal terms.
- The terms of purchase do not require the seller to provide any management assistance after the sale.
- The buyer agrees to give the seller some "outside" collateral, and the buyer's wife agrees to sign the promissory note.
- buyer will agree to pay "current replacement value" for all retail inventory instead of "seller's original cost" as he originally offered.

In exchange for the buyer's acceptance of certain terms that the seller perceives as favorable, the seller might agree to certain terms that are more favorable to the buyer. For example,

- If the buyer will give outside collateral, the seller will reduce the purchase price in his original counteroffer.
- If the buyer will assume the $20,000 balance due on one of the newer company vehicles, the seller will accept the $50,000 down payment the buyer originally offered.
- If the buyer will close within thirty (30) days, the seller will provide sixty days of management assistance.
- If the buyer will increase the down payment from 30 percent (30%) of the purchase price to 40 percent (40%), the seller will agree to finance the balance at 5 percent interest rate instead of the 8 percent requested in his first counteroffer.

JACK (JOHN V. M.) GIBSON

- If the buyer will give the seller a long-term lease, perhaps ten years, on the business premises (which seller owns), seller will accept the buyer's original offer and agree not to increase the rent during the full ten years.

Now, with these thoughts in mind about some of the many possible terms that can be added to an offer (to make it more appealing and to increase the odds that the seller will find an offer acceptable), let's move from the *valuation process* to the actual *contract preparation process*.

Letter of Intent

Before preparing and submitting an offer or formal purchase agreement, sometimes it is sensible to submit what is called a **letter of intent**.[60] These "letters" are quite brief and set forth in very straightforward language, the basic terms, under which you want to buy a business. Such a letter is easier for the seller to understand and respond to than a more formal and lengthy legal document. In the case of Doozy, a letter of intent might be no more detailed than the one on the following page.

Note that the letter can be a binding or nonbinding offer. The purpose of the letter is to see if there is a meeting of minds between the parties regarding key points, such as **price and terms**, before going to the trouble of preparing the detailed contract. In the case of a binding letter, the buyer is "binding" himself only to prepare and submit a formal purchase contract within five days if the seller accepts the price and terms exactly as set out in the letter. If the letter were nonbinding, the buyer would have no obligation.

Of course, a seller is free to accept the letter offer subject to a few changes. The seller, for example, in paragraph 2 might scratch out $50,000 and substitute $40,000 or in paragraph 6 scratch out $150,000 and insert $160,000. In paragraph 7, he might increase the down payment to $60,000, and in paragraph 9, he might increase the interest rate to 8 percent. The seller would initial each of the changes in the letter, and the seller would sign the letter before it is returned to the buyer.

---

[60] There are pros and cons to using a letter of intent when acquiring a small business. It is often preferable to eliminate this step, except where the buyer is requesting unusual "terms," which cannot easily be set out in a standard contract because of their length or legal complexity.

Sample Simplified Letter of Intent

Dear_____,

By means of this (binding) (nonbinding) letter, I am conveying to you my intent to offer to purchase the following assets of Doozy Manufacturing Co. (hereafter, Business) for the price and under the terms set out below.

1. *All equipment and tools used in operation of Business.*
2. *Raw materials with an original cost of $50,000.*
3. *All goodwill and rights to all trade names and logos.*
4. *Unfilled work orders in hand at closing totaling $80,000.*
5. *You will enter into a noncompete agreement and a management assistance agreement with me.*
6. *The price will be $150,000 before adjustments, if any.*
7. *The down payment payable at closing will be $50,000.*
8. *The balance will be paid in sixty equal and consecutive monthly installments of principal and interest.*
9. *The interest rate will be 7 percent annual percentage rate.*
10. *Before the closing, I will inspect all equipment to see if it is in good working order and will count and value the inventories. If the inventory value is less than $50,000, the price and down payment will be reduced by the shortage.*
11. *The closing will be thirty days after we sign a formal purchase agreement.*
12. *Prior to closing, you will continue to operate in the normal manner*

If these terms are acceptable to you, please signify by your signature and return to me. Within five (5) days of receipt of your signed letter, I will present you a purchase contract on the price and terms set out above together with earnest money in the amount of $10,000.

Respectfully,　　　　　　　　　*Agreed:* _____

　　　　　　　　　　　　　　　　John Smith, President, Doozy Mfg. Co., Inc.

_____　　　　_____

John Doe (Purchaser)　　　　　*John Smith, Individual*

Date: _____　　　　*Date:* _____

Closing Costs and Service Deposits

During the *negotiation process*, the buyer must keep a sharp eye on his available cash reserves. If he has, for example, only $60,000 available, he should not spend the entire $60,000 on the down payment. Some must be kept for closing costs, some for working capital (if the business does not "cash flow" from the first day of ownership) and some for deposits that a buyer may have to put up in order to maintain service with service providers, such as a telephone company or utility company. These costs can vary from market to market. Learn what they are in your market.

Many buyers neglect, or do not think, about the cost of the "service" deposits. In a standard contract (see Stipulation 11 in Purchase Contract), these deposits remain the property of the seller. Of course, the buyer may request in his offer that all such deposits be included among the assets to be conveyed at closing at no extra cost. If a contract does not explicitly state that deposits will be conveyed to the buyer, the buyer is wise to determine the amount of such deposits and include this amount in his closing budget. Some sellers forget that there are deposits on account with these providers and, therefore, leave them in place.

If a buyer has to obtain a new lease on the business premises, the landlord may require a deposit also, typically one month's rent, sometimes both the first and last month's rent. Even though closing costs and service deposits are relatively modest, it would be wise to hold $10,000 in reserve. See other costs in the Settlement Sheets in the Appendix.

Counteroffers

Whether the buyer first submits a letter of intent or omits this step and submits a formal purchase contract to a seller, the seller is likely to respond with some changes. This "response" is called a counteroffer. Often, the requested changes are quite modest. The buyer then must (1) determine how to respond to the seller in his counteroffer or (2) notify the seller that he (she) has no interest in proceeding. If the buyer accepts the seller's changes, he (1) initials them on the original letter, or contract, and (2) returns a properly executed copy to the seller.

This exchange of counteroffers may go back and forth several times. Typically, a buyer's response is to reply to the seller by saying, in effect, "I will give you what you are asking if you will give me something else, perhaps some additional inventory or some additional management assistance after the sale." Try to keep in mind what you would like the seller to do for you.

With each exchange of offers and counteroffers, the gap between the price and terms offered and the asking price and terms gets narrower and the agreements between the parties begin to reflect more fully the individuality of the business. When agreement has been reached on all points, you, as buyer, then begin to prepare the formal purchase contract. If the negotiating has been done via letter of intent, be sure to observe the clause regarding how many days you have to submit the contract. Sometimes, the signed letter is turned over to your attorney or broker who will draft the contract.[61]

TIP: Using preprinted Contract forms provided by a broker might save a lot of money and speed up the contract preparation process. Attorneys might require several days to prepare a contract, while a broker will be able to fill in the blanks in a preprinted contract form while you are in his office. If you choose to use a preprinted form, it is wise to let your attorney review it before it is submitted to the seller. If you wish to incorporate, you can also save some money by applying for a charter directly from the Secretary of State in your state. It is not required that an attorney do this for you. Review Purchase Contract in Appendix. **An attorney, however, must prepare closing documents.**

Seller's Authority to Sign

If the owner of the assets to be purchased is a corporation (like Doozy), a corporate officer, as well as the owner individually, will sign the letter, or contract. The secretary of the board of directors of the selling corporation should sign a **corporate resolution** authorizing the president (or other officer) to enter into an agreement to sell the assets of the business. This resolution can either (1) authorize the sale on specific terms, (2) accept an offer to purchase on the terms offered, or (3) authorize the president to enter into negotiations (sometimes exclusive) with a specific named buyer. It could be as simple as the following resolution:

---

[61] Brokers cannot "draft" contracts. Instead, they use preprinted contract forms that were prepared by attorneys and simply fill in the blanks.

Resolution

*"**Be it resolved** that the undersigned shareholders of Doozy Manufacturing Corporation (Company) authorize James P. Doozy, president, to offer for sale the stock or assets of Company on the following terms (specify terms)."*
And, if it is agreed:

"The shareholders further authorize James P. Doozy to retain the firm of _____ as exclusive agent to represent Company in the marketing and sale of Company."

If you, as buyer, want **exclusivity**, another sentence should be added to the letter of intent (and to any contract that follows), substantially in the form set out below:

"During the term of our negotiations, you will not enter into any negotiations with any other party nor accept any offer to purchase business from any other party."

Even when the assets (or business) you are planning to buy are owned by a corporation, some parts of a contract or letter of intent contain promises that the officers or shareholders of the corporation cannot make in their corporate capacity. For example, item 5 in the Sample Simplified Letter of Intent states, "You will enter into a noncompete agreement and management assistance agreement with me."

Does *you* refer to the corporation or to one or more of the officers or shareholders of the corporation? If, for example, the buyer expects the management assistance to be performed by an individual, then that individual must sign the contract or letter in his or her individual capacity as well as in corporate capacity. In other words, that person must sign twice. This is why, at the bottom of the sample letter, there are two signature lines for the seller. More about signatures will be covered in the following sections.

PART II
THE PURCHASE AGREEMENT

When you have decided to try to buy a business and how to structure your offer, the next step is to prepare an offer to purchase. An attorney or experienced broker will have professionally prepared blank purchase contracts and will gladly go over them with you to assist you in structuring your offer.[62] The broker's assistance can be invaluable during this process because he knows the seller's requirements. He has probably gone over several different "structures" with his client. The broker will try to help you for another very basic reason: he will not receive a commission unless a sale is successfully consummated.

Importance of Legal Assistance

It is recommended that you hire your own attorney to review any purchase agreement (or offer to purchase) before you sign it, or sign it subject to review and approval by your attorney. Your job is to agree on the price and terms of acquisition. Your attorney's main job is to be sure that the wording of the agreement will protect you. After signing it, you, your broker, or your attorney can present the offer to the seller, his agent, or his attorney. Submitting unsigned offers generally does not get the seller's full attention. And if you have questions about financial and tax implications, consult your accountant before signing and submitting it as well.

Taking Title

An attorney can also advise on how to "take title" and how to file for a charter if you wish to operate as a corporation.[63] Title is taken in the name of the entity that will buy the business. Generally, this entity is a person (individual) or a corporation. If it is to be a corporation, a corporate officer must sign the purchase contract.[64] You can buy and own (take title to) the business in one of three ways: (1) as **a sole proprietorship** (you are the sole owner), (2) as a **partner** in a

---

[62] When selecting an attorney, it is wise to remember that attorneys have specialties. Try to find one experienced in handling the sale of businesses.

[63] It is not required to retain an attorney in order to apply with your secretary of state for a charter, but every corporation needs a charter to become incorporated. As part of this process, your attorney will prepare corporate by-laws and provide you with a minutes book.

[64] Sometimes, offers to purchase are submitted before a corporate charter is issued. In such a case, a purchase contract will include language like, "buyer reserves right to take title (at closing) in corporate name."

partnership (if you wish to have partners), or (3) in **corporate name,** if you own or wish to form a **corporation**. An existing corporation, of course, can buy and own more than one business. The "partners" could be or become shareholders in the owning corporation.

If you have decided to have partners or other shareholders, it is highly advisable to enter into a **preliminary operating agreement** or **preincorporation agreement** with them before you submit your offer. They may have opinions about the price and terms you offer. And it is highly advisable that they specifically authorize you in the agreement to buy the assets (or stock) of Doozy before you enter into a binding contract with the seller. Failure to have appropriate agreements between the partners or shareholders in place can result in costly and unfortunate disputes after a business is purchased. Problems between shareholders and partners could fill many books. They generally arise because (1) no formal written agreement sets out the parties' financial responsibilities to each other or (2) how to resolve disputes when they arise. Specifically, each partner or shareholder is entitled to know (1) how profits will be distributed and (2) how each will be paid in the event the company is sold or liquidated or if a shareholder or partner dies. Let me cite an unfortunate case.

Case History – SHAREHOLDER DISPUTES

Three shareholders (members) in an advertising company had signed an operating agreement. Their original intent was that there be four members. The agreement was not specific enough to offer clear guidance about how to resolve disputes, but it did state that all votes required approval of 75 percent of the members. For better or worse, since there were only three members, nothing could be achieved without unanimity. Any member could request binding arbitration however. All three members were employed by the corporation, but the member who had been elected president had all the financial authority. Not wanting to use attorneys (because of the cost involved and to avoid irritating the president), the other two members took no formal action to resolve the disputes that arose. Three months later, the corporation (an LLC) had lost over $200,000 and the two minority members were still hesitating to involve an attorney.

Moral 1 – draft all agreements to fit the facts, i.e., the number of actual members.

Moral 2 – don't hesitate to get help as soon as disputes arise. You could lose a lot of money by waiting.

As is the case with a seller, a buyer also must have proper authority to buy a business or to enter into a binding agreement to buy a business. Therefore, in addition to a preincorporation agreement, the shareholders or members of a corporation should adopt a **corporate resolution** that specifically sets out the authority of the person making an offer. Let's assume that you have agreed to purchase Doozy for $160,000 with a $100,000 down payment but only have $60,000 in available funds. Four friends agree to back you and put up $10,000 each. The preincorporation agreement states that stock will be issued to all five shareholders and that all five must put up their money by a certain date. This agreement might go on to state that the money would be used to purchase a specific business.

After the corporation is formed, the shareholders should adopt a resolution authorizing you to enter into a contract with the business owner. It could be as brief as the following. The adopted resolution would be entered into the corporate minutes book.

Resolution

*"**Be it resolved** that John Doe is hereby authorized to offer to buy the assets of a business known as Doozy Manufacturing Corporation with principal place of business at (insert address) on the following terms (or at a price not to exceed $_____)...*

ATTEST, Secretary of _____ Corporation on this ___day of ____ (month and year)."

DESCRIPTION OF PURCHASE AGREEMENT

The basic blank purchase agreement (generally referred to as **purchase contract**) used by brokers is an uncomplicated two- or three-page document that has been prepared by an attorney. It simply sets forth in binding legal language the same points of agreement listed in the letter of intent. In addition, there are almost always attachments to a contract. These are referred to as **exhibits** and **schedules**. They are always referenced in a contract and therefore become part of the contract. On larger or more complex transactions than the sale of Doozy, the contract might run to many more pages than the sample in the Appendix.

The schedules, generally, list or describe in detail what assets it is you are agreeing to purchase, such as,

- Schedule of furniture, fixtures, and equipment (FF&E)
- Listing of customer accounts
- Schedule of trademarks and trade names
- Depreciation schedule (necessary for a stock sale)

The exhibits, generally, are existing documents that set out in detail legal matters relating to the intended transaction. These may include

- Lease on business premises
- Equipment leases (on company trucks, for example)
- Employment contracts
- Supplier agreements
- Closing balance sheet for business (vital for a stock sale)
- Noncompete agreement
- Management assistance agreement
- Price sheets

There are some points in a purchase contract (and in the schedules and other documents attached to or incorporated into a contract) that only an attorney experienced in corporate law will know how to draft. These may include the seller's **warranties and representations**, escrow arrangements, noncompetition agreements, and the like. The covenants and warrants in the body of the sample contract plus the brief warrants listed in Special Stipulation 8 of the sample contract are adequate for many small business sales. In addition, there are "closing documents" that an attorney should draft, such as any promissory note that the buyer will give the seller. Despite efforts to standardize the form and content of many documents, certain documents that are valid in one state may not be valid in another state.

Notice that at the bottom of the Purchase Contract, there are two signature lines for the seller: the first for his signature as an individual and the second for his signature as a corporate officer. If the Seller is not a corporation, one signature line may be adequate to protect the buyer.

Filling Out the Purchase Agreement

If a broker or attorney is assisting you, he or she can help. A broker will normally ask you questions and fill in most of the blanks in the agreement for you with your answers and add helpful suggestions. Sometimes, filling out the purchase agreement is very straightforward. In any event, I suggest that you start by filling out the sample contract. It is helpful in some cases to go through the exercise of filling out a preprinted contract several times before signing it or submitting it to the seller.

In the middle of the first page of the sample contract are seven blank lines where you can enter the classes or amounts of each asset you intend to buy. This is the so-called "allocation of purchase price." The total of the "allocations" equals the price you are offering. Begin by filling in the price you wish to offer. Then enter the known quantities. Some of these are shown on the seller's offering document, i.e. the amounts of inventory the Seller offers to include. Next, you might enter the total value shown on Schedule A. The difference between these known amounts must then be allocated among other specific classes of both tangible and intangible assets.

Do not forget to assign realistic values to the management assistance and to noncompetition agreements. The balance (or unallocated value) is generally assigned to goodwill. Finally, it may be useful to divide the goodwill into various classes of intangible assets—the trade name, trademarks, and customer list, for example.

The next section deals with the method of payment. The total of the down payment and the deferred payments must be the same as the total shown under the allocation section. During the *negotiating process*, there may be some changes in both the allocations and the price. But, the total in the final contract and the values you allocate are shown on the starting balance sheet of your new business. And the total of the payments is shown on the seller's ending balance sheet. In other words, the purchase price equals the selling price.

Since the two most costly components of most acquisitions are the equipment and the inventory, carefully review all items of FF&E on the Schedule A. Determine whether Schedule A is complete and if the value shown for each item is reasonable. Then turn your attention to the inventory you are buying.

Classes of Inventory

The allocation of inventory will be different for virtually every business. There are many different kinds of inventory, and for your protection, each might need to be treated as a separate item in the purchase agreement. Typical classes of inventory are listed below. Most will not be shown on a seller's balance sheet or on the offering document or profile, but they may have substantial value and be on hand in substantial quantities. Some of these are the "hidden assets" mentioned earlier in the book. More importantly, these may be things that are critical to the smooth operation of any business. In a small retail business, it may be adequate to list and assign value to only the "supplies" and "resale merchandise." A possible allocation for Doozy is shown on Table 14. Following Table 14 is a possible "allocation" for a larger business.

Shop supplies	Office supplies	Cleaning supplies
Rental inventory	Resale merchandise	Raw materials
Work-in-process	Finished goods	Parts inventory
Shipping and packing supplies	Printed materials of many kinds	Intellectual property of many kinds

There are two critical factors to keep in mind: (1) the problem of mismatched or obsolete inventories and (2) the problem of running out of critical items soon after taking over ownership of a business. Assume your purchase agreement states that there shall be on hand at closing a combined value of $100,000 in resale inventory and supplies, and when the inventory is counted the evening before the closing, there is in fact $100,000 worth on hand. Things seem to be in order to proceed with the closing (see Part II of the next chapter). But the next day, with customers standing in line, you discover several small problems; there is no extra cash register tape, no extra toner cartridge for the copier, and no packaging materials of a certain size.

They may be larger problems as well. Let's assume that you have bought a liquor store that historically had equal daily sales of wine and of spirits. But the owner/seller had been preoccupied with the upcoming "closing" on the sale of the store, and the wine inventory was now well below desirable levels but the inventory of spirits was above normal levels. Not only will you probably lose some sales to regular customers, you may lose some of these customers who have been loyal patrons of your store. Worse, from a cash flow standpoint, you may have to immediately replenish the wine inventory at an immediate cost of, perhaps, $25,000 or more. Read **Case History: Mismatched Inventory** in Chapter 7.

Obsolete inventory is a separate problem. Often, this problem can be avoided if, before preparing your offer, you can walk through the store or plant with the owner and carefully observe the different quantities and classes of inventory. I am reminded of a furniture plant that, from time to time, changed designs of various items carried in its catalogue. However, carefully stored away were table legs and other parts for items that had been discontinued. All of these obsolete items had been included in the inventory and were included on the company balance sheet, but they had little or no value to the buyer of the business. In similar situations, the purchase agreement must spell out some remedy for the buyer.

Distinguishing between rental inventory and resale inventory deserves some attention also. Many businesses receive income from the rental of equipment even though rental income may not appear as a separate revenue account on the income statement. A ski shop, a forklift dealer, and a business providing staging services for concerts and conventions and many other types of business all (typically) rent a lot equipment. This equipment is carried on the balance sheet as is the other inventory, but rental equipment to their customers is depreciated as it wears out. It is wise to separate the values assigned to these two different classes of inventory in the purchase agreement. Understand the business you are buying so that your agreement reflects the distinctions between the classes of inventory that are critical to the smooth transfer of ownership and operation of the business in the critical period following the change of ownership.

Terms of Management Transition Assistance

Filling out the other sections of the purchase agreement does require some careful attention. Again, an experienced broker or attorney can be a big help. But the business will, hopefully, become your business and must reflect your needs and wishes. Think through what needs to be included in each of the special stipulations. Look, for example, at **Stipulation 2: Management Assistance.**

How many hours of assistance do you feel you need? What days of the week or hours of the day will work best? Can the assistance be provided (1) by telephone, or (2) will it require the seller's presence at the place of business? Or is some combination of the two preferable? Some of the assistance may specifically require the seller to introduce you to key customers and suppliers. Of course, if some part of this stipulation (or other special stipulation) requires amplification, insert wording like,

> *"As set out in the Management Assistance Agreement attached as Exhibit A."*

Be sure to include wording that will protect you in the event seller does not complete his obligations. Note in the **purchase agreement (portion)** following Table 14 that $50,000 is allocated to management assistance. The $50,000 is payable in a one-year note without interest. If assistance is not provided as agreed, the buyer could—if appropriate language is included in the agreement—(1) "hold back" some of the $50,000 until the assistance is completed or (2) deduct a sum that reflects the value of the uncompleted assistance or (3) in writing inform seller that he is in noncompliance and the $50,000 note is rescinded.

Dates in a Purchase Agreement

The sample contract has three key dates for every buyer to observe: **offer date**, **acceptance date**, and the **closing date**. An offer only remains "open" until the acceptance date. If the seller has not accepted the offer by that date, the offer expires. Other dates are also important. Some are discussed later in this chapter and some in the next chapter. These include dates for fulfillment or removal of each of the contingency clauses, dates for making deferred payments to seller, default dates (which are set out in the promissory notes), notification dates (between the parties) of various events, dates for performance of management assistance by seller.

In the course of the *negotiating process*, it may be necessary to change several of the dates. In the signature block also are dates after each of the parties' signatures. The buyer may sign (offer) on one date, and the seller(s) sign (accept) on another date.

Signature Block and Attachments

Often, only the buyer and seller sign the purchase agreement or contract, both acting in their individual capacities. If either buyer or seller is also acting in his or her corporate capacity, it is necessary that he or she sign as a corporate officer. The name of the corporation and the title of the officer must be shown. If the agreement refers to the spouse of either party, then the spouse must also sign. Sometimes, also a third party will sign if the third party is guaranteeing the deferred payments due seller. Below the signature block is space to list separately all attachments that are mentioned in the agreement.

CONTRACTS AND THE LAW

Contracts are written for the purpose of protecting the parties to the contact. To me, this means two things:

1. The parties to a contract each receive what they thought they had bargained for.

2.   The contract contains adequate remedies in the event that something unforeseen arises after the sale.

In most cases, if a contract has been professionally drafted and fully explained to the parties, there are no problems or misunderstandings. When problems arise, it generally is because of a poorly drafted contract, not because of conscious intent to defraud or deceive. But occasionally, one party or the other, more often the purchaser, is damaged financially in some way. So it seems sensible to examine the possible causes of damage. These are (1) the concealment of pertinent or material facts, (2) the nondisclosure of pertinent facts, and (3) the misstatement of material facts.

An example of "concealment" might be the seller's failure to tell the buyer that that there were several pending lawsuits against the selling corporation. An example of "nondisclosure" might be the omission of the fact that a corporation has several shareholders who were not aware that the majority shareholder was in negotiations for the sale of the company. An example of misstatement might be for the seller to accept an offer that clearly stated that "all assets will be conveyed free and clear" when he knew that there were outstanding loans secured by some of the assets (cars, trucks, computers, etc.).

Another area that is open to misstatement involves a seller's customers. A seller may say that he has, for example, $100,000 in orders on the books when he knows that this is a guess or is untrue. If such a statement is a material inducement to the buyer, the buyer should check it out and include in the contract some statement from the seller, binding him or making him legally liable in some way for any misrepresentation. What remedy, for example, would you have if, at closing on the purchase of Doozy, unfilled work orders total only $65,000 instead of the $80,000 asked for in the letter of intent above?

A prudent buyer should be aware of several facts regarding concealment and nondisclosure. First, in most "arm's length" commercial transactions, neither party has a duty to disclose to the other party all information that may have a bearing on an intended transaction. Second, a misstatement of information must result in injury or financial loss, and third, a misstatement must have been relied upon.[65] It must have been a material inducement for the buyer to go forward with the purchase.

Only an imprudent buyer would say to himself that, if it turns out that something the seller said is wrong, "I can just sue him and collect damages." A

---

[65]   Bergh, *Business Law*, 59–61.

buyer must do his own investigations and, if some representation seems important (material in legal language), require that the representation be included in the warranties and representations section of the contract. In other words, the buyer must "take the seller up" on what he says if his statements have a bearing on the buyer's decision to buy or upon the price the buyer decides to offer.

Uniform Commercial Code and the Bulk Sales Act

Much fraud in the past revolved around the sale of inventory. If, for example, a company sells you its inventory for, say, $300,000 without informing you that the inventory had not been paid for, the suppliers of that inventory may have the right to come to your place of business and repossess their "goods" even though you had paid for them when you bought the business.

For reasons like that, the U.S. Congress in 1948 adopted the Uniform Commercial Code, which had as its objective not only the protection of the buyer from fraud but also the elimination of variations among the state laws governing the sale of "goods" (merchandise and other business assets). A part of this code is the Bulk Sales Act, which was subsequently adopted by many states. Even states that did not adopt the act *in toto* have adopted statutes that include many of its provisions.[66]

One of the purposes of the adoption of this code was to prevent buyers from being scammed: business owners could sell their businesses, together with the goods that comprised them, to unsuspecting buyers before they had paid their suppliers. The suppliers could then repossess their "goods," and the buyers would be left with little recourse. For this reason, many states require that, before a sale takes place, sellers give buyers signed affidavits listing all their creditors and the amounts owed to them.

It is then the responsibility of the buyer to notify the creditors of the impending sale and ask them to confirm the amounts the seller listed on the affidavit. In most cases, notification is handled by the closing attorney, so the buyer has little knowledge of the amounts owed. The important thing is to be sure that the seller is in a position to pay off these debts before the closing or simultaneous with the closing from the buyer's (your) down payment. Check both the accounts payable balance and cash balance on seller's latest balance sheet. If your state has adopted the Bulk Sales Act provision of the Uniform Commercial Code, notification of creditors must be at least ten days prior to the closing.

---

[66] Bergh, *Business Law*, 440

If the seller is not in a position to retire these debts and convey the assets "free and clear," the buyer may consider assuming some of these debts as part payment of the purchase price. Assumption of debt is a common way to finance a business acquisition, particularly larger acquisitions, but it should not be done unless the buyer has all the facts and is protected by a "right of offset" clause in the purchase contract. See Stipulation 8 (**Seller Warrants**) in the sample contract and following discussion.

Sellers' Warranties and Representations

A good contract does more than set out the terms and price that a buyer is offering. It also contains certain promises that the seller makes to the buyer regarding the condition of the business (or assets) being offered for sale. These promises are referred to as "**warranties and representations**." The seller must warrant, for example, that he (she) has good and marketable title to the assets and will remove any defects from title or bill of sale to make it marketable. Read carefully the paragraphs at the bottom of the first page of the sample contract and also seller's warrants on pages 2 and 3.

The seller also is expected to warrant something about the condition and quality of these assets and the accuracy of his (or the business') financial statements, with language, such as,

"All equipment is in good and working condition or will be by the time of the closing."

"Seller warrants that accompanying financial statements for years _____ and _____ are true and accurate to the best of his knowledge." (Include specific time periods.)

Every buyer should think of other aspects of a business that the seller should warrant since they may not all be included in a standard purchase contract or in the sample in the Appendix.

If the contract states that certain terms and conditions must be met before a business is sold, the precise terms must either be attached to the contract or spelled out in the contract itself. For example, if the buyer observed that a certain piece of equipment was not working when he visited the plant, the contract should state that there will be a reinspection before closing. It might include the following or similar language:

"If any piece of equipment is not working at time of closing, either (a) the closing will be delayed until seller repairs it or (b) seller will reimburse buyer the cost of having equipment restored to good working condition."

There should be no ambiguity about the obligations each party assumes as a condition of a sale. A failure to spell out these obligations in detail in the contract and to spell out how and when each obligation will be satisfied could result in serious and costly problems after the sale has been completed. Sometimes, contracts include penalties for failure to complete an obligation in full or on time.

Some "attachments" to the contract are considered **closing documents** and are not available at the time the original contract is entered into between the parties. These attachments are documents that reflect what the parties have already agreed to but which need to be put into proper legal form and, therefore, must be drafted by an attorney. An example mentioned above is the promissory note.

In addition to a detailed description of the four classes of business assets (listed in Chapter 3), it is normal that the purchase of a business includes two other very important assets that are not found on the balance sheets of most businesses:

- **A noncompete agreement, or restrictive covenant,** in which the seller agrees not to compete with the buyer for a period of time (often three to five years) within a certain territory and in certain product lines or activities
- **A management assistance agreement** under which the seller agrees to provide certain specific services to the buyer after the sale for a certain period (perhaps several days or weeks at the place of business scheduled over one to three months, plus several hours of consultation by telephone during and after the completion of the "hands-on" phase)

These two agreements are often vital to the success of a new business owner. They must be included in, or attached to, every purchase contract if the buyer requests them to be. If the seller resists entering into such agreements, it is normal to expect the price of the business to be reduced. Note that the performance of these two assets (agreements) relies upon the owner of the business individually. These agreements cannot be performed by the business itself. Care should, therefore, be taken to identify in the contract who will perform the requirements of these two agreements and how much value will be allocated to them in order to protect you, the buyer, in the case of the seller's nonperformance.

The terms of these additional agreements should be as specific as possible so that there is no misunderstanding after the sale has been closed regarding the seller's specific obligations or the penalty for his nonperformance in whole or in part. If, for example, the seller proceeds to open a competing business after the sale, the seller may win back an exclusive product line or may take several of your key customers. Either of these events could reduce the value of the business and make it difficult for you to meet your or the business's financial obligations. For this reason, many contracts contain language stating that all or part of the deferred payments due seller will be waived if seller is in noncompliance or in violation of these agreements (or certain provisions of the agreements).

Conduct of Business Pending Closing

This section refers to how the parties expect the seller to conduct (operate) his business between the acceptance of a contract to sell his business and the closing on the sale. Seller's "conduct of business" during this period can be critical to a buyer's success and should be covered adequately in a contract. Obviously, a buyer would not want significant changes to occur without his knowledge or approval or would not want the seller to be unavailable for consultation or delivery of documents.

The purchase contract in the Appendix touches on this important point only twice. See the sentence at the end of paragraph 1 on page A-11. It states that the seller covenants that his "business will remain open during normal business hours." This covenant is not adequate to cover many things that could occur in a business between the date of signing a contract and the date of conveyance to the buyer. See also Stipulation 8.e., which refers to "conducting business in the normal course" and lists several "normal" business practices. The standard way to cover issues concerning operation (or conduct) of the business is simply to place prominently in the contract the following important sentence:

"The business will be conducted in the normal course pending closing."

However, each situation is different. The *normal course* clause above is adequate for many situations, but what is *normal* may need to be spelled out in some detail in the case of the business that you are buying. The management of inventory and the sale or purchase of expensive pieces of equipment, for example, can be issues in many acquisitions. Issues regarding employees and payroll can also be important. If a business takes on additional (and unanticipated) expenses (or debt) during the preclosing period, the buyer's cash flow projections and, possibly, the price the buyer is willing to offer will have to be revised. The business owner may, for example, buy a new truck. This and similar issues can be handled by adding additional specific **warranties or covenants** (such as the following). In some cases several warrants may be needed. See **Seller Warrants** on page A-13

"All inventories will be replaced on an as needed basis by seller."

"Seller can make no material changes to the conduct of business, including the hiring or dismissing (key) employees with express written consent of buyer."

It would not be unusual for the seller to reduce inventories or, perhaps, run them down dramatically, if not prohibited by contract. Some sellers tend to relax during this period of ownership transition; they feel their work is done, and they can simply wait to pick up a check at the closing. If the seller does not replace the inventories when the items are sold, the amount of "cash on hand" will increase and, in effect, increase the down payment the seller will receive at closing. This is very favorable to a seller but could put a buyer into a very difficult situation. Not only would a buyer need some additional funds (working capital) to replenish the inventories but a buyer might also lose some sales or have to slow down production (in the case he lacked some of the necessary raw materials).

Buyer's Warranties

Buyer warranties are not the "standard" but buyers are expected in some situations to give warranties to sellers. Such warranties are generally intended to (1) make the seller feel more secure, and (2) assure seller that buyer will not "bleed" the business, that is, remove assets such as excess cash from the business while still indebted to seller. If a buyer pays himself $100,000 for example, rather than $50,000 during his first year of ownership, the business will have $50,000 less cash flow available to meet debt obligations.

These warranties often evolve during the *negotiating process*. A seller may agree to certain more favorable **terms of purchase** (such as a lower down payment) if a buyer "warrants that he will limit his personal compensation to "no more than $75,000 per year for the first three years following closing." Or perhaps, if there is a lease in place on the business premises that the buyer wishes to assume (rather than attempting to negotiate a new lease with the landlord), the seller might require a **warrant** that the buyer will personally hold him (the seller) harmless from any future lease obligations.

Another reasonable warrant for a seller to request is one regarding insurance. Such a warrant may be worded:

> *"Buyer warrants that until the promissory note held by seller is paid in full to keep all assets fully insured at their market values."*

The more willing a buyer is to offer a seller reasonable protection, the more willing a seller generally is to accept "terms" in lieu of a "cash" contract. Frankly, in my experience, many sellers do not fully understand the types of financial and legal protection that may be available to them if they accept a sale on terms in lieu of cash. They must be educated before they will feel comfortable extending substantial amounts of credit to a buyer, particularly to buyer with little industry experience.

When purchasing stock (instead of assets), the seller is expected to warrant the net worth of the corporation. Let's say the net worth, after completing an audit, is $800,000. If the buyer buys the stock on terms, the seller might require him to warrant that "he will at all times following closing maintain a net worth of $800,000, or not less than the balance owed to seller, whichever is greater" or "maintain a net worth equal to 110 percent of the balance due seller." The extra 10 percent requirement is to protect seller from absorbing the costs of liquidation or of paying a broker to resell the company in the event of a default by buyer.

Remedies for Nonperformance by Seller

What will happen if (1) seller does not do everything he has promised to do in the purchase agreement or if (2) some of the promises (warranties) turn out to be overstated or false? Does a buyer have any remedies? Can the buyer return the business to the seller and get his money back? The broad answer is that "the contract does the talking." If the contract is silent on how to handle misrepresentations, the remedies may be limited to hiring an attorney to bring suit against the seller for the damages the buyer has suffered as a result of the misrepresentations. Of course, pursuing legal remedies can be a costly and lengthy affair.

It is far better to spell out **remedies** in the purchase contract. See, for example, Stipulation 8 (b) in the sample contract. It reads, in part, as follows:

> *"There are no undisclosed liabilities, claims, or pending or threatened litigation, and seller will defend and hold Purchaser harmless from same if any shall arise from actions which took place prior to the closing."*

This is the so-called "**hold harmless**" clause and it should be in every contract in some form. Of course, this stipulation could be more detailed, spelling out different remedies for different infractions.

One of the most effective remedies is what is referred to as the **right of offset**. This is a right that lets a purchaser "offset" certain costs against future payments due the seller. For example, if seller warrants that "there are no undisclosed liabilities" and it turns out that seller (1) owes the landlord money, perhaps for common area maintenance (CAM) charges that had not been billed by the time his business was sold or (2) owes money to the tax authorities (for nonpayment of the prior year's personal property tax, for example), what could a purchaser do?

It is normally prudent for a purchaser to pay **undisclosed liabilities** because failure to do so might seriously interrupt your business. There is often not time to dispute the charges with the former owner or in court. For this reason, most contracts includes language that lets a purchaser pay the charges and deduct or "offset" the charges paid against future payments due the seller.

Before exercising this **right of offset**, Purchaser must first inform the seller that he has received a bill that he did not agree to assume (or a bill that was more than the debt he agreed to assume) and give the seller time to either pay the bill or dispute it. Many contracts have wording like,

> *"If the disputed item remains unpaid ten (10) days after notification, buyer has right to pay same and deduct amount paid from next payment due seller."*

The possible existence of undisclosed liabilities (even when Seller has signed all the appropriate warranties) is one important reason to always hold back some portion of the purchase price. Of course, the buyer's best remedies are (1) to be thorough during the analysis and due diligence phases, (2) draft the purchase agreement carefully with professional help, and (3) review the results of the **lien search** which all experienced closing attorneys will perform during the *closing process*.

Another "remedy" is to prorate certain predictable expenses at the closing. Most closing attorneys will always do this and show each party's share of the prorated expense on the Settlement Sheet, but **prorating** bears mention here as a remedy. The monthly rent, the payroll, payroll taxes, real estate, and personal property taxes and insurance premiums are predictable. Ask the attorney to split, or prorate, these expenses between the parties at the closing. If, for example, Seller has paid the monthly rent of $2,000 and the closing is on the fifteenth, buyer will be expected to reimburse one-half, or $1,000 at closing. However, if the rent had not been paid, Seller should reimburse buyer $1,000.

Earnest Money

The purpose of earnest money is to "bind" a seller to a buyer. For this reason, earnest money is often called the binder. By accepting the earnest money and letting a third party hold it on his behalf, the seller is generally agreeing not to negotiate with or even talk to other potential buyers for a certain length of time.

In virtually every case, an offer to purchase a business is in writing and accompanied by an earnest money check.[67] This check is normally held by the broker (if the seller is represented by a broker) and deposited in the broker's escrow account upon acceptance of all the terms of the offer by both buyer and seller. The broker in such cases would be the **escrow agent**. However, you might elect to have the seller's attorney or your bank hold the **earnest money**. There are many options for how and where the earnest money is held.

The amount of earnest money that is appropriate is the subject of some ongoing discussion among professionals. It seems safe to say that the standard is between 5 percent and 10 percent of the offering price. Thus, in the case of Doozy, the **earnest money binder** might be around $10,000. Conventions vary from city to city. The purpose of the earnest money is to let the seller know that you are a serious buyer. A larger binder always makes the buyer appear more serious to the seller.

At closing, the earnest money is paid to seller as part of the down payment specified in a contract. In practice, the escrow agent gives the check to the closing

---

[67] It is advisable to "let the contract do the talking." It is not advisable to ask a seller directly if he or she will accept an offer of, say, $100,000. There are too many unknowns at this stage in the negotiations. Even if a seller says, "Yes, I will accept it," the seller may not realize that your verbal offer includes (in your mind) the entire inventory. The seller may intend (in his mind) to sell the business for $100,000 plus the value of the inventories.

attorney who disperses checks to the seller. The earnest money cannot be spent prior to the closing; it is simply held in escrow.

Earnest money is not "at risk" of being lost or forfeited until all the "conditions" of the offer or purchase contract have been met. If any conditions cannot be met (within the times or dates stipulated in the contract), the escrow agent must return the earnest money to the buyer, in full, when asked to do so. Be sure that the seller understands the importance of adhering to these times or dates. However, if all conditions have been met and the buyer does not close by the agreed-upon closing date, the earnest money is "at risk" and could be forfeited.

Every condition must have a specific date set out by which it must be completed or removed by the responsible party. If the responsible party has not met the terms of a condition by the date specified, the other party generally has the right to withdraw from the contract, or the contract may be deemed null and void, depending upon how the contract is drafted. The thought of reading and signing a purchase contract can be intimidating, but it is simply your offer to buy the assets or stock of a business. The essence of a contract is something like this,

> *"I'll offer you a price of $X and a down payment of $Y, if you will sell me your business, sign an agreement not to compete with me for five (5) years, and stick around after the sale for two months to train me, provided that I can meet certain conditions (see below)."*

Any offer should (1) identify the specific assets you wish to purchase (with dollar amounts for the "countable" items, such as inventories) and (2) set out all the "conditions of sale." Review the first page of the contract in the Appendix. In this contract, the FF&E is itemized in an attachment to the contract referred to as Schedule A.

Contingent Nature of Contracts

It is quite common for a contract to include a few conditions that must be met before a sale will go forward. These "conditions of sale" are generally referred to as **contingencies**. The most common involve a buyer's ability to accomplish certain important tasks before a contract is enforceable, especially the task of arranging financing to meet the terms set out in the contract. Thus, an offer will include language like,

"This offer is contingent upon purchaser's ability to obtain or to sat-isfy the following specific conditions."

These conditions do not necessarily pertain to Doozy, or to any specific business, and are not intended to be all-inclusive, but each of them could be important. Review with your broker and attorney, or other trusted adviser, the conditions you feel should be included in your contract. There may be others important to your particular situation.

THIS CONTRACT IS CONTINGENT UPON PURCHASER'S ABILITY TO: (SAMPLE)

Lease on Business Premises: Secure on or before a certain date (insert date) a lease on premises, say, for five years at $10 per square foot (or at the lease rate the business now pays) from the owner or landlord.

Acquisition Financing: Obtain by *insert date* a bank loan of at least $200,000 (sometimes a specific bank is named) at an interest rate of not more than 8 percent annual percentage rate (APR) secured by personal assets of the buyer, with "interest only" paid for the first six months after closing.

Working Capital Loan: Borrow the sum of $100,000 at 8 percent APR from *name of bank* with the inventory and equipment included in the sale as collateral for the loan.

Appraisals: Obtain qualified appraisals on the real estate, equipment, inventory, etc., giving a combined value of at least $300,000.

Approvals: Receive from seller's suppliers (customers) written approval at least ten to twenty days prior to the stipulated closing date for purchaser to assume or obtain (contracts) (dealerships) (lines of merchandise) on the same terms now in force.

Permits and Licenses: Obtain all required permits and licenses from the various governmental authorities. (It is useful sometimes to list the required permits individually.)

Earnings Confirmation: Confirm the representations on seller's financial statements and tax returns for the past two fiscal years and do other related analyses and "due diligence."[68] Or purchaser's ability to confirm that adjusted pretax earnings last year, calculated on the accrual method, for example, is at least $50,000.

Compliance: Inspect business premises and determine that all equipment is in good working order and the facilities are in compliance with all applicable regulations. When buying a business that includes real estate, compliance with environmental regulations is especially important. Example: "*Sale is contingent upon confirmation that property is above flood levels.*"

Inventory, Work-in-Process, and Work Orders: Obtain a count and valuation of all inventories (using current vendor catalogues, supplier price lists or invoices) immediately prior to closing and, if their total value is less (or more) than the value offered in the contract, reduce (or increase) the purchase price and down payment by the amount of the shortage (or overage). It is most unusual for the amount of inventory set out in a contract to match the amount on hand at closing. Thus, some adjustment to the purchase price at the closing will be necessary.

Accounts Receivable and Accounts Payable: Confirm account balances with customers or vendors.[69] Generally, a buyer will not assume accounts payable or other current liabilities and will not purchase the accounts receivable. If he does either, the offer should include provisions requiring the seller's personal guarantees regarding (1) collectability of the receivables and (2) remedies in the event that the assumed liabilities are greater than agreed. These points are necessary to mitigate the buyer's risk. Review the discussion about the "hold harmless" clause.

Failure to include important contingencies into a contract or to remove or satisfy a contingency can cause problems down the road. Many sellers and buyers have become impatient and decided to move ahead and close. The refrain "we

---

[68]   The term *due diligence* cannot be defined specifically. It is not an accounting term. It refers to the process of doing the investigations and analyses necessary to determine that a business is in fact in the condition it was represented to be in and that all contingencies and other conditions of sale have been or can be met. See Glossary.

[69]   Sometimes, all the confirmations are not available at time of closing. Audit or other financial records as of the day of closing cannot be prepared until those records have been compiled. Contracts, therefore, stipulate that there will be adjustments made when those records are available, generally within five or six weeks of closing.

can take care of that later" still rings in my ears. The following story illustrates the potential dangers in taking that approach.

Case History – THE IMPORTANCE OF PERMITS AND LICENSES

The purchaser of a security guard business failed to obtain a license from the governing state agency. In fact, he had not been told that a license was necessary. When a customer asked to see his license, the buyer was red-faced. But he promptly called the state agency and asked if it would allow him to stay in business if he promptly enrolled in the required prelicensing class. Fortunately, the state authorities agreed, but the buyer was operating "outside the law" for several months. The licensing process cost this buyer considerable time and money. An offer should always be "contingent" upon buyer's ability to secure the specific permit or license needed.

Moral – find out what licenses are required and include a suitable contingency clause in your offer.

Acquisition Financing and Liens

If a contract is contingent upon third-party financing, it is wise to identify specifically the assets that will be offered as collateral because the lender, may require a **first lien** against them. Seller will have a **second lien** on those assets behind that lender if he finances some portion of the sale. He may not agree to subordinate his lien rights. Doing so would particularly complicate matters (in the seller's mind) if he had to take the business back. A good counterargument is that the bank will be seller's best watchdog; the bank will do everything possible to prevent a default, including reviewing the buyer's financial statements and, maybe, limiting buyer's compensation. This potential problem may be resolved by giving the bank first lien on some assets and the seller first lien on others.

Observing Dates for Removing Contingencies

As in all contracts, dates are very important. Just as the contract specifies that the closing must occur by a certain date, so each contingency should have a specific date for its completion, satisfaction, or removal. The completion dates may be the same as the closing date agreed to in the contract. However, most buyers would want to know as soon as possible if a contingency will be met. Therefore, certain contingencies may have earlier (and possibly different) dates for their completion.

The time between contract acceptance and closing is not a time for a buyer to sit back and watch the grass grow. A thirty-day period for removing the contingencies can go by very quickly. The danger to the buyer is, if the seller becomes convinced that the buyer has not made a "good faith" effort to remove the contingencies, he will not agree to a contract extension and may, in fact, be legally entitled to enter into a contract with another buyer. You cannot simply tell the seller on the thirtieth day that you could not get a necessary bank loan and expect your earnest money returned.

Any offer should spell out in detail all necessary conditions of sale. This means conditions imposed upon buyer or seller. If any condition imposed upon the seller is not met by the date set out in the accepted offer, you would have the legal right then either to (a) restructure your offer or (b) request return of your earnest money. Whether you choose *a* or *b*, do so promptly and do so in writing so that there can be no misunderstanding. If you do not notify seller, it can be assumed by your silence that the conditions have been met to your satisfaction and that the closing date does not need to be extended. However, you must be diligent in attempting to satisfy your conditions if you expect your earnest money to be returned.

Remember that your contract may include "by reference" some schedules, or exhibits. If these are not attached to the contract, the contract is generally not enforceable until all parties have received and approved every document that has been made part of the contract.

Allocation of Purchase Price

As stated above, a contract or offer should specifically identify the nature, quantity and value of each asset (or class of assets) to be sold. It is understood that assets not specifically identified in the offer will be excluded from a sale, but sometimes, it is helpful to also identify any assets that the parties agree to exclude.[70] This process of assigning values in the contract is referred to as the **allocation of purchase price**. If it is not written out, there can be costly misunderstandings because allocation has income tax and other implications for both parties. For you, as a buyer, the values allocated are the value that are shown on your starting balance sheet and are used as the basis for your future depreciation.

---

[70] It is normal practice for the broker to provide the buyer with a complete description of the FF&E when the buyer is introduced to a business. See Schedule of Day Care FF&E and Description of Rental Equipment in Chapter 1.

Let's look at a possible allocation included in an offer to purchase (the assets of Doozy. The values given each class of assets are close to their estimated market values. From the buyer's point of view, the objective to is "write off" the entire purchase price—that is, to deduct from future earnings as much of the purchase price as possible. This means assigning larger values (when possible and when acceptable to the IRS) to assets that can be written down, depreciated (**tangible assets**) or amortized (**intangible assets**), and smaller values to others.

For example, you may want to add value to the FF&E to reflect the purchase of Doozy's new $15,000 truck. The seller may resist because he wrote off the entire $15,000 cost as a Section 179 expense. As a consequence, the full value allocated to the truck will be taxable to him as ordinary income. The seller, quite logically, wants to minimize the income taxes due from the sale, so there is often some negotiation surrounding the allocation issue. Note that the allocation in Table 14 below shows considerably more detail about values than the letter of intent. This is quite normal and very appropriate.

If the seller does not accept the initial offering price of $150,000 and you want to raise your offer, the price must be reallocated. In this situation, you may assign value to other assets, to the trade name Doozy, for example, or add value to the assets shown below. The allocation, including values assigned to goodwill, must always equal the purchase price.

Table 14. Allocation of Purchase Price in Doozy Offer

Value of Raw Materials Inventory	$20,000
Value of FF&E, Tools and Dies (fixed assets)	45,000
Value of Miscellaneous Supplies	5,000
Value of Management Assistance	20,000
Value of Restrictive Covenant (4 years)	30,000
Value of Work-in-Progress Inventory	20,000
Value of Finished Goods Inventory	10,000
Possible Offering Price:	**$150,000**

The allocation of purchase price for a business larger and more complex than Doozy may include many different classes of both tangible and intangible assets. Likewise, the payments to the seller(s) may be allocated differently. The hypothetical "allocation" below is for a bonsai nursery with two shareholders. The purchase agreement may read something like the following:

Purchase Agreement (Portion)

On the dates herein stated, Purchaser agrees to buy, and Seller and its share-holders individually and in their corporate capacities agree to sell, the following classes and quantities of assets of ABC Bonsai located at 400 Main Street, Anytown, USA (hereafter, Seller, or Business) being all the tangible and intangible assets necessary for the normal and proper operation of Business:

Allocation of Price

Furniture, fixtures and equipment (see schedule A)	$100,000
Leasehold improvements (see schedule B)	90,000
Shop and yard tools	20,000
Raw materials, potting soil and mulch	10,000
Bonsai trees and plants	200,000
Other trees and plants	60,000
Resale merchandise	40,000
Inventory of containers (for potting)	10,000
Packing and shipping materials	10,000
Office and shop supplies	10,000
Customer list	30,000
Inventory of current catalogues	10,000
Rights to use of trade name	50,000
Goodwill	60,000
Noncompete agreements (2)	100,000
Management assistance	50,000
Total	**$850,000**

Allocation of Payments

Earnest money	$ 50,000
Balance of down payment	250,000
Noncompete agreement no. 1 (5 years at 5%)	60,000
Noncompete agreement no. 2 (5 years at 5%)	40,000
Promissory note (five years at 5%)	400,000
One-year note for management assistance	50,000
Total	**$850,000**

All deferred payments will be evidenced by promissory notes to be prepared by the closing attorney. The interest bearing notes will be paid in monthly installments. The one-year note will carry no interest.

The closing attorney will also prepare a security agreement, which will give Seller a first lien against the tangible assets listed above and against rights to use of trade name of Business.

In some cases, the breakdown of assets (listed in an offer) needs to be shown in greater detail than shown above. The categories used will normally be also shown on the starting balance sheet of the buyer or buying corporation, so the categories should be those which are useful in the ongoing management of the business and in the monitoring and timely reordering of inventory. Because some stores have too much inventory of several kinds but too little of other kinds, a buyer may want the allocation to specify a desirable or normal mixture.

TAX TIP: Some tax advisers recommend allocating as little value as possible to goodwill and other nondepreciable assets. Federal tax rules change from time to time. Today, in order to write off goodwill, the owner must show that the goodwill has been impaired—that is, it is worth less than a business owner paid for it. Useful tax information can be found at IRS.gov/uac/Tax-Topics.

Case History – MISSING ALLOCATION OF PURCHASE PRICE

The parties did not want to hold up closing, so the closing attorney added this language to the contract: "Parties have agreed to handle the allocation of the purchase price outside of closing." The seller wanted certain allocations "low" so he could keep his income taxes low. The buyer wanted some allocations higher so he could write off more depreciation. The parties never came to a meeting of the minds. As a result, the buyer could not set up his starting balance sheet and the seller could not file his federal tax return. The seller's attorney became upset with the buyer and sued him. The combined legal fees far exceeded any tax savings either party may have enjoyed from receiving a more favorable allocation.

Moral – don't forget to allocate the full purchase price in the purchase contract before the closing. Failure to make an allocation can lead to problems.

Deductions from Pretax Income

In the years after buying a business, the buyer can probably take tax deductions from earnings in the amounts set out below in Table 15 or slightly more.[71] The amount of the deductions depends upon several choices every buyer must make. The most important of these choices is generally how to depreciate the fixed (or depreciable) assets acquired in a sale.

In the Doozy contract, **fixed assets** are assigned a "contract" value of $45,000. You, as buyer, can depreciate the $45,000 in several ways. If the value is written off over five (5) years, tax deductions are $9,000 per year (so called **straight-line depreciation**). You could write off 150 percent or even 200 percent of the "straight line" amount, which is **accelerated depreciation**. In Doozy's case, at 200 percent, your first year write-off would be $18,000. Depending upon the useful life of each asset (or class of assets), the buyer might decide to write them off in less than five years or to take a longer write-off.

If you choose to take **accelerated depreciation**, the amount of depreciation you can take will decline each succeeding year. Many buyers accept this trade-off because it is important in the early years of ownership to reduce or postpone expenses, including the expense of income taxes. Income taxes can be reduced also by increasing the owner's salary. A salary of $50,000 is used in Table 16. I am opposed to increasing owner salary too quickly because I believe it is beneficial in the long run for your company to have **retained earnings**—that is, to build up **equity** in your company.

If forecast earnings for the first year are no more than, say, $36,000, there will be no income tax due. After taking $42,900 in deductions in Year 1 as shown in Table 15 below, in fact, there will be a tax loss of $6,900. This loss can be carried over to Year 2, thereby increasing Year 2 tax deductions from $21,700 to $28,600. It is important to your **cash flow** to allocate the purchase price in a manner that will reduce taxable income in the years following the purchase. Remember that depreciation is a noncash deduction; it is a write-off. The other three items (values assigned to management assistance, restrictive covenant, and interest) are generally paid in cash in the year in which the tax deduction is taken. Review Tables 16 and 17 in conjunction with Table 15.

---

[71]   It is advisable to ask the advice of a CPA before agreeing to an allocation of purchase price for tax reasons because the IRS has guidelines concerning what is reasonable and defensible.

Table 15. Total Deductions

Noncash and Other Deductions	Year 1	Year 2	Year 3	Year 4
Depreciation ($45,000/5 years)	$9,000	$9,000	$9,000	$9,000
Management assistance	20,000	0	0	0
Restrictive covenant	7,500	7,500	7,500	7,500
Interest on $100,000 note	6,400	5,200	3,800	2,400
Total Deductions[73]	$42,900	$21,700	$20,300	$18,900

The fact that most of the purchase price of a business can be written off, or expensed, over time, as appears to be the case with Doozy, supports the use of pretax income instead of after-tax income when estimating the **earnings value** of a business. Some appraisers disagree on this point. Use of after-tax earnings might be more appropriate when valuing businesses that (1) are larger than Doozy and (2) sell for several times more than their book value.

If you elect to buy stock instead of the assets, the situation is different because you will use the same **depreciation schedule** that the present corporation has been using. In Doozy's case, the **fixed assets** have been fully depreciated, so there would be no depreciation deduction available to you until new depreciable assets are purchased. The other deductions on Table 15 will be available.

Because some "to be purchased" assets may be owned individually (not by Doozy Manufacturing Co., Inc.), several "parties" must sign the contract, even if they are the same person. This person signs in two capacities: as president of Doozy and as an individual. If the noncompete and management transition agreements are in separate documents, they must also be signed. The contract should clearly state which of the deferred payments (if any) the buyer will pay to the business (the corporation) and which will be paid to the owner (or other parties) personally.

After making an offer, you will probably receive a counteroffer, as happened with the **letter of intent**.[73] This is normal. There are often several exchanges of offers, counteroffers, and responses. Even if the price and terms of payment

---

[72] Buyers should be aware that this book does not offer tax advice. It is advised that they seek the advice of a CPA to determine permissible deductions since tax laws change frequently.

[73] The (your) original contract will contain wording like, "This offer is open for acceptance until (insert specific date)." Be careful to observe and to enforce the dates in your offer because an acceptance received after the specified date will not be binding unless negotiations between the parties to the contract have continued by mutual agreement after that date. If there are questions about this point, talk to an attorney.

offered are accepted, there are often other "terms" that require further negotiation. In these cases, the business broker can be your best ally. He knows the seller and will understand the meaning of all terms used in your offer. If there is any uncertainty about the meaning of any part of the written offer, consult an attorney because the written word controls. Verbal agreements are not enforceable and should be avoided.

Suggestion—if it is still difficult to determine what price to offer, see if there are similar businesses on the market in your trade area. Review the Business for Sale classification in local publications. Check prices at which they are offered. If they are listed through a broker, consult the broker to learn if they are similar to Doozy in terms of annual sales, earnings history, asset value, and the like. Brokers want to be helpful because you may become a client if you find them to be helpful.

But for the moment, let's assume that your offer to buy Doozy has been accepted on the terms set out below and we can move to the *due diligence process* and the *closing process*.

> ## Summary of Offer to Purchase Doozy Manufacturing
>
> **Price**: $150,000, with a down payment of $55,000.
> **Balance**: payable in two five-year notes at 8.5% annual interest.
> > Note 1—$50,000 note secured by the various inventories.
> > Note 2—$45,000 note secured by the fixed assets.
> **Monthly Principal and Interest payable to seller:** $1,949

Negotiating the Final Contract

This process should not be intimidating. It might be more intimidating if the seller accepted your offer without changing a word. What usually happens is that the seller signs the offer with some changes: he marks through several items in your offer, inserts new wording, initials the changes, and gives the offer back to you. This is his **counteroffer**. Some of the requested changes may be words; some may be numbers. In some cases, the seller or his broker or attorney may insert a new paragraph covering some point that you had not addressed in your offer. Some typical changes involve price, down payment, earnest money, closing date, terms of any promissory note, and the date for acceptance of the offer (or counteroffer).

You then review the requested changes. It may be prudent to share the counteroffer with your attorney, particularly if the changes are lengthy or complicated. If you agree with the requested changes, simply add your initials beside the seller's initials. Then promptly deliver the contract with the initialed changes back to the seller. If both parties have initialed all changes and are in full agreement, the offer becomes a binding contract. It is an agreement between two parties subject, of course, to the fulfillment of the conditions set out in the contract. If you feel that you cannot accept some of the changes in a seller's counteroffer, mark through them, insert the language you prefer, and initial.

Responding to counteroffers may involve several exchanges of documents and, sometimes, requests for additional information. If there is a broker, the broker goes back and forth between the parties. It's his job to work out the details. For larger businesses, this negotiating process may take several weeks. For smaller businesses, the process is often resolved in two or three days. In most cases (where there is a broker), you will have given the broker some idea what your negotiating positions are. This helps move things along. During this time, it may be necessary to change the dates set out in your offer: the "acceptance" date and the "closing" date. See the last two paragraphs of the sample purchase contract.

In some situations, the seller will not accept your offer or make a counteroffer. This occurs very infrequently, usually when the parties are far apart in their opinions of the fair value of the business. Your offer then expires if your offer or purchase contract includes these (or similar words):

> "This instrument is open for acceptance until noon on the __ day of _____ (month and year)."

If an offer or counteroffer has not been accepted by the acceptance date, the buyer and the seller are free to enter into negotiations with other parties. For this reason (among others), it is important always to be aware of dates in an offer and in a contract (after the offer has been accepted).

It is very important that your offer (or counteroffer) not remain open indefinitely. You may want to make a run at trying to buy another business, but you do not want to end up contractually obligated to buy two businesses. In every case, after the **acceptance date** has passed, you are entitled to a full refund of your **earnest money**.

Even after you receive the full refund of your earnest money, a seller can have a change of mind and decide that your offer was acceptable. He might, in fact, sign and initial it and return it to the broker. At this point, things can occasionally become complicated, so remember how important it is to include an "acceptance date" in your contract *and* to inform the seller in writing that your offer has expired and your earnest money has been returned. If you have continued to negotiate after the "acceptance date", you and the seller may have some continuing contractual obligation to each other. Check with your attorney.

Sometimes, you (the buyer) feel that the seller's last counteroffer is still too high. You have adequate cash to make the down payment, pay the closing costs, and handle short-term working capital requirements. Your concern is being able to meet on time the deferred financial obligations you will owe the seller. Often, the key to resolving this concern is to point out to the seller the anticipated cash flow problems and the months in which you expect them to occur. Ask the seller (again) to alter the schedule of payments to fit the reality of his business. One suggestion is shown below:

Suggestion—if the seller will not agree to modify the terms of payment, offer to pay **all-cash** in exchange for his agreement to accept a reduced price. This might entail taking out a loan from a commercial bank and, thus, deferring the closing until you can close on your loan. But the seller at this point may be relieved that he will not have to worry about not receiving the deferred payments on time. After all, very few sellers want to ever be in the position of having to take over ownership again after having been retired for a while (and perhaps having moved to another city) in the case a buyer defaults.

Summary Checklist for Contracts

This is a review of the essential components of an offer. Does your contract (letter of intent, draft contract, offer or purchase agreement) include, at a minimum, the following information?

1. Seller's warranty that all assets will be conveyed in fee simple free from any and all defects.
2. Selling price (have you calculated the **present value**?).
3. Down payment at closing plus any deferred portion.
4. Amount of principal and interest to be paid to seller, to bank or others.
5. Dates on which all payments are to be made.
6. Dates on which each payment becomes delinquent or incurs a late charge.
7. Collateral for each of the deferred obligations.
8. Terms and conditions for reducing or releasing collateral.
9. The closing date on the sale of the business.
10. List of contingencies and dates for their fulfillment or removal.
11. Right of offset clause (in case of undisclosed liabilities).
12. Addresses to which all payments are to be sent or made.
13. Allocation of selling price, including all assets to be conveyed.
14. The earnest money. Who will hold it? When can it be returned?
15. Where and when will the seller's management assistant be provided?
16. Under what conditions may the stated selling price be adjusted?
17. Procedures for valuing the inventory.
18. How to contact Seller after the sale is complete.

Does the contract spell out each party's rights or remedies in event that

1. Payment on any note or other deferred obligation are late.
2. A loan or note is in default.
3. Buyer fails to close on the sale on the date stipulated.
4. Seller refuses to close (sell) on the date stipulated.
5. Inventory value(s) differ from values shown in the Allocation of the Purchase Price section of the signed (final) contract.
6. Certain assets are not on premises or in good working order at closing.
7. Seller does not provide all management assistance as promised.
8. Seller violates some part of the noncompetition agreement.

Finally, if the business, like Doozy, is holding customer deposits, the contract should state clearly:

1. How the deposits are to be shared among the parties and
2. When and in what form the buyer's share will be transferred.

Suggestion— Register your tradenames. The name of your business and other names used "in trade" may be your most valuable assests. The act of incorporating will protect your rights to the exclusive use of the business name in the state of incorporation but will not prevent businesses in other states from using the same name. Also, it will not prevent others from using the names of products (or product lines) that you sell. For assistance, go to *uspto.gov.trademarks*.

CHAPTER 7

THE CLOSING ON THE SALE

PART I
THE DUE DILIGENCE PROCESS

After a purchase contract has been negotiated and signed by the parties, and all changes inserted in the contract in longhand have been initialed, original copies are given to each party. Then the *closing process* begins. It consists of two distinct parts: the due diligence part, which begins as soon as the contract is signed (perhaps thirty days before the closing), and the actual closing part, which begins after the contingencies and conditions of sale have been satisfied. With smaller businesses, the *due diligence process* may take only a week or two. With larger businesses, the process may require well over a month, especially if approval from suppliers, bankers, or other third parties is needed.

The *due diligence process* was touched upon in the previous chapter. It essentially is the process by which the buyer

(1) confirms the representations and other promises made by the seller in the contract and

(2) removes or satisfies contingencies set out in a contract. Remember, a sale is almost always contingent upon the satisfaction of certain conditions requested by buyer and/or seller, such as "buyer's ability to obtain a lease (or lease extension) on the business premises" from the landlord or seller's ability to confirm

or back up some verbal representation he made about profit or cash flow as an inducement to the buyer (to submit an offer).

The buyer of Doozy believes that the business during the last fiscal year earned $31,000 (after deducting the owner's salary) on sales of $300,000. The buyer also believes that Doozy's physical plant is adequate to handle sales of about $463,000 without the need to purchase any new equipment. It is obviously important that the buyer to be able to confirm these assumptions. However, the contract is silent on these matters. Why? Because the buyer was advised not to draw attention to what the business could do in the future since the seller may at the eleventh hour conclude that he "underpriced" the business and, therefore, wants to take it off the market.

Buyer was, instead, advised to focus on two things during his *due diligence process*:
(1) the financial results the business in the past and
(2) on the values of the assets to be conveyed.

The signed contract contained only five contingencies (all fairly typical) that had to be satisfied during the due diligence period. The contract stated,

> *"This contract is contingent upon buyer's ability to satisfy the following conditions:*
>
> 1. *Confirm that last year's sales were at least $300,000.*
> 2. *Obtain a new lease on the premises for five years at a gross rent of no more than $1,800 per month.*
> 3. *Obtain an independent appraisal confirming that the FF&E has a value of $45,000.*
> 4. *Confirm that Doozy had in hand at time of closing bona fide signed customer work orders of at least $60,000 and unbilled work-in- process of at least $24,000.*
> 5. *Confirm that there are on hand inventories (of resale merchandise, raw material, and finished goods) with a book value, contract value, or original cost of at least $30,000."*

After analyzing Doozy's financial history, the buyer chose to keep the contract as simple as possible. He felt he would be adequately protected if the five conditions set out above were met or exceeded. Note that:

(1) the $1,800 monthly rent in Condition 2 exceeds Doozy's current $1,500 monthly rent shown on Table 7, and

(2) the $24,000 work-in-process exceeds the $20,000 value allocated in the purchase price in Table 13.[74]

The seller may or may not agree to all these conditions, especially Condition 4. However, the buyer felt that there might be more work-in-process in the shop than the seller had told him originally. Besides, there is no harm in asking. Condition 4 could be a useful negotiating tool. Contingency clauses for some businesses are lengthier and more numerous.

The typical buyer's greatest fear is that the earnings or sales of a company have been overstated, so often, there are several "contingencies" dealing with past earnings. If it turns out that earnings were overstated, the buyer may be hard-pressed to meet his debt service requirements or to pay himself an adequate salary, so clearly, it is important to be able to confirm that earnings are equal to or greater than represented. The following case history is fairly typical.

---

[74] A comment on Rent—if the buyer were fortunate enough to secure a new lease at less than $1,800 per month, the savings would increase projected income. Also, rent is what is called a "fixed expense." It will probably not change over the next five years. Most expenses are what are called "variable expenses." They will generally rise at least with the rate of inflation. When preparing your budget, always distinguish between the two.

Case History – NEED TO CONFIRM EARNINGS

A wholesale distributor reported pretax earnings of $500,000 for the past twelve months, an increase of $100,000 over the prior year. The buyer, relying upon this representation, offered $2,700,000 and inserted into the contract a condition that he be able to confirm the $500,000 in reported earnings. Seller agreed. However, due diligence turned up the following concerns:

1. Rent of $6,000 for the last month had not been paid.
2. Outstanding commissions and profit sharing obligations of the company totaled $150,000.
3. At least $150,000 of the accounts receivable from the past year seemed to be uncollectible.

There was no explanation for why rent had not been paid. The profit sharing was not due until ninety days after the end of the year and was not recorded in past years until it was paid. Since pretax earnings equaled 10 percent of sales, the $150,000 in doubtful accounts receivable represented overstated earnings of about $15,000. Adding the unpaid rent, preliminary earnings were overstated by $21,000, or 4.2 percent, which is not very serious. The serious part is the $150,000 in accrued obligations. It turned out that the company recorded $110,000 in accrued obligations the year before. Thus, a negative adjustment of $40,000 appeared in order ($150,000-110,000). The total of the three adjustments is $61,000, or over 10 percent of the reported earnings. The buyer felt that the adjusted earnings of $439,000 ($500,000 less $61,000) were inadequate to support the price he had offered, so he requested the owner to reduce the price from $2,700,000 to $2,400,000. The seller would not budge from the original price. Fortunately for the buyer, the contingency in his contract giving him the right to confirm the company's earnings let him withdraw from the contract.

Moral – be sure the contract gives buyer the right to confirm seller's financial representations. Without it, this buyer would have been in trouble (or lost his binder).

Bank Loan Approval

In the Doozy contract, the seller has accepted the buyer's request for "owner financing." The majority of small businesses are sold with some owner financing, but this is not always the case. Often, buyers must obtain outside financing.

When this is so, a sixth contingency must be added to the contract. The wording may look something like the following:

> *"This Contract is contingent upon buyer's ability to secure a loan of not less than $100,000 with a five-year maturity at an annual interest rate of 6.25 percent APR or less from a commercial bank. Written loan approval must be secured no less than fifteen days prior to the scheduled closing date."*

Banks will want to see a copy of the final contact. They will expect the buyer to prepare a business plan with projected earnings and cash flow. And banks will want some collateral as security for a loan. Often, the collateral is in the form of a first lien against the assets of the business plus the buyer's personal guarantee. If the seller has agreed to offer some seller financing, the seller must then accept a second lien behind the bank. Sellers, of course, do not want to be in second position, so the form and amount of collateral may become a subject for negotiation. Banks, in my view, are often good watchdogs, so in effect, a diligent bank may also protect the seller's interests as well as its own.

Banks may do something else that could protect a seller; they may put a cap on the amount of compensation that a buyer may pay himself. In the case of Doozy, this may be an annual salary cap of $50,000. Of course, the original cap may rise or be removed under certain conditions. In the case of larger or more complex businesses, banks can also be expected to add additional covenants as conditions for their loan approval. If you are unable to secure a loan commitment, you are probably entitled to full refund of your earnest money.

TIP: If you have done your homework and have prepared a good business plan, securing a loan will generally not be difficult. While banks are in the lending business, they are not in the risk business. They want your business to succeed. Your banker should be your friend. Stay in touch with him. However, when you approach a banker, be prepared to explain how the business operates and why you feel you can manage it successfully. Also, be prepared for tough questions from your banker. Tough questions do not mean the banker has no interest in your proposal; it means the banker wants to see if you've done your homework and how you react under pressure. Your business broker probably maintains a list of which banks are currently lending.

When Financial Statements Are Missing or Incomplete

From time to time, the unincorporated sole proprietorships will have incomplete financial statements. Performing due diligence is a little different when the statements are not as complete as Doozy's (or in the case of the business discussed above), but it is still very important. In fact, it is vital to "buying a business without being had." As a buyer, you might hear a seller say that he earned, say, $50,000, but according to the only available financial statement, the seller's business showed a small loss. Let's assume that you have found such a business and, in fact, are ready to submit an offer. How should you proceed? What kind of contingency clause or other protection should you put in your contract?

The *due diligence process* is often quite simple, especially when the buyer has experience in the industry. For example, buyers of convenience stores, which are all-cash businesses, are usually concerned only with the top line—that is, the gross sales. This is because buyers with extensive industry knowledge know exactly what the **cost of goods** is from their experience with similar stores and they know what their **operating expenses** will be.[75] They know the rhythm of the sales—that is, the times of the day or week when sales are normally high and when they are normally low. And they know that an average sale is exactly, for example, $8.52. They estimate that the cost of goods for beverage products is 20 percent and that beverage products generally comprise 70 percent of gross sales. These buyers know a lot about the businesses they are looking at, so the sole contingency might read,

> *"This contract is contingent upon buyer's ability to confirm that current weekly sales total at least $20,000. If buyer does not notify seller to the contrary by (insert date), it is agreed that this contingency has been satisfied in full."*

To satisfy this contingency, a buyer can count the number of customers entering the store during certain hours and watch what products the customers leave the store with. A buyer can also look at the record of purchases in a store. That's easy to do if all purchases come from one or two sources (vendors). If the

---

[75] The cost of goods should generally be a relatively fixed percent of gross sales. To calculate the percent in many small businesses, it is sufficient to divide the purchases made during a period of time by the sales (or revenue). However, when it is believed that the sales figures are incomplete, it is important to get atypical costs of goods percent from other sources or from other similar businesses. In larger businesses, the cost of purchases and cost of goods may differ substantially because of changes in inventory levels.

cost of goods is 20 percent, then gross sales are estimated to be five times purchases. If purchases are expected to be 40 percent of sales, multiply by 2.5 to get sales, and so on. This system isn't perfect, but is very useful when the owner of a business pays cash for some purchases. Simply adding up the checks posted to "purchases" in such a business will not work.

Some buyers want to count the daily receipts or review daily cash register tapes (or records) to determine sales. This is quite accurate unless the owner has paid any vendors in cash for certain purchases. If sales receipts appear low, ask the owner if he has paid vendors from the cash register and ask if he has kept a record of such purchases. If purchases (or cost of goods sold) appear low, ask if he ever pays vendors from some other accounts (or from his pocket).

During *due diligence process*, one seller boasted that "this business put my four kids through college," but the business showed only a modest profit. Fortunately, the office manager (who did not want to lose her job) was very cooperative. She had a complete record of purchases and knew exactly what the cost of goods and gross profit margins were. After speaking with her, the buyer was satisfied that the seller's representations about profitability were accurate. To see how another buyer satisfied the contingency about sales, see case history below.

Case History – DUE DILIGENCE WITHOUT FINANCIAL RECORDS

A convenience store had no reliable records of sales or earnings. The buyer did, however, know some employees at the beer and gasoline distributors that supplied the convenience store. They told him what the value of weekly shipments had been. To these figures, the buyer added the standard markup to derive an estimate of sales of these products. To determine miscellaneous sales, the buyer and his brother sat in their car in the parking lot and counted the number of walk-in customers who entered the store during selected periods. The customer count was more than satisfactory. In fact, based upon this information, the buyers determined that actual weekly sales were well in excess of the $20,000 estimate provided by the seller.

Moral – when reliable financial records are not available, there are still ways to perform extensive and accurate "due diligence."

Obviously, you should proceed cautiously when the only available financial statements appear misleading or suggest that profits are less than the owner tells you they are. However, there are almost always ways to reconstruct statements and to confirm with considerable accuracy the sales and gross profit of a small business. The basic lesson learned through trial and error by many buyers is never to buy a business without putting adequate contingency clauses in a contract to protect them in the event that it is not possible to confirm sales, cash, flow, profit, or other key financial criteria.

Renegotiation

If changes in the purchase contract, in the price or in the terms of purchase, are indicated by factors that come to light during due diligence, further negotiations are needed. Since the original contract has been negotiated and accepted, I call this process **renegotiation**. The *due diligence process* may bring to light factors that make a business appear more profitable or less profitable to the buyer. Often, due diligence brings to light positive things about a business that even the seller did not know. In such cases, no renegotiation is needed.

When due diligence suggests that earnings are overstated, renegotiation is called for. Many sellers will agree to a downward adjustment in the price. Some will not. But do not hesitate to ask. And always, put your request in writing. If the seller fully understands why you have concluded, or feel, earnings are overstated, he may be more inclined to accept some favorable adjustment. However, as you might expect, the seller's first reaction often is to become defensive. If you want to buy the business, it is important to respect seller's feelings and not lose heart.

Further negotiations, over time, may open up ways to bridge the gap between the price the seller wants and the price that you have determined is fair. Ask the seller to respond to revised offers in writing. In the seller's responses, he may reveal things he would like added to the contract. These become a basis for tradeoffs. At this stage in the *negotiating process*, the total price that the seller receives from a transaction is not always the foremost thing on his mind. Listed below are a couple of responses that may lead to a successful conclusion of the renegotiation process. For example, the seller might say:

"I will agree to reduce the contract price by $30,000 if you will

1. *Accept $20,000 less inventory (or some other value)*
2. *Permit me to exclude a new vehicle from the sale*
3. *Keep me (and my family) on the medical insurance policy during the management assistance period*

4.   *Reduce the term of the promissory note (for the balance of the purchase price) from five years to four years*

5.   *Increase the down payment by $20,000."*

Whatever the seller says in his responses, a written response indicates that he still wants the sale to go through. My advice is, hang in there and continue to seek imaginative ways to bridge the gap. Some trade-offs involve only price and terms, but others involve strategies that might reduce the income taxes a seller will owe as a result of the sale. Some involve things that seem to make the transition of ownership smoother from the seller's perspective. Changing the method for valuing inventory may be helpful. Frankly, most sellers do not know what the stumbling blocks are until after an exchange of offers. Some renegotiation may occur in a verbal exchange, but after some agreements have been reached, be sure to have them appended to the contract and initialed.

Compliance with Bulk Sales Act/Notification of Creditors

After both parties have signed the contract, often the first task is to notify creditors. Get a copy of their addresses and send them a notice (at least ten days before closing) stating what the seller says the account balance is. The creditors will only respond if the account balance in your notice is not as shown in their records. If the contract does not indicate that you are assuming some trade debts, this step may not be necessary, particularly if you are sure that the seller has (or will have at closing) adequate funds to pay off the outstanding balances due his suppliers.

PART II
THE CLOSING PROCESS

The *negotiating process and the due diligence process* have both ended satisfactorily. All contingencies have now been removed or satisfied. There was no need (in the case of the Doozy purchase) to secure bank loan approval since the seller has agreed to carry (take back) notes for the balance of the purchase price. It appears that the sale will go forward and that you are now ready to purchase the business you have found. The *closing process* is the last step in buying a business. It is an exciting time but a time to be careful as well. This process begins with preparing a preclosing checklist that lists the specific tasks that a prudent buyer must complete before taking title to his new business. A list of these tasks may include those listed on the following preclosing checklist as well as some additional items:

Preclosing Checklist
Tasks to Be Accomplished by Purchaser Prior to Closing

Check (✓) when done

☐ Complete any work needed to mend or update your credit scores
☐ Transfer (establish) telephone service
☐ Transfer (set up) electricity and water service
☐ Obtain business license and other licenses needed—County Courthouse
☐ Determine closing costs from your agent or closing attorney
☐ Open checking account and get checks printed, if an asset sale
☐ Obtain cashier's checks for down payment and closing costs
☐ Arrange for Visa or MasterCard service in business name
☐ Apply for approval to assume distributorships or dealerships
☐ Arrange for yellow page ad (new directory cut off is August 31) or Google business ad
☐ Obtain a federal ID number from your local IRS office
☐ Obtain general liability insurance binder
☐ Obtain other insurance (or binders) as indicated
☐ Arrange times and personnel to take preclosing inventory
☐ Inspect premises and determine if all FF&E are on site and in good repair

☐ Obtain landlord's approval to assume current lease or obtain new lease

☐ Be sure all contingencies in your purchase contract have been completed by the dates stipulated in the contract

☐ Determine the time and place of the closing

☐ Obtain Certificate of Use and Occupancy from city hall

☐ Ask your accountant to set up a starting balance sheet

☐ File application with the state for your corporate charter (if indicated)

☐ Arrange times with seller for training and to tell employees of sale

☐ Call your agent for assistance if you have questions

Suggestion—buyers tend to focus on getting documents that the seller or closing attorney is responsible for providing. They tend to forget that they have chores to tend to as well. Do not forget to pick up a signed copy of your lease on the business premises, to pick up an insurance binder from your agent, and to get all required permits and licenses. Someone at the closing table may want to see these. If a banker is involved, he will certainly want evidence that these tasks have been completed. See Preclosing Checklist above.

TIP: Because it is sometimes difficult to know which assets to insure or at what values to insure them, some purchase contracts include language requiring the seller to keep all insurance in force at his cost for thirty (30) days following the closing. Inventory levels, for example, may change substantially.

Taking and Extending Inventory

Closing normally begins the day (or evening) before the actual closing with the "taking" and "extending" of the inventory. The parties need to know if the actual value of inventory on the day of closing is more or less than the value set out in their contract. Sometimes, the parties elect to use a professional inventory service (as in the case of liquor stores) and split the very reasonable cost. Inventory services may use handheld computers and can count, value, and extend the inventory in an amazing brief time. Sometimes, the parties take and value the inventory themselves. Taking inventory is a three-step process: (1) counting the items in inventory, (2) putting prices (or costs) on the items, and then (3) extending the inventory.

Because the prices are visible in retail businesses, extending inventory usually begins with the "shelf" price. In a manufacturing business, there are no "shelf" prices, but there should be price sheets showing the prices at which the products are offered for sale. In every case, the "sale price" must be converted to a cost. The results of the inventory, using a retail liquor store as an example, may look something like the following:

No.	Description of Item	Unit Cost		Total
4	1.5 liter bottles of XYZ	@ $7.85	=	$31.40
7	1.5 liter bottles of ABC	@ .50	=	66.50
9	1.5 liter bottles of ABC	@ 9.50	=	66.50
8	.75 liter bottles of ABC	@ 5.25	=	42.00
	Total Retail Price			$178.15
	Less Markup at 50%			59.38
	Seller's Cost			**$118.77**

When a larger business is sold, often, personnel from the accounting firm representing one or both parties monitor the process by "spot checking" the inventory count. If the inventory is large, inventory sheets are prepared a few days in advance. Sometimes, these sheets show current or replacement costs for each item. In other cases, the values of many inventory items are not known when the count is taken. In these cases, the inventory sheets are taken back to an office the following day and priced out from suppliers' catalogues or price sheets. It is always helpful if the method for pricing (costing) inventory is set out in the contract. There can be a big difference between the original cost and the current or replacement cost of an item.

After the items in inventory are counted, the inventory must be valued to determine its cost.[76] There are several ways to do this, among them:

1. **Discount the retail price.** For merchandise in a typical retail store, take the "shelf" price of each item and discount it by the average

---

76 Extending the inventory on larger businesses may take several days or more, so some of the normal closing tasks cannot be completed by the day of actual closing or the transfer of ownership. This is not a problem. However, if you feel this will occur in your case, it is wise to review the implications with an experienced attorney.

markup. If the shelf prices of the wine in a liquor store total $30,000 and the average markup is 40 percent, the cost basis of the wine is $21,428:

Calculate: $30,000 divided by 1.40 = $21,428.

2. **Use recent supplier price lists.**

3. **Check original purchase invoices**. Always do this, for example, in the case of automobile or equipment dealers that have large ticket items in inventory.

4. **Discount shelf price by gross profit margin.** If a drugstore or furniture store has an inventory value of $500,000 (using the retail sticker prices) and has a gross profit margin of 35 percent, the cost basis (original cost) of the inventory is about $325,000. Often, different margins are used for different classes of inventory.

   Calculate: $500,000 × .35 = $175,000 Gross Profit.
   $500,000 less 175,000 = $325,000 Cost Basis.

5. **Calculate the percentage of completion.** A cabinet manufacturer or manufacturer of armored truck bodies may have work-in- progress, so each item or job may have to be priced individually.

The method for pricing and extending inventory is fairly standard within a given industry or market, but it must be spelled out sufficiently so that the parties know they are in agreement. To do this, a contract might include language like one of the following provisions:

1. *"Inventory will be valued at the lower of seller's original cost or current replacement cost."*

2. *"Inventory will be valued at the shelf price less 25%."*

3. *"Inventory will be valued using prices on suppliers' latest price sheets."*

Adjusting the Purchase Price

Difficulties can arise when the value of the extended inventory differs considerably from the value set out in the purchase contract. If there is an overage, you may not have available funds to purchase the excess. If the value is less than called for, the buyer (you) may immediately after the closing have to purchase additional inventory in order to have sufficient inventory on hand to meet normal customer requests or, in extreme cases, to stay in business. It is prudent to include in your contract provisions that explicitly cover these situations, such as,

1. *"The value of inventory on hand at closing will be at least $100,000."*

2. *"If the value of inventories is less than the value set out above (in the contract), the purchase price and the down payment will be reduced by the deficiency."*

3. *"Inventories in excess of the value set out in this contract will be discounted by 10 percent or excluded from the sale, at the purchaser's option."*

4. *"If the inventory value exceeds $100,000, the excess value will be added to the purchase price and to the promissory note held by the seller. The down payment will not increase."*

In larger transactions, your contract may include some wording like,

> *"No adjustment to the price will be made unless the value found during the inventory count differs from the contract amount by more than $20,000"*

or

> *"Value will be between $2,000,000 and $2,100,000."*

Note that in the first provision, the buyer would have the right to walk away from the sale if inventory is short. The seller would have to purchase additional inventory prior to closing at his cost to make up the shortage (or agree to convey to buyer at closing cash equal to the deficiency). The key point is that all possible scenarios should be anticipated and remedies spelled out in the contract. Unfortunate things can occur when the values of inventories or distribution of items within a category of inventory are different than expected.

Case History – MISMATCHED INVENTORY

On the evening before the closing on the sale of a dress shop, there seemed to be far more dresses in stock than the buyer had recalled. When the inventory was counted and valued, the "overage" totaled $20,000. Since the contract was silent on how to handle overages, the buyer paid the extra $20,000. It turned out that a large percentage of the dresses were in petite sizes (the seller's size). The seller had returned "borrowed" items to the shop before the inventory was taken. The buyer soon learned, to his dismay, that "petites" were hard to sell.

Moral – put clauses in the contract on (1) how to handle overages and (2) handle mismatched inventory.

The purchase price is also adjusted for reasons other than shifts in amount and cost of inventories. Review the following:

1. **Lost or misplaced items of FF&E**—the easiest way to resolve this is to deduct the values shown on the description of furniture, fixtures, and equipment attached to the prospectus (or given to buyer later) or in a schedule attached to the contract.

2. **Damaged equipment or merchandise**—parties should get estimates of the cost of repairs and reduce the purchase price (and down payment) by that amount.

3. **Dated merchandise**—for example, unsold summer merchandise should be discounted if still in inventory in December. However, if a contract is silent on this point, buyers may have no recourse.

4. **Insufficient earnings**—see "Case History: Need to Confirm Earnings.

5. **Failure of seller to satisfy other contingencies**

Tip: A contract does not need to provide for an upward adjustment in price in the event of excess inventory. It can simply state: "The contract is contingent upon purchaser's ability to confirm that the inventory value on hand at time of closing totals at least $*(fill in blank)*." When the buyer has counted and valued sufficient inventory to be comfortable that the contingency can be met, the counting is suspended. Thus, the seller does not know what the final value is, and there is no danger of there being an unwelcome upward adjustment to the purchase price.

If possible, the count sheets are fully priced in time to give the closing attorney an exact inventory figure. The attorney can then adjust the purchase price and other closing documents, such as the promissory note, if the final figure differs from the figure in the contract. If the count and pricing are complicated, the inventory valuation may take several days to complete. However, closing normally proceeds as scheduled and revised closing documents are distributed to the parties when the inventory valuation has been accepted.

Role of Closing Attorney

Today, most small business sales are "closed" by a "neutral" closing attorney. This is an attorney who specializes in business closings; he represents neither the buyer nor the seller. He represents the contract that has been reached between the parties. Closings on the sale of larger businesses require attorneys representing all parties be present to handle different parts of the closing and represent their client's interests each step of the way.

Sometimes, something can go wrong at the closing. It is at the closing that any misunderstandings between buyer and seller need to be worked out. For this reason, the closing attorney will read aloud the purchase contract, bill of sale, and other closing documents in the presence of the parties. It is a time to be vigilant and be sure you understand every word. Ask questions. After the closing is completed, it may be too late to "straighten" something out.

Present at the closing are the closing attorney (and/or personal attorneys), the brokers, the parties, and sometimes their spouses. If the buyer is giving the seller a promissory note, the buyer's spouse may be expected to sign the note. Sometimes, there are two closings: one with the bank from which the buyer has borrowed some of the closing funds and then a second closing during which the parties sign (execute) the closing documents. It helps if a list of these documents has been distributed in advance.

In the previous chapter, the terms *offer* and *contract* were used interchangeably. Once the offer and the revisions to the offer have been accepted by both buyer and seller (referred to jointly as the "parties") the offer becomes a contract. A contract is an agreement that is legally binding on both of the parties who have entered into an agreement. An offer, or counteroffer, however, is binding on only the one party who has made the offer, and it is only binding until the **acceptance date** set out in the offer.

Importance of Dates

A binding agreement, such as a signed contract, must include the specific dates by which different parts of the agreement must be completed. The date for closing on the sale (and conveying the business to the buyer) is the most important date. If the contract does not clearly set out a date for handing over the business, it is not a contract because there would be no way to complete the contractual obligation. The dates for removing contingencies and completing the due diligence are also important and should be observed carefully. Normally, the contract states that the buyer "takes title" to the business from the start of closing day. Thus, he is responsible for expenses incurred from that time forward and is entitled to all income received.

The original offer may be worded in layman's terms, somewhat informal language, rather than in a more formal language found in a legally binding document. This is generally okay. However, informal documents often include language that is not very precise. As a result, the parties may interpret parts of the agreement quite differently from each other.

After an offer has been accepted, it is often redrafted by an experienced business attorney, generally an attorney retained by the buyer, and then submitted for the other party's attorney to review. It is very important not to assume there is understanding between the parties to a contract if these "understandings" are not explicitly written down.

Although the **closing date** is an essential component of any contract, with the approval of the parties, that date is often rescheduled to permit one party or the other to complete or remove a contingency listed in a contract. For example, titles to automobiles or real estate may not be ready by the original closing date, the accountant may not have prepared a closing balance sheet, the inventory process may not be complete, or an attorney may request more time to draft some required document. Some party whose approval to the sale is necessary (a banker or franchiser, for example) may not have sent in the approval. In such circumstances, it is prudent to extend the date until these documents or approvals have been prepared, received, and reviewed. However, with advice of your attorney, it is not at all unusual to proceed to complete the sale, leaving some legal details in the hands of the attorneys.

Lien Search

Remember that a seller must convey clear and unencumbered title to all assets that are to be sold. Thus, as part of the *closing process*, the closing attorney(s) will conduct a lien search to learn if any creditors have filed a notice at the local courthouse (or statehouse), advising the public that the business owes money. It is normal that banks, finance companies, and mortgage companies file a public lien against the assets that were financed. Sometimes, suppliers and other business creditors also file liens against certain assets. These creditors are referred to as lien holders. Occasionally, a lien holder does not remove a lien (even after having been paid in full), so you, as buyer, need to be vigilant.[77]

The seller (or seller's attorney) must arrange to pay off any liens against the business that might affect your ability to obtain a clear and unencumbered title to the assets that you are buying. If there is a neutral closing attorney, finding and removing liens (the lien search) becomes part of his or her normal responsibilities.

If the closing funds are inadequate to satisfy an unpaid lien, (1) the buyer can accept the asset subject to the lien and deduct the amount of the lien from the down payment and purchase price or (2) exclude the lien item from the sale and reduce the price of the business by the value of the item. This value is often shown on the schedule of FF&E attached to the contract or in the **allocation of purchase price** shown on the face of the contract. It is always wise for the closing attorney to inform seller immediately upon finding a lien so seller can arrange to pay it off in a timely fashion.

The Actual Closing

The actual closing occurs when the papers are signed and the exchange of ownership takes place. Closings can take place in the closing attorney's office, in

---

[77]   If there is evidence of payment, closing attorneys will remove the liens before or immediately after the closing. Or the attorney might pay off an existing lien from closing funds.

your broker's office, or at your bank. Your attorney may prefer that closing take place in his office. All are fine. The key is for you to be sure that all closing documents have been received and reviewed several days before the scheduled closing, are fully understood by you and your attorney, and are faithful to the understandings of the parties. **Do not proceed with closing if you or your attorney has not reviewed all closing documents in advance.** If you arrive at the closing table before an attorney has completed some required document, you might feel rushed to move forward with the closing without enough time to comfortably review the document. The attorney may feel rushed as well, and so the document may contain errors and must be reviewed carefully.

Be sure that the results of the inventory count and the inspections of the facilities and the FF&E have been made known and that your attorney and the closing attorney are aware of any need to adjust the price set out in the contract. These adjustments can easily be made on the closing day. The primary reason for adjustments is the change in inventory value that occurs almost daily. The final inventory value rarely matches exactly the value(s) set out in the contract.

The closing attorney lists all monies expected to be received and dispersed at closing on a **settlement sheet**. (There may be separate settlement sheets for the buyer and for the seller, such as the ones in the Appendix.) This document is very important. Every buyer should review it carefully in case there are errors or surprises, such as costs that you did not anticipate. Ideally, the closing attorney should distribute a copy a few days before the scheduled closing for you and your attorney to review. Do not be hurried and do not be hesitant to ask questions about any entry on the settlement sheet. The broker should be able to tell you exactly how much your closing costs will be. Ask him to pick up a copy for you when he picks up copies of the other closing documents. The closing attorney will probably also give both buyer and seller a **schedule of payments** for your convenience. This schedule will show "how much" and "when" loan payments are due.

From time to time, there are mistakes. Sometimes, even attorneys are unclear about how adjustments should be made or about other matters that buyer and seller have discussed and agreed to. The settlement sheet also lists any expenses that will be split, or prorated, between the parties—such as rent, payroll, personal property taxes, or legal fees. Normally, after a sale has closed, it is difficult to get from the seller payment for items that should have been prorated, and it may be too late to adjust the purchase price. Be very careful. Ask questions, and take your time. Do not let the excitement of ownership cause you to move through the closing process too quickly.

Depending on the size of the business being sold, the actual "closing" can last several hours or more. During this period, usually neither buyer nor seller is at the place of business minding the store. Arrangements should, therefore, be made for someone to handle the daily tasks, such as making deposits or writing checks. In regard to the day of closing, it should be very clear whether closing is effective at the start of business on the closing day, which is customary. If so, all sales receipts from that day are property of the buyer.

If the receipts are cash and checks, they should be deposited into the buyer's bank account. If checks are mailed to a post office box, the buyer or his agent must have a key to the post office box and arrangements must be made for the buyer to enter the business the next day. For these reasons, **it is helpful for the seller to bring with him to closing all keys necessary to operate the business.**

The buyer must bring checks to cover the closing costs and the down payment. The latter should be a cashier's check. The closing attorney should let each party know several days in advance what their share of the closing costs will be. They are often unexpectedly high, if real estate is included, so be prepared.[78] Without the purchase of real estate, these costs are surprisingly modest; the largest item is generally the closing attorney's fee, which in most markets is today equally divided between buyer and seller. If the seller has a broker, he or his firm is paid the commission from the closing funds by the attorney.

Finally, do not leave the closing table without firm agreement about some practical matters concerning the transfer of the business, such as,

1. How and when the seller will provide the agreed upon management transition assistance. Set some firm dates.
2. Whether receipts from business sales will be deposited to your (new) account or to the seller's (existing) account.
3. How much **petty cash** (or working capital) is necessary to operate the business and how much is on hand at the business.
4. Exactly when the transfer of ownership becomes effective.
5. Where the keys are (including keys to mail boxes), what they are for, and who (which employee[s]) has copies.

---

[78]   This is because some jurisdictions require that a portion of the annual real estate taxes (city and county) be paid or escrowed at time of closing.

There may be other similar issues. Carefully think through with the seller the mechanics of transferring both the ownership and management of the business before leaving the closing table.

After checks have been exchanged, the attorney gives you the **bill of sale**. This is your title to the business and a receipt for the money paid or owed to seller. The parties shake hands and the business is finally yours.

Yet some work remains to be done behind the scenes by the closing attorney. The attorney may have to pay some creditors and to record some documents. If vehicles are involved, he may still need to get new titles. Follow up with your attorney (or the closing attorney) after closing to be sure that he has not been distracted and his tasks have been completed. There have, unfortunately, been closings when important tasks were somehow overlooked, such as the recording of a deed to real estate or recording a **security agreement**, which tells the world that there are liens against certain assets. See **Confirmation and Bill of Sale** in Appendix.

PART III.
WHEN IS THE RIGHT TIME TO BUY

Anytime is a good time to buy if the price is right. Let's compare the market for small businesses with public stock markets first. People buy shares of stock in virtually every publicly traded company every day that the markets are open for trading. Why do they buy? They buy because the price, as quoted on the stock markets, appears attractive. They also buy because of the feeling that future earnings will grow, and as a result, the value of the stock, or business, will rise. This applies to small privately held businesses as well.

Business Cycles

Whenever buying a business, it makes sense to learn where the economy is in the business cycle. What phase of the cycle are we in now? Does this suggest you are buying at the "top of the market" or at the bottom or somewhere in between? Obviously, if you feel the market is about to slow down, offering a lower price makes sense because revenue and cash flow may fall sharply. If the market is expected to come out of a recession (or economic slowdown), a higher price may be warranted.

No cycle is identical to another, but some characteristics are fairly similar, such as the length of a typical cycle. From 1945 to 2015, there have been twelve cycles with the "contraction" on average lasting eleven months, each followed by an "expansion" lasting on average fifty-nine months.[79] The most recent contraction, which began in December 2007, lasted for eighteen months and, as of October 2015, has been followed by seventy-five months of expansion. There is no way to forecast precisely when a contraction or expansion will begin or end, but there are economic indicators that can be helpful in determining where in the cycle we are. The sales and earnings of some businesses follow the business cycle fairly closely while other businesses are largely unaffected. Some, in fact, are countercyclical—that is, they may grow while the economy is slowing down and vice versa. Determining which "indicators" would be helpful guides to timing the purchase of your business will probably require a little study.

---

[79] This data may be found on the website of the National Bureau of Economic Research (NBER): *www.nber.org/cycles.htm.*

Economic Indicators

Traditional indicators include the following six. Be sure to check them for your city, state, or market area.

1. Changes in the various rates of inflation
2. Changes in the unemployment rate
3. Number of persons filing unemployment claims
4. Change (growth) in the gross domestic product
5. Monthly changes in sales tax receipts
6. Changes in various interest rates

Some local area indicators, especially those relating to real estate and construction, can help a business buyer spot trends in his market area early in a cycle. Look for

1. Changes in vacancy rates in commercial real estate (shopping centers and office buildings)
2. Changes in current "per square foot" rental rates
3. Changes in number (and value of) building permits issued

In addition, there are many more industry specific indicators, such as the number of new houses sold, new cars manufactured, or changes in the prices of certain commodities (sugar or wheat if the business is a bakery, for example). Some indicators are so-called leading indicators because they could predict what is about to happen in the economy or in a specific industry. My favorite economic indicator (which I could watch and measure from my office window) is the number of cars lined up each day at the drive-thru window of a major chain fast-food restaurant at noon. I learned that this was a very precise measure of the propensity of the average consumer to spend or to save. When the line got longer, the economy, in my opinion, was on the mend, and when the line got shorter, the economy was contracting.

Additional information about indicators can be found at various sources and including U.S. Department of Labor (*www.dol.gov*), Bureau of Labor Statistics (*stats.bls.gov*), the U.S. Department of Commerce (*commerce.gov*), and the Census Bureau (*www.census.gov/econ/*).

The markets over time adjust the price of each business to meet the realities of current or anticipated market conditions. Sometimes, of course, the market for smaller companies does not adjust as quickly as the public markets. And the prices at which smaller businesses change hands do not seem to fluctuate quite as widely either. It is for this reason that sometimes, sellers take quite a while to lower the asking prices of their businesses. Another factor to keep in mind is that when the economy slows, sellers are much more willing to offer buyers more attractive terms, such as seller financing, as well as lower prices.

Motives for Selling

The reality in the markets for all companies, small and large, is that they trade hands when they appear to be worth more to a buyer than they are to a seller. Why would this be so? Let's look at several reasons that sellers might be willing to sell for a price less than an informed buyer might be willing to pay.

1. The seller may have an opportunity to open a new business in a different industry, perhaps with friends or with children.
2. The seller may wish to retire and move to Florida or to travel with his wife.
3. The seller may be looking forward to having more time off to pursue other investments or to pursue hobbies, such as participating in the Senior Olympics or sailing a boat around the world.
4. The seller may have simply achieved the financial goal of having sufficient means to allow him (or her) not to have to work anymore.
5. The seller may have discovered that the business, in order to grow and remain competitive, requires the investment of substantial capital (persons nearing retirement age are often loathe to invest substantial new capital in their businesses).
6. The seller may be in somewhat of a rut: operating the business every day may have become boring or lonely.
7. Changes in the industry or marketplace may have persuaded the owner that he (or she) is no longer qualified to operate the business successfully.
8. The seller may be tired or facing an illness that requires him or her to cut back on the hours spent at the business.

Regardless of their age, sellers always have a motive for thinking about selling. Sometimes the motive is valid and sometimes not. Selling a small business, therefore, is really little different than saying, "I think IBM will rise more rapidly than AT&T." So the AT&T stock is sold, and the proceeds are used to purchase shares of IBM. This does not mean that AT&T is unprofitable, or is in financial trouble. It means, rightly or wrongly that, in one person's opinion, IBM is expected in the future to grow more rapidly than AT&T or will be able to pay a larger dividend. The needs, expectations, and motives of buyers and sellers are different, which is exactly what makes sales happen.

Motives of sellers are often difficult to ascertain, so **it is smart to try and buy when a seller is ready to sell and to learn what a seller's reasons for selling might be**. Some sellers really do not want to sell, particularly if they have nothing to look forward to in retirement except staying at home every day. They may enjoy negotiating simply to discover what the market feels their business is worth. If a seller is not sincere about selling, it is often wise to look for another business.

Owners may simply want to sell because managing the company does not seem to be as much fun or as challenging as it used to be. It may become more difficult for owners to make normal business decisions as they near retirement age. Some owners hesitate to invest in new equipment. These are both symptoms that their companies may be ready for "second-generation" ownership. However, a seller may not always see these factors as reasons to sell. Some, particularly long-time owners, are very reluctant to retire. They tend to resist change. They logically worry about what they will do if they no longer have the business to run.

These symptoms may also indicate that the seller is not as content as in past years spending so much time managing the business perhaps because he (she) has made enough money from the company to live comfortably. Simply put, this breed of seller no longer needs to work as hard as he (she) used to. In these cases, prospective buyers who tour a company often immediately begin asking, "Why isn't the owner doing this or doing that?" "Why hasn't he computerized inventory?" "Why are no incentives built into employee compensation?"

These apparent lacks are more often signs that a business is worth exploring seriously, rather than signs that a business is not worthy of further study. Buyers generally ask these questions because they have substantial experience or knowledge in areas where the sellers do not. This is a good "buy" signal, but a buyer is advised to share these questions with the broker (or his financial adviser) first because the seller might become defensive if his competence is in any way questioned by a younger and seemingly less experienced buyer.

The fact that buyers see opportunity for change is a strong indication that they "bring to the party" resources that a business may lack. For that reason, the set of assets that comprise the business may produce a greater return in future years than it has produced in recent years for the seller. Therefore, the business is worth more to a buyer than it is to a seller, and a deal (or sale) can be crafted that is acceptable to both parties.

Conversely, if everything about a business appears to be in great shape, it may be a signal to proceed cautiously and to do additional analysis. The seller may be aware of pending changes in his market or industry, such as the entry of a large, well-financed competitor into his market, or important changes in technology that may adversely affect the business. Or the business may simply be near the end of a normal business cycle. See following story about potential problems of growth.

Case History – THE PROBLEM OF UNBROKEN GROWTH

I recall a situation in which a buyer purchased a business that had shown virtually unbroken growth of over 10 percent for many years. The buyer assumed that this growth would continue and purchased the business at a price that reflected this optimism. The Federal Reserve had just begun increasing interest rates charged to its member banks, and the economy soon cooled off. The buyer was not able to meet his obligations and liquidated the business about two years after the purchase. Fortunately, there were adequate assets to cover all debts, but he did not recover his full investment.

Moral – if the business follows the cycles of the broader economy, try to anticipate when the growth will slow and make your offer accordingly.

As you approach the closing date, keep in mind the following questions, questions sometimes asked or remembered by buyers only at the closing table or after the closing has occurred.

Final Checklist

☐ Did you receive in advance of the scheduled closing (in time to review them carefully) copies of all contracts and other closing documents?

☐ Did you read and understand the contents of all documents? If not, did you ask your broker, attorney, or the closing attorney to explain the points that you did not fully understand?

☐ Did you observe all dates for removal (fulfillment) of the (your) contingencies?

☐ Did you carefully monitor the inventory process (the count and extension)?

☐ Did you remember to bring a cashier's check for the down payment to closing?

☐ Did you remember to bring other required documents to closing, such as proof or insurance?

☐ Have you scheduled management assistance with the seller?

☐ Have you scheduled a time for the seller to introduce you to all critical employees, customers, and suppliers?

☐ Do you know where all the keys are? And who has duplicates sets?

☐ Have you asked the seller about procedures for handling and depositing checks?

CHAPTER 8

CONCLUSION

Many people share the dream of someday owning their own business, yet a relatively small percent accomplish this dream. Some have looked at businesses. Some have even looked at many businesses over many years yet did not get to the point of submitting an offer or closing on a sale. Why? My experience suggests that that were fearful of "being had" in some way. They did not know whom to trust and were concerned about making a costly mistake. They lacked the tools to help them make a wise choice—the choice about what kind of business to buy and the choice about what price and terms to offer.

Let's review briefly some of the more common motives that lead people to want to own their own business.

1. Meet a family's financial needs
2. Obtain, or to "buy," a job
3. Provide employment for family members
4. Build a nest egg for a retirement
5. Serve as a stepping-stone to greater financial success
6. Become one's own boss (I'm tired of working for someone else.)
7. Achieve financial wealth and independence
8. Enjoy the freedom that comes with self-employment
9. Achieve the respect of your peers and community

These are compelling motives, so the reasons that so many people do not follow through on their dream must be equally compelling. It is prudent to understand the opportunities, risks, and challenges that come with business ownership. But the main objectives are (1) to determine with reasonable assurance that the business being studied will meet your personal financial needs and (2) to feel comfortable that the business will also be able to meet the financial obligations incurred in buying the business. There should be a fair price at which these objectives can be met. But many buyers lack the skills to determine that price with confidence. If you develop those skills, you will be able to buy with confidence and without overpaying.

A Brief Recap

It will be helpful to remember the results of the financial review of the business you have decided to purchase as well as the financial goals that you have set. These might be summarized for Doozy as shown in the table below. The **actual result** shown is after making adjustments to the financial statements.

Ratio or Factor (after Adjustments)	Desired Goal	Actual Result	Grade or Pass/Fail
Seller's ROE (pretax)	35%	90%	A+
Your desired ROI	40%		
Seller's annual sales growth	15%	nil	??
Seller's gross profit	30%	47%	Pass
Sales per employee	$100,000	$75,000	Fail
Sales per sq. foot	??		
Cash flow ÷ sales	20%	12.3%	B
Income ÷ sales	10%	10.6%	Pass
Other (?)			

A business does not have to "pass" each of these goals. But it is wise to keep your goals in mind, particularly during the *negotiating process*. Be careful not to pay more than the fair price. At the same time, if the business is attractive, it may be foolish not to be a little flexible about price and terms. Understanding the various processes or steps listed in the Introduction and discussed in the succeeding chapters should give one the confidence to make a wise choice and to feel secure after the choice is made. Let's recap these steps.

Note that there are now eleven steps. A new, number 6, the *pricing process*, has been added because "determining value" can be quite different from deciding what price and terms to offer. You might logically offer less than your opinion of fair market value.

1. The *search process*
2. The *study process*
3. The *financial review process*
4. The *adjustment (recasting) process*
5. The *valuation process* (and reconciliation of values found)
6. The *pricing process* (determining an offering price and terms)
7. The *contract preparation process*
8. The *negotiating process*
9. The contingency removal/fulfillment, or *due diligence process*
10. The *closing process*
11. The postclosing or *management transition (assistance) process*

Unlocking Value

In addition to these eleven steps to buying a business, there are some other steps that are useful in preparing a buyer to make a wise choice and in negotiating a good contract. Each buyer should ask if a business will meet his or her specific goals. The first step is what I call unlocking value. Can a buyer find more value in a business than the seller can? We have previously discussed a few ways to do this. Below is a recap with a few additional suggestions.

1. A business may have hidden assets, assets such as underutilized plant capacity or work-in-process.
2. There may be potential outlets for some products or services that the current owner for some reason has not identified or developed.
3. There may be more efficient and up-to-date ways to manufacture or market company products or services, such as more fully utilizing the power of computers or social media.
4. There may be related products or services the business might economically market to its present customers.
5. There may be surplus assets, such as excess inventories of some items that can be sold and converted to cash, thereby reducing the effective purchase price of the business.

6. A buyer may unlock value by improving operations in some fashion, perhaps by increasing output per man-hour or by adding performance bonuses to compensation.

7. Employees and customers may have valuable ideas about improving many aspects of the business. Talk to them. Many first-generation owners have not talked to their customers or employees in a long time.

8. Owners may have been overpaying for equipment or for resale merchandise or making unnecessary purchases. In Chapter 1, review Schedule 1. Would you have paid $1,200 for your desk? Review the **case history** at the end of Chapter 1. How much did this landscape contractor overpay for his merchandise by using credit cards?

Thoughts from Seasoned Buyers

The second useful step is to talk with seasoned buyers before making your decision. Let me share some guidelines that business buyers say they found helpful or wish they had heeded. Some were learned from painful experience.

1. Beware of buying a business if you are not able to perform or complete the full due diligence process after your purchase contract has been accepted.

2. If you can verify seller's financial statements, and if the statements have been audited, the business may be worth a premium. If the statements cannot be verified, the business may be worth a little less than your analysis suggests. Proceed cautiously.

3. Don't automatically pay a premium if the business has had years of unbroken growth. It may be at the top of its natural business cycle. "My advisers told me," said one disappointed buyer, "to look for a business that has had double digit growth each year for at least five years."

4. Before the sale, be sure to review the accountant's **opinion letter** for any comments about the way financial statements have been compiled. One buyer says, "I didn't know that accountants were supposed to attach an opinion letter to the financial statements, but I sure wish I had read it earlier." If there is no opinion letter, it may be wise to ask why.

5. Remember that a business's value depends upon the return it will give after the sale. What a business earns in the future is far more important than what it has earned in the past. Because it made money in past years does not mean it will make money in the future.

6. Beware if key documents, such as corporate resolutions, have not been prepared and signed in advance of the closing or if signatures are missing on closing documents.

7. Small businesses are different from large ones. The work rhythm is different. In larger businesses, there is often time to study problems at length before making or implementing a decision. In small businesses, decisions need to be made promptly.

8. Focus on the business. Do not be distracted because time is of the essence (as stated in most standard contracts). Customers, suppliers, and employees can quickly sense if the new owner is "in charge" and paying attention to business.

9. It is helpful if seller will (1) inform the employees that there has been (or will be) a transfer of ownership and then introduce you to the employees in an open meeting and (2) introduce you to key suppliers and customers. Introductions are often more effective if made in person. "I wish I had put these stipulations in my contract," says another buyer.

10. Calculate carefully your working capital needs. After the sale is closed, it may be too late to borrow more money.

11. Find a knowledgeable lawyer to prepare your closing documents, but try to avoid the need for more lawyers or going to the courthouse after the sale. Most legal problems arise because the original documents are not fully understood or drafted in sufficient detail.

After the Sale

The third step is to keep your eyes open after the sale has taken place. Keep track of your forecast budget, and monitor the cash flow carefully. Keep track of questions you wish to ask the seller during your management assistance time and schedule the first management assistance session before leaving the closing table. It may be useful if the contract gives you specific permission to call the seller at home after work hours when you have time to talk without distraction. Ask him to give you both daytime and "after-hours" telephone numbers and travel schedules, in case some questions need prompt answers. Here's one reason why:

Case History – BANK ACCOUNT PROBLEM

The purchaser of a day care center wondered why she had not received reimbursements from the state for certain "scholarship" children. It turned out that the state had sent all reimbursement checks to the previous owner's bank account, and that, immediately following the closing, the former owner had left town on vacation. This resulted in such a lack of cash flow during the first month of ownership that it almost bankrupted the business.[81]

Moral – before closing, let customers know how to remit future payments, or require Seller to tell customers where to remit.

The first weeks or months after the sale has been completed are not the time to be distracted. A new owner needs to take charge and to act decisively yet not change the "old way of doing things" without careful thought. The first case history (in Chapter 1) illustrates this point.

The following case history illustrates how important it is for the buyer to be ready to take over management of the business upon taking ownership.

Case History – SCHEDULING MANAGEMENT ASSISTANCE

The owner of a dress shop was fortunate to have found a buyer; she was nine months pregnant when the closing occurred. The buyer opened the shop on Monday and discovered there were no employees at work. Desperately, she looked for phone numbers but could find none. She tried to contact the seller, but alas, the Seller had gone to the hospital to deliver her baby. And the buyer had important appointments scheduled that took her away from the shop. It was several days before she found the phone numbers and could work out a schedule with her new employees.

Moral – be sure you know what will happen your first day of business and plan for it in advance.

---

[80] Some management assistance agreements (or the paragraphs in the purchase contract) spell out exactly when and for how long a buyer may talk with the seller. And they also spell out penalties if the seller violates his part of the agreement. Sometimes, the penalty is simply forfeiture by the seller of the money allocated to this agreement.

This next case shows that there can be strong resistance to changing the "old ways." This is especially true when employee compensation is threatened or when illicit behavior may be involved.

Case History – BIG SURPRISE AFTER CLOSING ON THE SALE

The purchaser of a hair salon and spa already knew that the former owner was not a hands-on manager. She was a stylist and had her own chair. The purchaser had reviewed the financial statements for the business and already knew that the reported cost of goods (for supplies sold to patrons) was abnormally high, a problem she intended to correct as soon as possible by implementing some basic controls. When the purchaser informed the six other stylists, several became defensive. She watched them for several days and concluded that all six were pocketing some or all of the sales proceeds when patrons paid in cash. When confronted with the evidence, all but one of the stylists resigned (actually, they left without giving notice while the new owner was out of the salon) and took some salon equipment and supplies with them. Instead of solving a problem, the new owner had created a larger one.

Moral – (1) pay attention to the "red flags" before agreeing to buy, and (2) be cautious in how you implement change.

Forecasting (Again)

Carefully forecast your annual and monthly sales and expenses. These forecasts become your budgets—a twelve-month budget and a monthly budget. Your expenses will be different from the seller's. Include your anticipated **debt service** in the forecast. Revise your monthly operating budget every month for a few months after the sale. Do not rely solely upon a budget prepared before or immediately after the acquisition because there are always surprises. And reserve in the budget enough cash for the lumpy expenses, such as annual business taxes and insurance premiums. The first budget prepared by Doozy's buyer is shown in Table 16. Finally, remember that in a small business, **the owner gets paid last.**

One of the reasons for going forward with the purchase of Doozy is your hunch that under your leadership, both sales and profits could increase by 10 percent per year during the next few years.[81] Since our analysis (refer back to

---

[81]   Ten percent growth may seem high. In reality, this "growth" number is the sum of the rate of inflation plus real growth. If inflation is 5 percent, real growth is only 5 percent. And part of the real growth is

Table 9) suggests that Doozy had an adjusted pretax income last year of $31,000, this means you project that Doozy will earn $34,100 (before income taxes) the year after you buy the business. Now, test this projection by preparing a twelve-month budget showing your anticipated revenue, gross profit margin, and operating expenses as shown in Table 16.

The forecasts in a preacquisition income and expense statement are a good starting place for preparing a statement showing projected monthly income (pretax) and cash flow. Table 16 only shows an annual budget. A more useful budget may include more expense accounts than are included in Table 16. For example, each type of insurance and tax expense might become a separate line item since these items are paid in different months. Try preparing an income statement using several revenue accounts and cost of goods assumptions as well. Using your estimates, it appears that Doozy may earn $34,354, slightly more than the projected 10 percent increase. The $34,354 is calculated before any interest or principal payments due to the Seller are deducted.

Sources of Data

Preparing accurate forecasts is very important and should be done carefully. Buyers tend (in my experience) to focus more on forecasting revenue than on forecasting the expenses. Buyers often say that they do not know where to find accurate data involving expenses and insert guesses or estimates into their projections. This can be a critical mistake. I recommend that buyers include a footnote showing the **source of data** for virtually every entry in the forecast. Start by talking to your broker; he wants a sale to take place. Revisit the offering documents and some of the websites mentioned throughout this book. Trade journals and trade associations can be helpful. While this book is not a guide to preparing a business plan, a detailed business plan will be necessary if bank financing is needed. Citing the sources of your data will always give banks and others more confidence that the plan and all forecasts are substantially accurate and reliable. Of course, all data in your original forecasts must be updated as newer or more accurate data become available.

---

from management changes, rather than from an expanding economy.

Table 16. Purchaser's Twelve-Month Income and Expense Budget (Projection)

	Amount	Percentage Change
Revenue from projected sales	$330,000	+10%
Cost of Goods Sold at 24%	79,200	+10%
Gross Profit Margin at 76%	$250,800	+10%
Owner salary	50,000	+4%
Employee wages (excluding owner's wife)	71,060	+10%
Part-time office worker	6,000	New
Payroll taxes at 10% of payroll costs	12,705	+6%
Rent (new five-year lease)	20,000	+11%
Bookkeeping service	1,800	New
Insurance—all policies	11,000	+10%
Utilities	15,840	+10%
Telephones	4,410	+5%
Office supplies	2,640	+10%
Taxes and licenses	2,860	+10%
Gasoline	3,300	+10%
Advertising (including yellow page ad)	2,730	+5%
Part-time shop employees	4,400	+10%
All other expenses (including reserve)	2,000	+100%
Subtotal	**$210,746**	
Depreciation	5,000	0%
Total Expenses	**$216,446**	
Projected Income (pretax)	**$34,354**	
Income as % of Revenue	10.4%	

Suggestion—some costs may be greater for a new owner than for a previous owner. Payroll taxes and insurance premiums come to mind. Check both carefully before preparing your budget. Older businesses over time earn a lower SUTA (state unemployment insurance) tax rate than you would qualify for if they have a favorable unemployment claims history. New businesses start at the highest rate. In regard to insurance costs, contact several carriers. See if buying all policies with a single carrier will result in lower aggregate premiums. Do not automatically continue the policies or levels of coverage the seller had in force since it may have been years since he "shopped" different carriers. However, if your premiums or other costs will increase, make the owner aware of this; it may help in your negotiating.

Some people do pay too much for a business (or buy on overly restrictive terms) and quickly run into difficulties. They often say they are drowning in debt service. This is really just another way of saying that a business did not meet a buyer's cash flow expectations or that the buyer did not forecast carefully enough. Do not let this happen to you.

To prevent a cash flow squeeze in the first few months of ownership, some prudent buyers put a clause in the purchase contract stating that payments due the seller will not begin until sixty or ninety days after the closing. The best way not to be "had" when buying your business is to do your homework. Forecast carefully.

Forecast monthly revenue and cash flow as well as expenses. If your business carries accounts receivable (as Doozy does), actual cash received each month may be much less than the forecast revenue. Revise the forecasts as results of operations become clearer. One key to a business like Doozy is to learn how much working capital you will need before the next job is completed, shipped, billed, and paid for. This could be a different amount every month.

In most retail businesses, sales occur daily and are paid by customers in cash. In a custom manufacturing business, there may only be one or two sales a week.[82] Thus, a new owner will need sufficient working capital to pay bills and wages in the meantime. Be careful not to spend all your available cash on the down payment. **Just because Doozy has positive earnings does not mean that Doozy will have a positive cash flow every week or month of the year.**

The timing, the price, a cooperative seller, reliable financial records and careful financial analysis—these are important parts of the answer to "how to buy a business without being had." But often, the most important is to find a business that feels comfortable to you in terms of your unique set of skills, resources, experience, and expectations and one that you feel will be able to grow under your management and direction.

Five Years after the Sale

You might ask yourself, "If you could buy Doozy for $150,000 with a $50,000 down payment and achieve 10 percent annual growth in sales, what

---

[82] In Doozy's case, customers must give Doozy a deposit when an order is placed. This deposit should be transferred to the buyer in whole or in part when the business is sold if a customer's order has not been completed. Sometimes, this deposit is split between the parties according to the percentage of the work that has been completed at the time of the sale.

would my financial situation look like five years later?"[83] Well, three good things would have happened as you can see on Table 17 below.

1. You would have paid off the $100,000 promissory note held by the seller, and you would own Doozy free and clear of debt.
2. If things went according to plan, your business would have **retained earnings** of $95,177 (see Cumulative After-Tax Income in Table 17), and
3. You would have **cash on hand** of $99,582. Subtract the estimated income taxes of $16,798 payable over the first five years from the cumulative cash of $116,380 shown at the end of Year 5.

Pretax Income for Year 1, your first year of ownership, is projected to be $34,100. See Part I of Table 17 below. Refer back to Table 11. With 10 percent compound annual growth, pretax income is projected to be $49,926 by Year 5. The Deductions shown in Part IIare taken from Table 15. They include $9,000 in depreciation expenses each year under your ownership ($45,000 for the FF&E ÷ 5 years = $9,000) plus interest due seller on the $100,000 purchase money note (or two notes) that the seller will carry if he accepts your offer. Both the projected EBITDA and projected cash flow in Table 17 are the same because your projected depreciation charges are included in the Deductions in Part II. The "old" depreciation of $5,000 is replaced in Part II by your "new" depreciation of $9,000, which is included in the Deductions.

---

[83] If there is no growth beyond the first-year projection shown in Table 16, there would still be adequate cash flow ($39,354) to cover the principal and interest due the seller (P&I on $100,000 at 8 percent paid over sixty months is $24,332/year). This is less than two-thirds of the forecast cash flow.

Table 17. Buyer's Projected Five-Year Income and Cash Flow

Part I	Year 1	Year 2	Year 3	Year 4	Year 5
Pretax Income	$34,100	$37,510	$41,262	$45,387	$49,926
Depreciation	+ 5,000	+ 5,000	+ 5,000	+ 5,000	+ 5,000
Cash Flow	39,100	42,510	46,262	50,387	54,926
Debt service (P&I)	- 23,761	- 23,761	- 23,761	- 23,761	- 23,761
Cash balance	16,339	19,749	22,501	26,626	31,165
Cumulative Cash Pretax	$16,339	$36,088	$58,589	$85,215	$116,380
Part II					
EBITDA (lines 1 and 2 above)	$39,100	$42,510	$46,261	$50,387	$54,926
Deductions (see Table 15)	42,900	21,700	20,300	18,900	17,400
Taxable Income	(3,800)	20,810	25,962	31,487	37,526
Income Taxes, estimated	0	-2,552	-3,894	-4,723	-5,629
After-tax Income	(3,800)	18,258	22,068	26,754	31,897
Cumulative After-tax Income	($3,800)	$14,458	$36,526	$63,080	$95,177

The **cash balance** left after debt service and income taxes (the portion not needed for working capital or new equipment) could have earned interest. See line 5 of Part I. This potential interest income is not included, but if it were, the income and cash flow would be greater than shown.[84] The **cash flow** shown above in Part I is based upon your assumption that there were no major capital expenditures, or other unforeseen expenses, during the first five years of ownership. If this is so, after five years, the business (and you) would have cumulative cash, after deducting estimated federal income taxes of $99,582.

Calculate: $116,380 - income taxes of $16,798=$99,582.

This is almost a 100 percent return (**ROI**) on your original $50,000 investment (excluding closing costs). Since the full cost of Doozy has been paid off and you own the company free and clear of debt, we must add the value of Doozy to the cash to find the true **ROI**. The best part is that Doozy will probably have grown in value above your purchase price. If these assumptions regarding projected earnings turn out to be true, and the 5:1 P:E is still applicable, Doozy after five years may have a market value of over $250,000.

---

[84] At an estimated 2 percent annual interest on the collected balance, projected interest income after five years would be between $4,000 and $5,000.

Calculate:

1. EBITDA after Year 5 $54,926 \times 5 = \$274,630$
2. Pretax Income Year 5 $49,926 \times 5 = \$249,630$

All in all, it is not a bad return on a $50,000 down payment (or on a $60,000 investment for that matter) if the seller required the larger down payment. Your investment has enabled you to create a business asset and cash that after five years of ownership are together worth $350,000 or more. This is a potential ROI of 600 percent, and this is why people want to own a business.

Calculate: Forecast Cumulative Cash	$99,582
Forecast Value of Doozy	250,000
Total Return (rounded)	**$350,000**

During the past five years, the budgets had room for increases in owner's salary. The first year salary was budgeted at $50,000. If the salary grew each year by 8 percent, it would now be $68,025. Perhaps some of that cumulative cash could have been paid to the owner as additional salary or bonus.

SUMMARY

While the numbers used in analyzing and reviewing Doozy Manufacturing Co. may seem modest to some, the processes and strategies used in valuing Doozy and in forecasting Doozy's income are applicable to business acquisitions of all sizes. A $100,000 investment in Doozy may have turned into a business worth $700,000 five years later (with the projected Cumulative Cash shown in Table 17). Perhaps a $1 million investment in a larger company would turn into a $7 million business.

Five years after the sale, most businesses are doing fine. The purchasers of those businesses have been able to retire their debt (pay off the loans they took out to help finance their purchase) and pay themselves a steady and growing salary. Although many of the case histories in this book deal with problems, they do not represent the norm. Purchasers who did their homework, sought professional assistance, and had properly drafted purchase contracts, avoided most of the problems outlined in these case histories—at least the problems associated with the purchase of their businesses.

Contract problems and problems stemming from misrepresentation normally occur early in a purchaser's period of ownership. Most contracts provide for after-the-sale adjustments that protect the purchasers from financial loss or from "being had" in some other way. However, sometimes, even five years later, problems can occur. This is the subject of the final Case History below.

Case History – SIGNATURES AND SHAREHOLDER LIABILITY

The buyer of a business had two minority shareholders. These two shareholders had loaned some money to the buyer and received shares of stock in exchange. Three years later, the business was sold. The new owner soon ran out of working capital and took the business through a bankruptcy. The court reduced the monthly payments on the note due the original owner. When he heard this, the original owner sued the minority shareholders, demanding the balance of the note be immediately paid in full. The judge agreed. It turned out that the shareholders had signed the original purchase contract as individuals rather than in "corporate capacity." Actually, it was not required that they sign in any capacity since they were not officers of the corporation. But because they had signed, the court held them personally liable.

Moral – always be careful what you sign, and do not sign if a signature is not required. It could be a costly mistake.

Many buyers whose investments did not turn out as well as they had hoped say that they wished they had taken more time before buying their business— time to study the business and its industry more in depth, time to negotiate more imaginatively, time to draft a contact more carefully, and time to perform more adequate due diligence.

Taking time is an important key to making a successful investment. Taking a little extra time to review the financial statements may reveal hidden assets, hidden income, or hidden inconsistencies or errors. Understanding a business, its industry, and its markets will always put a buyer in a position to negotiate more favorable terms of purchase and, perhaps, to be more successful in securing financing from skeptical investors or bankers.

If you like a business, do not be discouraged by the initial asking price or by your disappointment when you first look at a set of financial statements. Things are not always as they first appear. It is equally important to trust your judgment when an attractive opportunity is available. If your contract is well drafted and includes the necessary contingency clauses, you should be able to buy a business without being disappointed with the financial results.

Not all acquisitions will grow as rapidly as projected above for Doozy (an inflation adjusted growth rate of 5 percent a year). Some, of course, will grow much more rapidly, depending upon the markets they serve. Some few businesses will show no growth at all. Yet all of these can turn out to be successful investments if the owner/operator buys on the right terms, at a fair price, and keeps a sharp eye on cash flow.

How much to pay for goodwill remains a tough question for many buyers. Buyers want to see a lot of tangible assets, and their bankers want to see a lot of collateral. But remember that a business that makes more money with fewer assets is the better business. Finding creative ways to finance an acquisition without using a bank may be the answer. And remember also that in today's so-called information economy, the most important assets in a business may be knowledge assets: the contracts, data bases, contacts, customer files, software, specifications, manuals, and the collective memory of where a business has been and what it has learned. Be sure to identify and define these assets as carefully as you identify and count the inventory.

You have now completed the Ten Steps To Successfully Buying a Business. And you have taken a look at how your business might have performed during the five years after you bought it. There are, in conclusion, a few basic guidelines that seem to summarize the lessons drawn from the real-life experiences covered in this book.

Six Basic Guidelines to Successfully Buying a Business

1. **Do not overpay.** Try to determine a fair price (a fair value) to pay for your business. There is a small but important exception to this guideline: do not be driven by "leaving no money on the table." If your projections indicate that the business will have adequate cash flow, the price is probably fair. Remember that it might take a lot of time (and lost salary) to find another equally attractive business.

2. **Don't buy a business that doesn't feel comfortable to you** (even if you feel that the asking price is a great value). It is hard to define "comfortable." Think about whether you are comfortable with the products, the customers, the suppliers, the facilities, the employees, the location, and the size as well as complexity of the business, or in

other words, the more important nonfinancial characteristics of the business.

3. **Be sure that the purchase contract will protect you from unforeseen events.** Perhaps you discover a material misrepresentation by the seller. Or perhaps there is an economic slowdown or rapid rise in interest rates. Does the contract give you protection to the extent practical?

4. **Be sure that the seller has some financial interest in your success.** There are many creative ways to accomplish this. Some, but certainly not all, have been discussed in the preceding chapters of this book: seller financing, a solid management assistance agreement with the seller, and appropriate consequences in the event of violations of any of the seller's warranties and representations.

5. **Be sure that you are adequately capitalized.** Defining precisely how much capital will be adequate can be difficult or even impossible. The key is to think through various potential scenarios (events that are likely to occur at some time in the future) and to project how you could handle them.

6. **Finally, stay involved in your business.** Most businesses do not run by themselves; they need steady guidance. Usually, no area of involvement is more critical to your success than "watching the cash." Be sure that safeguards are in place to prevent overcharging by suppliers, malfeasance by employees, late payments by your customers, and the other basic aspects of good financial management.

After the closing, take time to learn the business in depth. This is often critical to success. Too many second-generation businesses fail for reasons far beyond the scope of this book. The price was right; there was a good, clean contract. The parties were able to satisfy the contingencies and honored their warranties. Yet some of these buyers did not achieve their goals. So I close with this advice:

Learn the business, meet your customers, and get to know the employees. Stay involved. You may put in some sixty-hour weeks while you learn how the business flows—things like when to reorder, when to staff up, when to lay off, how much advertising is necessary, and which ads are showing the best results. As stated above, too many new owners discover that businesses do not run by themselves.

These guidelines plus the Steps, Tables, Tips, Suggestions, and Case Histories, should help you to buy a business with confidence and avoid disappointment and unnecessary financial crises in the years ahead. Of course, managing your business prudently will be up to you.

GLOSSARY OF TERMS

Over many years working in the business brokerage industry, the author has observed that small business owners are not, in general, very concerned with accounting matters. Their objective is simply to run their businesses profitably. Consequently, business owners and the people who advise them (including business brokers) do not always use financial or accounting terms very precisely.

The author recalls one conversation with an owner who stated that his business had income of around $300,000. After some time, it became clear that the owner was using the term *income* to mean the "revenue" coming into the business. His annual "sales" were $300,000. He did not mean "bottom line income," or pretax earnings, as the author had at first assumed. There is a big difference between those two meanings.

It is important always to learn the definition of all terms used during the process of studying, valuing, and negotiating the purchase of a business. It is equally important to learn the definitions that other people are using. Consulting an accounting textbook is recommended. It is hoped that the layman's definitions in this Glossary (and used in the world of small business) will be helpful to you. Above all, do not hesitate to ask the meaning of any terms you hear; it can help you avoid some costly misunderstandings.

Accounting (keeping books)

Most businesses "keep books" in some fashion or other. Smaller, unincorporated businesses sometimes "keep books" quite informally. Corporations, however, generally keep books according to standard accounting principles referred to as GAAP. These "books" consist, at a minimum, of three documents: a statement of income, a balance sheet, and a cash flow statement. The balance sheet shows the current and fixed assets at the top and the current and long-term liabilities at the bottom. The cash flow statement shows changes in the "cash position" of a company from year to year. Books are kept on either the "cash" or "accrual" method, but in some small businesses, a combination of both is (incorrectly) used. Sometimes, tax returns are prepared on the cash basis while internal company books use accrual accounting. Thus the "income" on tax returns may (legitimately) not match income on the company books.

Book value

The book value of a business is found on a company's balance sheet. It is the difference between the book value of its assets and the book value of its liabilities. The book value of an individual asset is the original cost of the asset less any accumulated depreciation. Book values of individual assets generally differ significantly from their market values. In fact, the market values are generally considerably higher. In other words, the book value of a business should not be confused with its market value. Book value is a poor measure of a business's worth.

Breakeven point

We often ask how long it will take to reach breakeven. This is the point when revenue (cash) from the operation of a business has grown to equal the cash going out. A true breakeven must include among the "cash going out" a reasonable compensation for the owner/operator of a business.

Cash basis

The term *cash basis* refers to one of the two basic methods of accounting. Books are kept on the **cash** method or on the **accrual** method. If books are kept on the cash method (as they are in most small businesses), sales are reported when the cash payment is received and expenses are reported when they are paid. Thus, businesses could have many expenses (bills) that have not been paid and are, therefore, not recorded. In such a case, the book value may overstate the real value of the business. Likewise, some sales are not recorded when the sale is made if the purchase is not paid in cash (check or credit card) at the time the sale occurred.

Cash flow

The term *cash flow* generally refers to the sum of the reported earnings plus all "noncash expenses," such as depreciation and amortization, less two things: (1) payments for the purchase of depreciable equipment and (2) payments that reduce a company's debt. We can look at daily, weekly, monthly, or annual cash flows. Net cash flow would be cash flow less principal payments due on a company's debt and income taxes.

Consideration of sale

This term is often used by lawyers, brokers, and accountants. It refers to the price stated in an offer or contract. It is usually the sum of all the payments, or considerations, that a buyer agrees to pay the seller. In other words, the consideration of sale is the sale price of a business. It may differ from the present value if the full price is not paid at closing or if some of the "consideration" is in the form of noncash payments.

Cost of goods sold

On the financial statements of many smaller businesses, the gross profit is calculated (shown as) sales minus purchases. This practice can lead to inaccurate gross profits and, more importantly, incorrect gross profit margins. To correctly calculate gross profit, we must deduct the cost of goods sold from sales. If a business (during some time period) had purchases of $150,000 and the inventory (shown on the latest balance sheet) increased by $50,000, the gross profit could be understated by $50,000. Conversely, if inventory decreased by some amount, gross profit could be understated. The correct way to calculate the cost of goods (products/services) sold is, add purchases to beginning inventory and then subtract ending inventory. The idea is to calculate what it actually "cost" to produce the reported sales.

Thus, the cost of goods is sometimes called cost of sales, or cost of production. This is the cost of making, or assembling, the goods sold and may logically include the cost of factory labor and equipment depreciation, in addition to the purchase of resale merchandise and other supplies and materials. When comparing gross profit margins, be sure to learn what "costs" are included in cost of goods. If a business prepares financial records on the cash basis, be sure that all costs have been accounted for. A "cash basis" business may only report as purchases those items that have been paid for.

Debt service

Debt service is what it costs literally to "service" the debt(s) of a business. It includes both principal and interest payments, debts owed to the seller, as well as payments on debts owed to banks, finance companies, and other parties.

Due diligence

The term *due diligence* cannot be defined specifically. It is not an accounting term. It refers to the entire spectrum of analyses and investigations necessary to determine that a business is, in fact, in the condition it was represented to be in. Due diligence, more specifically, refers to investigations undertaken by a buyer, or his (her) agents, during the period between the acceptance of the purchase contract and the closing on the sale. The object of this process is to assure the buyer that all the contingencies and other conditions of sale can be or have been met. Sellers also occasionally conduct due diligence on the buyers, particularly if the buyer asks the seller to finance part of the purchase price of a business.

Earnings

The term *earnings*, as it is used in this book, is defined as the earnings of a business after paying a salary to the business owner that is consistent with present market salaries for persons in similar positions. Earnings, such as Doozy's, are also pretax earnings—that is, earnings calculated before paying or accruing federal or state income taxes but after deducting all business expenses (including depreciation expenses). The terms *earnings, income,* and *profit* are often used interchangeably. The term *net profit* (or *net income*) is earnings after paying (or accruing) applicable income taxes. When looking at "earnings" of an unincorporated business, be sure to learn if the owner has deducted any salary for himself (herself).

EBIT

EBIT stands for earnings before interest and (income) taxes. Some analysts use EBITDA (earnings before interest, taxes, depreciation, and amortization). The object of both is the same: to standardize the "earnings" of different businesses so that they may be more accurately compared. Some new businesses may be highly leveraged and pay lots of interest but pay little or no income taxes. Older businesses may have no depreciation, and therefore appear quite profitable and pay a lot of income taxes. In other respects, the businesses may be identical (and be worth the same).

Equity

In layman's terms, equity is what we have left over after all the bills are paid. We speak of equity in a house as the difference between the mortgage balance and the market value. In finance and accounting, the definition of equity is different; it is a balance sheet term. It is the difference between the book value of the assets and total liabilities. Equity consists of retained earnings plus proceeds from sale of stock. The market value of a business may be far different than the value of the equity shown on the balance sheet of a business.

Fair market value

It is the most probable price a buyer, ready willing and able, will pay to a seller—each informed of the important facts, neither under duress, and after the business has had reasonable exposure to the market. The length of time that represents a "reasonable exposure to the market" will vary with the type and size of business.

Financial statements

Businesses normally prepare monthly and annual financial statements. A financial statement always includes two parts: a statement of income and expenses, and a balance sheet and a cash flow statement, but often does not in the case of small business (ask if one can be made available). The term *"income statement"* means the same as "profit and loss statement", or P&L. Statements should also include an opinion letter from the CPA, or preparer, but rarely do. Be leery of relying heavily on statements if there is no opinion letter or if the letter has exceptions. Although many businesses do not compile statements on a regular or timely basis, this is generally not cause for alarm.

General ledger

Most businesses have a general ledger. It is a daily record of all transactions: receipts, disbursements, credits, and debits. It also shows daily cash balances and overdrafts. If a business's records are computerized, it is easy to generate a general ledger. Of course, this record contains confidential information, so it would not be freely distributed to buyers until the negotiating or due diligence process was well along.

Goodwill

The term *goodwill* used in its accounting sense refers the difference in value between the purchase price of a business and the value assigned to the assets included in the sale. Under this definition, it is well to remember goodwill can have either a negative or positive value. In a broader sense, goodwill refers to the general reputation of a business. However, it is advisable to try to specifically value the goodwill and to identify all the individual intangible assets that make it up. Sometimes, we look at goodwill as that collection of assets that do not appear on company's balance sheet. It can include logos, the trade name of the business, customer lists, work orders, contracts, catalogues, proprietary software, and many other assets essential to operating a business.

INDEX

BIBLIOGRAPHY

Books

Bergh, Louis. *Business Law.* 6th ed. New York: Ronald Press, 1964.

Berthelette, Eric, and Kresen, Frank, eds. *The Entrepreneur's Planning Handbook*, revised ed. Denver: Entrepreneurial Foundation, 1997.

Domash, Harry. *Fire Your Stock Analyst.* Prentice Hall, 2006.

Gerber, Michael E. *E-Myth Revisited.* Harper Business, HarperCollins, 2005

Gumpert, David E. *How to Really Create a Successful Marketing Plan.* 3rd ed. Boston: Inc. Publishing, 1996.

Lereah, David A. *The Rules for Growing Rich: Making Money in the Information Economy.* Random House, 2000

Morris, Joseph, and James N. Brendel. *Mergers and Acquisitions: Business Strategies for Accountants.* Hoboken: John Wiley & Sons, 1995.

Pratt, Shannon P., Robert F. Reilly, and Robert P. Schweihs. *Valuing a Business: The Analysis and Appraisal of Closely Held Companies.* 3rd ed. Chicago: Irwin Professional Publishing, 1995.

Price, Courtney, Mack R. Davis, and Richard H. Buskirk. *Sample Business Plans: Premier Fast Track.* Denver: Premier Entrepreneur Programs Inc., 1994.

West, Tom. *The 2003 Business Reference Guide.* 13th ed. Concord, MA: Business Brokerage Press, 2003.

Articles

Gibson, John. "The Need for Forensic Accounting in Valuing Small Businesses." *Allied Business Group*. 2004.

Gibson, John. "Notes on Value of Goodwill in Small Businesses." *Allied Business Group*. 1999.

Jones, Gary E., and Dirk E. Van Dyke. "Using the Black/Green Approach to the Build-Up Summation Method."

Miles, Raymond C. "Placing the Subject Business within the Range of Market Values." *Business Brokerage Press*. 2005.

DISCUSSION QUESTIONS, CHECKLISTS, AND STUDY GUIDES

Introduction

1. Why do some businesses fail?
2. Why are some buyers disappointed in the financial results of businesses they bought? Identify as many possible explanations as you can.
3. A business should have enough cash flow to cover four essential things. What are they? Discuss why each is critical to your success.
4. There are ten distinct steps to go through to successfully negotiate a fair price and purchase a business. Can you name them?

Chapter 1—Why Buy a Business?

1. Are there advantages in buying an established business rather than starting a new business? List them.
2. What are the differences between first- and second-generation businesses?
3. How can we find businesses that might be for sale?
4. Discuss and list some important differences between small businesses and larger, publicly traded businesses.
5. What is the role of a business broker? Are there advantages to the buyer in using a broker? How can the broker help the buyer?
6. What documents should a seller provide to a potential buyer, and when should he (she) provide them?

7. What should you look for in your first review of a set of financial statements?

8. Name some of the obvious (or potential) red flags related to the operation of a business? To the financial statements?

9. What are the advantages of preparing and analyzing "spreadsheets" during the study process?

Chapter 2—What Kind of Business to Buy?

1. What are the major types of businesses? Discuss the characteristics of each.

2. List some important nonfinancial criteria to take into account when placing a value on a business?

3. What are some of the factors that have led to the slowdown in growth in certain industries? Or to their eventual disappearance?

4. Why should it matter to you, as a buyer, what kind of business you buy?

5. List the financial criteria that best describe your ideal business.

Chapter 3—Business Valuations

1. List and discuss the three major approaches to valuing a business.

2. What secondary sources of data might be helpful in doing a business valuation?

3. Identify and discuss some common financial measures for (a) describing a business and (b) comparing one business to another.

4. Discuss whether Business 1, 2, or 3 (on page 26) is more valuable and why you think so.

5. Discuss how to determine if a set of financial statements has been prepared on the "cash" basis, "accrual" basis, or a combination.

6. List and discuss reasons why the reported sales or expenses (of many small businesses) may not be fully accurate.

7. Discuss how you might determine if some expenses have not been posted.

8. Why could there significant variations between the amount of expenses posted for some accounts in different reporting periods?

9. What differences can be found in the financial results of different kinds of businesses or businesses in different industries? (Think of the balance sheet as well as the income statement.)

10. Under what conditions would you expect a business to have no goodwill? Or negative goodwill?
11. If a business is growing, what is the real rate of growth (after adjusting for inflation)? Discuss methods of predicting future growth?
12. What earnings multiple is appropriate for each (type) of business? Discuss the reasons why different multiples are important.
13. Do you believe that so-called hidden assets should be considered when placing a value on a business? List some examples of hidden assets.

Chapter 4—Adjustments to Financial Statements
1. Discuss and list frequently encountered nonoperating expenses.
2. How can we tell when earnings (profits) have been overstated? List possible indications.
3. How can we tell when earnings may be understated? List indications.
4. What is the advantage of looking at monthly financial statements in addition to the annual statements?
5. When does it make sense to "weight" the earnings?
6. List and discuss some of the kinds of account entries that suggest it is necessary to make adjustments to the income statement.
7. Can you tell if the cost of goods and the Gross Profit is calculated accurately?
8. When should adjustments be made to the balance sheet of a company?
9. Recast the financial results for the day care shown on page 10. What is the actual pre-tax income, cash flow, and EBITDA for each year?
10. What, in your opinion, would be a fair price for the Daycare?
11. List in order the steps involved in "recasting" a set of financial statements.

Chapter 5—Earnings Capacity and Other Valuation Factors
1. Explain the concept and the importance of "earnings capacity."
2. Explain what the term *cash flow* means. Explain "cash flow from operations."
3. Explain the process of reconciling the "opinions of value" and why this may be important.
4. How can you spot items in the current operation of a business that should be changed? In your discussion, include financial and non-financial items.
5. Can you spot items that can easily be changed with new management?

6. What impact would these changes have on future cash flows? Profits?
7. What valuation factors or ratios could be red flags to a potential buyer?
8. What does the expression "let your contract do the talking" mean?

Chapter 6 —How to Structure a Purchase Agreement

1. What are the critical elements in an enforceable purchase contract?
2. What are some of the elements of a contract that each purchaser has control over?
3. What remedies does a buyer have when a seller defaults on some provision (the Seller's Warrants for example) in a purchase contract?
4. What remedies does a seller have when the purchaser defaults? Explain how these work.
5. Why is the "allocation of the purchase price" important, and what are some of the considerations that a buyer should focus on?
6. How can the allocation favor the seller, and how can it favor the buyer?
7. What contingency clauses should normally be in a contract? List them.
8. What warranties and representations should be in a contract? Which protect the buyer, and which protect the seller?
9. Describe the financial structure (terms) of a typical contract that includes "seller financing."
10. Discuss the circumstances under which you might buy the "stock" of a company instead of buying "assets."
11. Discuss the importance of the conduct of business pending closing clause (or section) of a contract.

Chapter 7—The Closing on the Sale

1. Explain the "due diligence" process. Why is it important to a buyer?
2. List and discuss what "approvals" may be necessary before the closing.
3. What are a buyer's options if the due diligence reveals that one or more contingencies have not been met?
4. List and then discuss the basic component of the closing process.
5. Discuss the more commonly encountered methods for taking and valuing the inventory of a business?
6. What does a "closing attorney" actually do? What should he do? List specific responsibilities.
7. What role should a buyer's attorney play in the contract preparation, due diligence, and closing processes?

8. Does it matter when to buy a business? When in the business cycle? When in the seasonal cycle of a business?

9. What specific duties (tasks) does a closing attorney perform?

Chapter 8—Conclusion

1. List in order the various "steps," or "processes," that should take place before the closing on the sale of a typical small business occurs.

2. Discuss the components of each process.

3. List the commonly cited reasons for buying a business.

4. Discuss how it might be possible for a purchaser to "unlock" additional, or "hidden," value in a business.

5. Discuss why positive cash flow is so critical to the success of a business purchase.

6. What are some of the things that should happen after the sale purchase of a business to help ensure each buyer's success?

7. How would you know if your purchase of a business has been a success?

8. Why do some businesses fail and some succeed?

Checklists

1. List and discuss the various documents and data that you would expect a business owner to provide to his broker or to prospective buyers when offering a business for sale.

2. List the red flags you might find in a set of financial statements, and discuss several appropriate ways to handle them.

3. List the various personalized sections (stipulations, covenants, or agreements) that you would require be added to a standard purchase contract. Discuss why they should be added. Do this for several distinct types of business.

4. List the usual attachments (Exhibits and Schedules) to a Purchase Contract (as well as some unusual attachments).

5. List and discuss the tasks that you feel must be completed (or questions that must be answered) before
   a. Scheduling the closing on the sale/purchase of a business, and
   b. Leaving the closing table.

APPENDIX

Buyer's Confidentiality and Noncircumvention Agreement

The undersigned prospective purchaser ("PURCHASER") hereby agrees not to disclose to or discuss with any third party, other than PURCHASER's employees, investors, and other professional financial advisers who shall also be covered by this agreement, confidential information provided by seller ("SELLER") or his agent, Allied Business Brokers Mid-south ("BROKER") with respect to a company identified through a summary profile titled: LIQUOR AND WINE STORE ("BUSINESS"), and dated February 3, 2011, and to keep confidential the company's business affairs including the fact that BUSINESS may be available for purchase.

PURCHASER warrants that he has contacted BROKER and is entering into this agreement for the purpose of considering an acquisition of a business.

PURCHASER agrees not to use confidential information provided by BROKER for competitive purposes and to keep in strict confidence all information relating to BUSINESS that could be used to the detriment of BUSINESS or its owners.

PURCHASER agrees to not circumvent or contact directly the owners, employees, suppliers, competitors, or customers of BUSINESS without permission of BROKER.

PURCHASER agrees to not make any offer to invest in or purchase the company except through BROKER and will be liable to BROKER for any fees that would be owed should PURCHASER circumvent BROKER.

PURCHASER acknowledges that serious monetary damage to BUSINESS and its owners could result from improper or unauthorized disclosure of confidential information, including the fact that the owners of BUSINESS are considering a sale of referenced business.

Upon request, PURCHASER will either return to BROKER all written confidential information provided and/or covered under this agreement, including original documents and all copies or reproductions, or certify that said confidential information has been destroyed.

Should SELLER or his agent find it necessary to engage the services of an attorney to enforce the terms and conditions of this agreement, prevailing party shall be entitled to collect reasonable attorneys' fees in connection with any successful enforcement activity.

AGREED & ACCEPTED _____ DATE: _____
                              Authorized Signature

PURCHASER NAME: _____
COMPANY: _____
ADDRESS: _____
TELEPHONE: _____

Value of Goodwill in Small Businesses

John (Jack) V. M. Gibson

Introduction

To many people involved in buying and selling businesses, determining the absence or presence of goodwill is a prevalent problem. The sale price of most successful small, privately held businesses includes a value in excess of the value of its tangible assets. In other words, the price for which successful businesses will sell (their market value) is expected to be greater than the market value of the individual assets used in the operation of each business.[1] This excess value is generally referred to in the courts and by others as goodwill. Sometimes, it is referred to as a *going concern* value. This latter term makes a distinction between businesses that are in operation and businesses that are going out of business.

Also, the values that appraisers assign to successful businesses are generally greater than the value of the tangible assets used in the operation of each business. There are, of course, lawyers, accountants, and others who argue this point. Further examination of the role and importance of goodwill reveals that in many cases,

1. The intangible (or goodwill) assets are very valuable,
2. Businesses could not function without these intangibles, and
3. The intangibles may be far more important and valuable than the tangibles, but
4. If a business has insufficient earnings, there may be no goodwill value when a business has many intangible assets.

The goodwill of a business can have many components. And these components can be easily identified in most cases if we look for them.[2] Trade name and specific items of intellectual property come to mind first. Software, licenses, copyrights, and various legal documents (such as a Buy-Sell Agreement between partners or shareholders) also have considerable value. Thirdly, franchise agreements and operations manuals and other how-to documents may be responsible for the efficient operation of a business and may, therefore, have considerable value as well. These examples do not cover the entire gamut of intangibles that are found in most small businesses.

How much goodwill value to assign to a business is always a matter of discussion.[3] The simplest yardstick I have developed is that the goodwill is expected to be about equal to one

---

[1] The word *assets* in this context refers to things that can be seen and touched. These generally appear on the business balance sheet and are referred to as tangible assets, i.e., inventories and equipment. These classes of assets are bought and sold in the market place and their replacement values are easy to ascertain. More difficult to ascertain is the value of the intangible assets that comprise the goodwill portion of a company's value.

[2] A good discussion of goodwill and negative goodwill can be found in Pratt, Shannon P., "Valuing a Business," 1996, Irwin Professional Publishing. See also the discussion on "going-concern value."

[3] Whereas the existence and amount of goodwill associated with each small business is debated, there is rarely much debate concerning goodwill in larger and especially publicly traded companies. These companies trade at many times their book values (assets minus liabilities). Attention is focused far more

year's adjusted pretax income. Of course, such a yardstick fits no business exactly. The actual or appraised value of the goodwill varies all over the place, even for outwardly similar businesses in the same industry. In fact, today, there are probably yardsticks for each major type of business—retail, wholesale, manufacturing, and service—and for many industries.

Another useful yardstick to keep in mind is that service businesses tend to have the fewest tangible assets and the greatest goodwill value (measured as a percent of the prices at which these businesses typically sell). Eighty percent of the sale price of a service company may be in the goodwill (intangible assets), while perhaps only 20 percent of the sale price of a small retail business may be in goodwill. These yardsticks are good starting points but not very reliable measures to use in preparing an appraisal.

Service businesses today form the largest sector of our economy. Many are traditional businesses, such as repair services. These may require large investments in equipment and rolling stock. Many newer service businesses, such as those that are outgrowths of the "information" economy, require fewer heavy fixed assets or other tangible assets. These businesses rely upon knowledge and information and other assets (such as licenses, trade names, copyrights) that do not appear on a typical balance sheet. As a result, these newer businesses may appear to have much more goodwill (and deservedly so) than many older traditional service businesses. The same yardstick or other shorthand valuation measure that is applicable one case may be totally unreliable in another.

Based on information from various business brokerage firms, about one half of all small businesses cannot be sold as going concerns.[4] They, therefore, cannot be expected to have any "going concern" value, or goodwill value, and will probably be sold for a price close to the value of the hard (tangible) assets. The most commonly observed reason for this situation is the lack of demonstrated and sustainable income. Here we are, using the term *income* to mean profit in excess of a normal salary for the proprietor or operator (if the operator is not the proprietor).

If we are being technical, the term *income* is really what is left over after

- Payment of a compensation package (including salary, payroll taxes, and other monetary benefits) equal to the "going rate" in each marketplace to hire someone who has the skills necessary to replace the operator, plus
- Paying a return on the value of the assets used by a business (the "return" is generally thought of as a sum equal to interest on the value of the assets at a rate at which a small business owner could borrow money).

Thus, a business can appear on paper to have some income and, therefore, at first glance, seem to merit some goodwill value in the marketplace. However, after subtracting a reasonable compensation package and subtracting a return on the value of the assets, this apparent income might disappear. Let's use the example of a business that during the most recent year

---

intently on earnings (the price-to-earnings ratio, or P:E) and the anticipated rate of growth in sales rather than on the loan value of the tangible assets.

[4]   What qualifies a small business to be called a "going concern" can be debated. For purposes of this discussion, a good definition might be: "a business that is sufficiently stable financially that a buyer would not have to inject additional working capital into it to keep it running."

- Paid a salary package of $40,000 to the owner,
- Showed pretax profit of $25,000, and
- Had tangible assets valued at $150,000.

If a competitive salary package in its market was $60,000, and we use 10 percent as the cost of money (interest), what looks like a profit of $25,000 becomes a loss of $10,000, and any potential goodwill vanishes.[5] Why? The answer is that few seasoned buyers would consider buying a business for more than the value of its assets ($150,000 in this case) if it did not earn at least enough to cover interest on the purchase price and reasonable compensation. This does not mean that such a business is not saleable; it only suggests that the sale price of such a business might not include any goodwill value. A buyer of such businesses may see real value in a bargain priced business because it could be a lot more expensive to start a similar business from scratch.

There are some other keys to determining the existence of goodwill value, and the value of that goodwill in a given situation, in addition to the existence of income.[6] Some of these other keys are the following:

Transferability

The goodwill must be transferable to a new owner. This means that the accounts, and other intangible assets, must survive a transition of ownership. If a new owner can keep the revenue and income stream (enjoyed by the former owner) intact after the purchase of a business, the goodwill is indeed transferred. Often, we should assume that some accounts can be transferred and that others cannot be. When some or all of the accounts cannot be smoothly transferred, the goodwill value can be expected to diminish over time, sometimes quite rapidly. Examples might be accounting and dental practices. A transfer of business ownership often appears to clients and customers to be a good time to look around for another service provider. In other cases, under new ownership, revenues and income will grow, and a business will flourish without the previous owner, in which case the value of goodwill might increase.

Organization

If the knowledge and business concept that produced the historic incomes in a business disappear when the owner, founder, or operator leaves, the goodwill value will evaporate very quickly. If, on the other hand, there is an organization in place, which consists of trained, competent, and loyal employees, a business may never miss the departure of the former owner (the goodwill tends to remain in place). In fact, a business may blossom under a new owner (the so-called "honeymoon effect") because (1) a new owner will listen to and respect the knowledge and ideas of employees and customers far more than the former owner needed to or cared to in many cases, (2) the new owners starts his ownership with new ideas and new energy, and (3) some customers were glad to see the former owner retire or sell out.

---

[5]   Be aware that interest rates charged for acquisition financing change frequently, but are often 3–4 percent points above the prime rate. Salaries, of course, also change. But the importance of the methodology sued in determining the amount or existence of goodwill should be a constant.

[6]   As used here, the terms *income*, *profit*, and *earnings* are interchangeable.

Contracts

Some businesses are fortunate enough or farsighted enough to have in place relatively long-term contracts with suppliers, customers, employees, landlords, or with other entities critical to the survival and growth of a business's revenue and income stream. If these contracts are automatically rescinded, or have to be renegotiated, when an owner leaves (or sells), there is uncertainty surrounding the continuation of the revenue and income and, therefore, of the goodwill. Some examples might be a line of credit with a bank, an exclusive distribution agreement with a supplier, or a long-term lease with a landlord. These factors are important examples of goodwill—each of which can be transferred, sold, or valued independently.

Let's consider for a moment what would happen to the income stream if the lease were about to expire and the landlord wanted to increase the annual rent by 20 percent or if a key supplier wanted to give the distribution rights to an established competitor. Both landlord and supplier may have been loyal to the former owner for years and, knowing he was considering retirement, held off on making any major changes. If the annual "below-market" rent the owner/seller had enjoyed was $60,000 a year, a 20 percent increase would raise the cost of rent to $72,000 and the income from the business would be $12,000 less. If 20 percent of revenue was from products purchased from the key supplier and no alternative supplier could be found, this loss could quite literally wipe out a business's bottom line (income). Business can survive this sort of double whammy, but it would reduce the value of almost any business and, thereby, eliminate most of the goodwill value.

Customer Contact

If customers rarely had personal contact with the prior owner, as is the case with many retail establishments, his or her departure would matter little. Also, there are some business-to-business establishments where there has been little or no personal contact between owner and customer. However, if the only contact between customer and the business is through the owner, it may be difficult and very time consuming for a new owner to obtain new orders or to build goodwill with longtime customers.

An example that comes to mind is a typical sales rep organization. The transfer of the goodwill of such a business is made easier if the former owner willingly signs a noncompetition agreement with a new owner. The former owner can also enter into a management contract with a new owner—under which there is an agreement, among other things, to introduce the buyer to all key customers. Such agreements become yet another intangible asset which forms part of the goodwill.

Another example of the value of customer contact is a business that has operated for many years under the owner's name. Even if the purchaser decides to continue doing business under this name, it is not the same business if the prior owner, a person familiar to most customers and whose name is on the marquee, is no longer on hand to greet customers. Many restaurants fall into this category and, as a result, have little or no goodwill value (and are also very hard to sell). The owner (and founder) was to a large degree the business; he or she greeted customers and could call them by name.

Name Recognition

How well known is a business's trade name within its intended markets? We all know the trade names Apple, Ford, McDonalds, and Amazon. How much money and how many years of hard work did it take to achieve almost universal name recognition? If the trade name of a business you are considering buying is well known throughout its market area, the name alone may be worth more than all the tangible assets used in a business. In fact, rights to trade names and to other intangible assets can be bought and sold in the same manner in which we sell equipment or inventories.

Conclusion

The determination of the existence of goodwill and magnitude of its value, we can see, depends upon many discrete variables. Each must be taken into account by the appraiser. However, overriding all other factors, it is the degree of probability that the income stream enjoyed by one owner can be successfully transferred to another owner that determines the existence and value of the goodwill. Markets dislike uncertainty, and if uncertainty exists regarding the prospects of an efficient transfer of the intangible assets, prudent buyers and investors will discount the value of goodwill that otherwise might seem to exist.

If it is determined that no goodwill exists, then we are left with selecting the proper asset value criterion. There are, in general terms, three separate criteria: (1) **value in use**, (2) **value in place**, and (3) **liquidation value**, which is the price that the assets will bring under a situation in which a business will cease operation and the assets must be sold off one by one, or in lots, and moved to another location. The asset value "in use" is far higher in most cases that the value that the assets would bring in a liquidation or "going out of business" sale. Also, the value in use is higher than the value of the assets "in place." The reasoning is that it costs someone time and money to assemble the aggregation of assets into a viable and smoothly operating business.

In a "going business," the equipment is installed, and the counters and shelving are in place and have been installed into a workable configuration. These assets clearly have a use and can be used efficiently and profitably. And the skill with which they have been assembled and installed can, to a very real degree, determine the profitably of a small business. Although it is not at first apparent to a skeptical buyer, these "configurations" evolve over many years of trial and error. A lot of effort and experience (translate, time and money) go into determining the optimal mix of assets as well as their most efficient configuration. The cost is often money well spent by a Seller and money that a buyer will not have to spend.

During this learning process (which may continue over many years), an owner learns which assets are essential and which are disposable. This is why good businesses (some with few apparent hard assets) can justify a goodwill value well in excess of the value of the business's tangible assets. In the cases of two very similar businesses, it could be that the one with fewer tangible assets is the more valuable. Such a business will have a much higher **return on assets**—that is, **profit divided by the cost of the assets**. This bodes well for any buyer because it suggests that relatively small investments in additional assets (such as inventory or new equipment) might yield a higher return than a similar investment in an asset-heavy business.

Bigger Cabinet Corporation, Inc. Spreadsheet 2001–2007

	2007	2006	2005	2004	2003	2002	2001
Gross sales	$4,365,729	$3,931,819	$3,180,802	$2,852,704	$2,677,929	$1,265,757	$2, 222, 255
Cost of sales	2,816,790	2,592,498	2,100,668	1,897,314	1,767,932	956,704	1,648,880
Gross profit	1,548,939	1,339,321	1,080,134	55,390	909,997	309,053	573,375
% Gross Profit	35.48	33.38	33.23	32.74	33.25	24.01	25.47
Operating expenses							
Advertising	69,386	79,630	67,431	32,372	22,787	11,719	21,127
Auto	4,812	5,509	7,713	6,831	7,383	2,518	4,707
Bad debts	6,204	58,312	(35,348)	2,508	25,874	0	(2,115)
Credit card fees	8,939	12,214	15,667	14,654	12,948	0	0
Bank charges	49	495	1,413	1,098	30	10	90
Canteen	507	1,477	1,409	(636)	(480)	(59)	(158)
Depreciation	31,677	18,701	15,262	14,039	12,715	2,766	4,609
Donations	900	575	0	0	120	350	250
Dues	820	775	925	805	805	30	30
Meals	846	502	207	227	21	18	73
Equipment rental	1,022	1,172	834	0	0	0	46
Insurance	121,373	130,009	142,869	147,559	122,573	78,242	122,146
Trash collection	1,152	989	2,381	1,512	935	647	1,093
Miscellaneous	75	135	1,094	174	623	0	487
Repairs	10,881	10,174	7,732	12,283	4,816	2,023	6,259
Office supplies	14,637	15,540	12,676	5,190	8,584	3,065	5,045
Temporary office	811	1,139	624	448	0	0	0
Payroll taxes	76,138	77,382	62,895	55,102	47,943	26,744	46,253
Pension/profit sharing	160,800	87,906	20,182	0	41,950	0	0
Professional fees	11,104	18,777	14,051	37,993	11,631	6,450	9,295
Postage all	6,280	5,971	5,461	30,531	37,038	20,270	31,534
Rent	60,000	60,000	60,000	60,000	60,000	30,000	50,000
Salaries							
-Owner	272,846	96,000	96,000	48,000	0	0	0
-Children	83,577	83,577	83,577	83,577	83,577	41,788	0
-Other	530,294	486,423	457,674	395,809	357,188	191,455	0
Taxes and licenses	8,873	9,678	15,840	16,020	15,350	128	12,408
Telephone	37,258	34,267	28,786	23,498	25,207	11,969	19,784
Travel	1,394	1,187	1,057	722	179	0	0
Utilities	19,679	25,687	18,860	18,830	22,925	10,384	20,147
Total expenses	1,542,333	1,350,205	1,107,990	1,009,194	922,722	448,327	42,633
Operating income	6,606	(10,884)	(27,856)	(53,796)	12,725	(139,274)	(169,258)
Miscellaneous income	(20,948)	(12,776)	(1,935)	(3,994)	(5,490)	(3,389)	(3,593)
Disposal of asset	6,177	(1,175)	6,375	12,213	5,297	0	0
Income taxes	6,264	2,945	269	0	3,307	3,400	3,400
Other income	9,523	11,006	(4,709)	(8,219)	(3,114)	(10)	193
Pretax income	$ 16,130	$ 122	($32,565)	($62,015)	$ 15,839	($139,284)	($169,065)

Notes

(1) The figures shown for Salaries—Owner, Children, are taken from W-2s. On income statement, Salary—Children is combined with Salaries—Other.

(2) Results shown for 2002 are for six months only as result of change of fiscal year.

WORKSHEET FOR FORECASTING REVENUE AND EXPENSES
(Dollars in thousands except as noted)

Example	Last Year	Year (1)	Year (2)	Year (3)	Year (4)	Year (5)	Percent Change
Forecast Revenue	$300	330	363	400	440	484	61%
Cost of Goods Sold @ 33%	100	100	121	133	146	161	
Gross Profit @ 66%	200	220	242	267	294	323	
Fixed Expenses	40	40	40	40	40	40	
Variable Expenses	150	165	181.5	200	220	242	
Total Expenses	190	205	221.5	240	260	282	
Pre-tax Income	$10	15	20.5	27	34	41	410%
% of Revenue	3.3%	4.5%	5.7%	6.7%	7.7%	8.5%	

Instructions for preparing Worksheet:

1. Forecast annual revenue and anticipated year-over-year growth rate (real growth + inflation)
2. Calculate Cost of Goods Sold as a percent of Revenue. Determine which costs to include in Cost of Goods
3. On separate sheet of paper, Itemize all expenses for current and next year to estimate Total Expenses
4. Identify fixed expenses including debt service where appropriate.
5. Subtract Fixed Expenses from Total Expenses to find Variable Expenses
6. Calculate Variable Expenses as a percent of Forecast Revenue
7. Forecast future Variable Expenses at same rate of growth as used in Forecast Revenue (10% in above Example)
8. Calculate Pre-tax Income as a percent of Forecast Revenue
9. Footnote all entries where possible giving source of data

	Year (1)	Year (2)	Year (3)	Year (4)	Year (5)
Forecast Revenue $	_____	_____	_____	_____	_____
Cost of Goods Sold @ ___%	_____	_____	_____	_____	_____
Gross Profit	_____	_____	_____	_____	_____
Fixed Expenses					
Owner salary	_____	_____	_____	_____	_____
Rent	_____	_____	_____	_____	_____
P&I	_____	_____	_____	_____	_____
Other	_____	_____	_____	_____	_____
_____	_____	_____	_____	_____	_____
_____	_____	_____	_____	_____	_____
Total Fixed Expenses	_____	_____	_____	_____	_____
Variable Expenses	_____	_____	_____	_____	_____
Total Expenses	_____	_____	_____	_____	_____
Pre-tax Income $	_____	_____	_____	_____	_____
% of Forecast Revenue	____%	____%	____%	____%	____%

FOOTNOTES:

Sample Promissory Notes
Promissory Note (with Installments)

$100,000

Dated: November 27, 2002

For value received, Johnny B. Buyer (hereafter, "Borrower"), 112 East 112th Street, New York, New York, 12231, promises to pay to Bob B. Bigger (hereafter, "Lender") the principal sum of $100,000 together with 9 percent (9%) annual interest on the unpaid balance.

Borrower agrees that this note will be paid in forty-eight (48) equal and consecutive monthly installments of principal and interest of with the first payment due on the 15th day of January 2003 and on the 15th day of each month thereafter until paid in full.

If any installment is not received within ten (10) days of the due date, Borrower agrees to pay Lender a late fee of exactly $100.00. Late fees not received by the due date of the next installment shall be added to the principal balance and accrue interest.

Borrower further agrees that in the event three consecutive installments are not received by the due debt, Lender, at his option, demand the entire unpaid balance of principal and accrued interest will become immediately due and payable.

If Lender brings suit against Borrower to recover an unpaid balance due and prevails in a lawsuit, Borrower will pay legal fees and court costs which the court finds reasonable.

Agreed: _____   _____

                  Johnny B. Buyer   Witness and Date

Promissory Note (Secured)

$100,000

Dated: August 15, 2004

For value received, Borrower, Thomas B. Buyer, of 201 Second Avenue, Syracuse, New York 22124, promises to pay to Lender, George A. Smith, of 505 East Elm Street, Syracuse, New York, 22134, the sum of one hundred thousand dollars and no cents ($100,000.00) together with interest at the rate of 8 percent (8%) on any unpaid balance.

Payments are payable in sixty (60) consecutive monthly installments in the amount of $ beginning the 1st day of October 2004 and on the 1st day of each month thereafter until paid in full.

This note is secured by a Security Agreement dated August 15, 2004, setting forth conditions agreed to by Borrower. Borrower acknowledges that default or breach of any of these conditions permits Lender, at his option, to demand full and immediate payment of any balance due under this note.

Note may be prepaid at any time in whole or in part without penalty.

_____   _____

                  Johnny B. Buyer   Witness Signature   and Date

Purchase Contract

STATE OF   **Tennessee**
COUNTY OF   **Shelby**

This **Purchase Contract** entered into this the _____ day of _____ 20 __,
by and between _____ (hereinafter, Seller)
with an address at _____,
and _____ (hereinafter, Purchaser)
with an address at _____.
Purchaser and Seller are hereinafter jointly termed the Parties. Purchaser has paid to Allied
Business Brokers (hereinafter, Broker) the sum of $_____, as earnest money
and part payment of the purchase price. On the dates herein stated, Purchaser agrees to buy
and seller agrees to sell all goodwill, trademarks, trade name(s), logos, contract rights, customer
lists, and other tangible and intangible assets, including but not limited to those listed below, of
the business known as _____ (hereinafter, Business)
located at _____ with the exceptions, if any,
of the excluded assets listed in Special Stipulation 1 on the next page:

All furniture, fixtures, and equipment as further described in attached Schedule A	$_____
Resale inventory and supplies (valued at Seller's cost) in the amount of	$_____
Leasehold improvements	$_____
Management Assistance (see Stipulation 3 following)	$_____
Covenant(s) Not to Compete (see Stipulation 4 following)	$_____
_____	$_____
_____	$_____
Total Price	$_____

The Purchaser agrees to pay to the Seller at closing the following:

Earnest money, above acknowledged	$_____
Payment by cashier's or certified check	$_____
And additional payments, or assumption of debt, as follows:	
1. _____	$_____
2. _____	$_____

making the **total purchase price** for business prior to adjustments, if any, called for herein in
Stipulation 8.
Total Payments to Seller $_____

The seller covenants and agrees to bind its heirs, executors, administrators, successors, or assigns, and to convey the said business and/or property to said purchaser or applicable heirs, executors, administrators, successors, or assigns, in fee with proper deed, capital stock, bill of sale, or title (whichever is applicable), with all marital and homestead rights waived (if applicable)—free from any and all defects or encumbrances such as liens, except such as are herein agreed to be assumed by the Purchaser. Seller agrees to pay for any action required to remove any defects from title or bill of sale or other instrument in order to make it good and marketable. Seller further warrants, represents, and agrees that Seller has good and marketable title to all of the real and personal property and other assets of the Business being sold hereby. Seller also agrees that from the date of acceptance of this purchase contract through the day of closing of the sale, that the Business will remain open during normal business hours.

Upon the tender of such deed, capital stock, bill of sale, or title, above mentioned, the Purchaser agrees to comply fully with the terms of this purchase contract. All taxes, assessments, rents, and insurance premiums are to be prorated to date of closing, by the Parties, outside of closing.

Time is of the essence. Parties agree to work diligently to satisfy all conditions and contingencies of the intended sale set forth in this purchase contract. This purchase contract constitutes the sole and entire agreement between the Parties hereto and no modification or amendment shall be binding unless in writing and attached hereto and signed by all Parties to this agreement. No representation, promise, or inducement not included in this purchase contract shall be binding upon any party hereto.

Purchaser agrees that its/his/her/their failure to comply with the terms hereof within the stipulated time gives Seller the right to retain the amount paid in escrow as liquidated damages, and Seller agrees to equally divide this earnest money with Broker for services rendered in regard to this Purchaser without any reduction of fees that may be due Broker on a sale of this business to another Purchaser. The Seller acknowledges that Broker cannot guarantee payment of check or checks accepted from the Purchaser as earnest money.

This instrument shall be regarded as a bona fide Purchase Contract by Purchaser or Seller who first signs to the other and is open for acceptance by the other until noon on the ___ day of _____2008, by which time written acceptance of such offer must have been actually received by Broker, who shall promptly notify the other party, in writing, of such acceptance.

If accepted as set forth herein, this Purchase Contract becomes **LEGALLY BINDING** upon both Parties and upon their heirs, executors, administrators, successors, and assigns.

The closing of this sale shall be on or before _____, 20____. The following **SPECIAL STIPUATIONS** are an integral part of this Purchase Contract and shall, if conflicting with printed matter, control.

SPECIAL STIPULATIONS TO PURCHASE CONTRACT

1. **ASSETS EXCLUDED FROM SALE** (if any): _____
    _____

2. **MANAGEMENT ASSISTANCE**: Seller will, for the consideration stated, if any, provide management assistance and training after closing consisting of _____
    _____
    _____
    _____

3. **COVENANT NOT TO COMPETE**: For the consideration stated, if any, Seller agrees not to compete for _____ years from closing as owner, part owner, investor, manager, consultant, or permanent employee (except as an employee of the Purchaser), without Purchaser's prior permission, in the following types of business within the area defined below:
    Type(s) of business: _____
    Restricted area: _____
    Other restriction(s): _____

4. **PAYMENT of CLOSING COSTS**: Parties agree to retain a closing attorney to prepare the closing documents and handle the closing and agree equally to share the attorney's fee and other closing costs and fees, provided they do not exceed $_____ each.

5. **CONDITIONS PRECEDENT TO CLOSE**: Seller agrees to meet the following conditions at its expense:
    _____
    _____
    _____

6. **SECURITY FOR DEFERRED PAYMENTS**: _____
    _____
    _____
    _____

7. **INVENTORY COUNT AND ADJUSTMENTS TO The PURCHASE PRICE**: _____
    _____
    _____
    _____
    _____

8. **SELLER WARRANTS**: Seller hereby represents, warrants, and agrees:
   a. All financial statements of Seller furnished relative to this agreement fairly reflect the financial position and results of operations of Seller for the periods indicated. (Parties may list these statements here:)
   b. There are no undisclosed liabilities, claims, or pending or threatened litigation, and Seller will defend and hold Purchaser harmless from same if any shall arise from actions which took place prior to the closing. If there are undisclosed liabilities, buyer may, after giving Seller ten (10) days notification to dispute or satisfy such liabilities, pay same and deduct amount paid from next payment or payments due Seller.
   c. All equipment to be conveyed to buyer will be in normal working condition at time of closing.
   d. All inventories to be conveyed to buyer will be in good and marketable (and current) condition at time of closing.
   e. Pending closing, that Business will to be conducted in the normal manner, replacing inventories and meeting financial and other normal obligations of Business when due.

9. **CONTINGENT NATURE OF CONTRACT**: Parties agree that this contract is contingent upon the satisfaction of the following conditions prior to the closing date set out above or amended by the Parties. However, Parties agree to be diligent in securing their prompt satisfaction.
   a. _____
   _____
   _____
   b. _____
   _____
   _____
   c. _____
   _____
   _____

10. **PAYROLL**: All payroll and payroll tax liability accruing to the close of the sale shall remain the responsibility of the Seller. Immediately from and after closing of this sale, all subsequent payroll expense shall be the sole responsibility of the Purchaser.

11. **DEPOSITS**: Any and all amounts currently on deposit for the benefit of the Business for utility service, phone, rent, etc., are the property of the Seller and are not included as part of the sale. Purchaser shall deposit such amounts as necessary to continue the operation of the business. Customer deposits held by the Business shall be divided as follows:

12. _____
_____

13. **INCORPORATION BY PURCHASER:** It is agreed that the Purchaser may elect to incorporate. In such event, the new corporation shall become the Purchaser, and the Purchaser shall cause the corporation to ratify all of the terms and conditions of this Purchase Contract. Further, Purchaser shall continue to be personally liable for the performance of this contract, covenants, andss agreements and the payments of any unpaid balance owed to Seller hereunder.

PURCHASER	**Witness**	**Date**

SELLER (individual signature)	**Witness**	**Date**

SELLER (corporate signature)	**Witness**	**Date**

Attachments to Purchase Contract (list separately)

Schedules: Schedule A, Schedule of Furniture, Fixtures and Equipment
Schedule B, Schedule of Contracts in House
Schedule C, Schedule of Accounts Receivable
Exhibits: Management Assistance Agreement
Non-Competition Agreement

Note that this Purchase Contract may call for certain Attachments, Schedules, and/or Exhibits. If so, this Purchase Contract will not be enforceable unless these documents are attached.

Sample Settlement Sheet
Purchaser's Account

SELLER: ABC Enterprises, Inc.,
(d.b.a. Amoco of Casino Strip)
and its Shareholders
6804 Casino Strip Blvd. Robinsonville, MO 31664

PURCHASER: Horacio Mendoza
5339 Horseshoe Trail
Jonesboro, AR 39115

CHARGES:	Sale Price	$194,000.00
	Legal Fees and Other Closing Costs	$1,000.00
	Proration of 2005 Property Taxes	$3,058.32
	Adjustment to Contract Price	$6,000.00
	Balance Due Bank	$3,993.00
	Filing Fees	$20.00
	TOTAL CHARGES	$208,071.32
CREDITS:	Earnest Money Deposit	$20,000.00
	TOTAL CREDITS	$20,000.00

BALANCE OF PURCHASE PRICE DUE FROM
PURCHASER AT CLOSING: $188,071.32

The undersigned has examined the above statement and hereby acknowledges that the same correctly reflects the disbursements made for his account and benefit, and the undersigned hereby states that this transaction has been consummated in accordance with his understanding and agreement with the Seller of this property.

March _____ 2015   Horacio Mendoza, Purchaser _____

Settlement Sheet Seller's Account

SELLER: Julius M. Barnstead
                1944 South Angela
                Memphis, TN 38104

PURCHASER: Greenspace Landscapes, LLC
                9847 Farmington Road
                Welllington, TN 38002

BROKER: Sam Cantor & Company

CREDITS:	Sales Price:	$110,000.00
	TOTAL CREDITS:	$110,000.00
LESS:	Commission to Broker	$11,000.00
	One-half closing attorney fee	$450.00
	Promissory note to Seller	$40,000.00
	UCC Lien Search	(est.) $150.00
Payoff Outstanding Liabilities:		
	Chase Auto Finance	$6,189.12
	Fifth Third Bank	$10,620.50
	Courier fees	$30.00
	TOTAL CHARGES:	$68,439.62
NET PROCEEDS TO SELLER AT CLOSING:		$41,560.38

I have examined above statement and hereby acknowledge that the same correctly reflects the disbursements made for my account and benefit, and I hereby state that this transaction has been consummated in accordance with my understanding and agreement with the Purchaser of this property. I further understand that the business is not shown on the City or County tax rolls for personal property taxes. In the event an assessment for such taxes is made after closing, I agree to pay all such taxes assessed for the period up to closing. Items marked as "estimate" are estimates only and are subject to change after closing.

Date: _____ Seller: _____

Confirmation And Bill Of Sale

FOR AND IN CONSIDERATION of the sum of one hundred fifty thousand dollars ($150,000) in hand and of which receipt is hereby acknowledged, John A. Ranger (hereinafter, "Seller") of 82 East 82nd Street, New York, New York 11223, does hereby grant, convey sell, transfer, and deliver to George B. buyer (hereinafter, "Buyer") of 112 112th Street, New York, New York 12233 as business know as Doozy Cabinet Manufacturing Company Inc., with an address of 123 32nd Street, Newark, New Jersey 12345 (hereinafter, "Business") under the terms of the attached Purchase Agreement dated August 14, 2007.

Seller warrants that he is the lawful owner of Business and has the legal right to sell same and will defend title of Business against any and all legal claims and demands.

Agreed this _____ day of _____, 2007

SELLER: _____ BUYER: _____

WITNESS:

     Signature _____

     Print Name _____

Blender of Dry Mixes for Dairy & Seafood Processors

This three-and-one-half-year-old company blends mixes that are used by both the dairy products industry and by fish and poultry processors. The present accounts are located in six states from Florida to Oklahoma. During the company's first two years of operations, the company blended mixes primarily for the dairy products industry. As margins declined, the owners curtailed shipments of dairy products in favor of formulating and selling product to meat processors. The last shipments of dairy mix were in October 1997. The largest volume blended since that time has been for catfish processors. As of June 1998, monthly sales are back to 1996 levels of about $100,000 per month. Sales for June 1998 exceeded $130,000.

ORGANIZATION

This company is a Tennessee corporation with nine stockholders who collectively pledged $231,250 at time of incorporation. As of June 30, 1998, pledges of $218,250 had been paid. The president of the company is the largest shareholder with 30 percent of the outstanding shares.

FACILITIES

After two and a half years of operation in Arlington, TN, the company moved in June 1997 to Ocala, FL, where it leases 3,000 square feet from one of the stockholders. This move was made because of proximity to several dairy accounts. Today, the largest concentration of accounts is in the Mississippi delta. After moving to Florida, much of the equipment was upgraded and replaced. Virtually all equipment is stainless steel and will meet EPA's strict standards. The balance sheet shows an original equipment cost of $232,000.

MANAGEMENT

The daily operations are managed by the president's son in Ocala. The president, who still lives in Tennessee, is responsible for sales and has been assisted by several commissioned sales persons who receive average commissions of 5–6 percent of each sale. Technical support is provided by a PhD chemist with many years experience in both meat and dairy products. In addition there are two and a half hourly personnel receiving an average of $7.50/hour and the president's daughter who was paid $20,000 for accounting and bookkeeping assistance.

REASON FOR SALE

Three factors are responsible for the decision to sell: the plant manager is going back to college in the fall; the president has recently had serious back surgery, and the landlord needs the space occupied by the company.

FORMULATIONS

The formulations are custom blended. They serve to reduce dehydration and discoloration of frozen products as well as extend their shelf life. The sale will include the rights to the use of all formulations. The trade names and formulations are owned by the founders of the company individually.

OTHER ASSETS IN SALE

A summary of assets to be sold and their approximate values are shown below:

Accounts receivable—guaranteed	$120,000
Raw materials and bags (at cost)—guaranteed	20,000
Finished goods at 80% of selling price	10,000
All furniture, fixtures and equipment	120,000
Rights to use of formulations and trade name	50,000
Management assistance & noncompete	25,000
Miscellaneous supplies, tools, etc.	5,000
	$350,000

RECENT DEVELOPMENTS

In January 1998, the company negotiated very favorable pricing with its largest raw material supplier. In May 1998, the company raised prices to its customers by about 2.5 percent. These two factors should improve the gross profit margin by 4–5 percent points.

ASKING PRICE—$350,000

If $250,000 is paid at closing, Purchaser may pledge accounts receivable and inventories to a first lien lender. Seller will carry note for balance at 9 percent.

MARKET ANALYSIS

Table 1
1995 U.S. AQUACULTURE PRODUCTION

	Pounds Produced	Pounds Sold
Salmon	34,000,000	80,000,000
Trout	55,000,000	61,000,000
Crawfish	55,000,000	33,000,000
Catfish	447,000,000	351,000,000

Table 2
U.S. CATFISH PRODUCTION
Pounds of Live Weight Catfish Processed

1997	524,959	1990	360,435
1996	472,000	1989	341,900
1995	446,686	1988	295,109
1994	438,269	1987	280,495
1993	458,013	1986	213,756
1992	457,367	1985	191,616
1991	390,870		

The industry (blenders of dry mixes) is driven primarily by the increase in the volume of shipments of frozen foods in recent years. Processors and retailers alike want the product to retain a fresh look and texture as long as possible. It is important also that the product not lose weight through dehydration while frozen. These factors are particularly true in the meat and seafood processing industries.

In the case of seafood, until recent years, most products were shipped and sold fresh. Therefore, sales were tightly clustered around seaports and coastal cities. Traditionally, fish like trout, bass, and salmon were served fresh; frozen fish had little appeal. This has changed radically, and now the average family as well as many schools and other institutions serve frozen boned filets and fish sticks. Fish today is easier to prepare and eat, and sales have soared. Demand has outstripped traditional sources of supply. Therefore, domestic production of pond raised fish (aquaculture) has become a large and growing industry. For recent U.S. production (1995), see Table 1.

In volume, the growth in catfish production has been the greatest. However, the increase in the percent of pond-raised salmon and trout is impressive. Table 2 shows the steady increase in catfish production by pounds

	Estimated 1996 Population	Pounds (000's) Consumed 1986	Pounds (000's) Consumed 1996	1996 Rank	Pounds Consumed Per Capita	1996 Rank
		Table 3 CATFISH CONSUMPTION BY GEOGRAPHY				
Texas	18,000,000	28,000	47,500	1	2.64	4
Illinois	11,500,000	14,000	23,500	2	2.04	6
California	30,500,000	6,500	16,200	3	.53	15
Louisiana	4,300,000	11,300	16,200	4	3.76	2
Tennessee	5,000,000	4,200	16,100	5	3.22	3
Arkansas	2,450,000	5,100	14,000	6	5.71	1
Florida	14,000,000	2,200	13,500	7	.96	12
Mississippi	2,700,000	7,000	11,000	8	.41	16
Alabama	4,100,000	6,000	10,000	9	2.44	5
Michigan	9,400,000	1,500	8,100	10	.86	13
Missouri	5,200,000	5,000	7,500	11	1.44	7
Georgia	6,800,000	5,000	6,750	12	1.00	11
Indiana	5,600,000	2,400	6,200	13	1.11	9
Kentucky	3,750,000	1,200	5,000	14	1.33	8
N. Carolina	6,800,000	1,400	4,350	15	.64	14
Oklahoma	3,250,000	2,500	3,500	16	1.08	10

of live weight processed since 1985. According to the Catfish Institute, average consumption nationwide of pond-grown catfish in 1997 had grown to 1.0 pounds per capita from .4 pounds per capita in 1985.

Because of this growth and the concentration of catfish consumption in the Mid-South, the Company decided in 1997 to concentrate on developing formulations for use by catfish processors. The owners now estimate that the Company has 50 percent of the catfish dry mix market after only one full year of production. Note on Table 2 that the consumption (by weight) has more than doubled in several states between 1986 and 1996 most notably in Texas, California, Tennessee, Arkansas, Michigan, and Florida. Most notable is the fact that several of the most populous states (Ohio, Pennsylvania, and New York) are not shown. Also note that California, our largest state, consumed only .54 pounds per capita. These data suggest that there is ample market for continued growth in catfish consumption.

Because of declines in catches in recent years, it seems fair to assume that pond production of other species (trout and salmon) will also continue to grow and that consumption of frozen fish will become more popular in many markets where fresh fish is not readily available.

Disclaimer

This report includes information obtained from sources believed to be reliable, but no independent verification has been made, and we do not guarantee accuracy or completeness. Opinions expressed are subject to change without notice. This report should not be construed as a request to engage in any transaction. The price and terms shown above are subject to change without notice.

Source of data for tables—The Catfish Institute 1997   *Profile JG-039-068*

ABOUT THE AUTHOR

Gibson holds degrees from the University of Virginia and Cornell. After stints on the graduate faculty at the University of Memphis and Florida State University, he founded and operated Allied Business Brokers for twenty-five years. He has been a frequent lecturer on the subject of business acquisitions and has been admitted to testify as an expert witness on business valuations in local, state, and federal courts.

In his community life, Mr. Gibson was president of the Economic Club of Memphis and served on the Board of the Fogelman College of Business at the University of Memphis. In retirement, he performs appraisals of privately held businesses and is a volunteer business counselor for SCORE.